Roleplaying in a Grimsical World of Fantasy

Lead Developer and Writer
SOPHIE LAGACÉ

System Developers
SOPHIE LAGACÉ,
MIKE OLSON,
SEAN NITTNER

Editor
KAREN TWELVES

Artists
JONATHAN HOFFMAN,
JENNIFER BACH,
DAVID WEINMAN,
NOAH BRADLEY

Graphic Designer
DALE HORSTMAN

Proofreader
JESSICA BANKS

Indexer
KRISTA WHITE

Creative Director
SEAN NITTNER

Micro Fiction
EDMUND METHENY

Project Managers
SEAN NITTNER,
STEPHEN BAJZA

Business Development Manager
CHRIS HANRAHAN

Marketing Manager
CARRIE HARRIS

War of Ashes Shieldwall and War of Ashes Shieldbash
ZOMBIESMITH

Creative Consultants
ROB DONOGHUE,
FRED HICKS,
ANTHONY BROWN,
JOSH QUALTIERI,
LEONARD BALSERA,
BRIAN ENGARD,
AARON BROWN

Based on the Fate Core System By
LEONARD BALSERA,
RYAN MACKLIN,
BRIAN ENGARD,
MIKE OLSON,
FRED HICKS,
ROB DONOGHUE

Additional Material from Fate Accelerated By
CLARK VALENTINE,
LEONARD BALSERA,
FRED HICKS,
MIKE OLSON,
AMANDA VALENTINE

An Evil Hat Productions Publication
www.evilhat.com • feedback@evilhat.com
@EvilHatOfficial on Twitter
facebook.com/EvilHatProductions

First published in 2015 by Evil Hat Productions, LLC.
10125 Colesville Rd #318, Silver Spring, MD 20901.

Softcover ISBN: 978-1-61317-114-1
Printed in the USA.

This is a game where people make up stories about wonderful, terrible, impossible, glorious
things. All the characters and events portrayed in this work are fictional. Any resemblance
to real people, fantasy adventurers, clerics of fickle and dangerous gods, or children's shows
with furry puppets is purely coincidental, but kinda hilarious.

Playtesters: Adam Gutschenritter, Alessandra Morgan, Alex Johnston, Anastasios
Tsoraklidis, ANIMAfelis, Anja Nittner, arphon, Benjamin Feehan, Bert Isla, Brennan
Bishop, Brian Kelley, Brian Lyngaas, Bry Hitchcock, Chris Scott, Christopher Anderson,
Colin Jessup, Crystaline Wright, Dani Laney, David "Ur-Kuld Lichender of the Dank
Cave" Miessler-Kubanek, David Leaman, Dorene Giacopini, Duncan Gray, Dyer Rose,
Edmund Metheny, Erol, EvoNerd, Fivos Athanasopoulos, Frank A. Figoni, Gabriel
Garcia, Genevieve Tocci, George DeLaMater, Gokce Ozan Toptas, Hamish Cameron,
Hermina, Jason Tocci, Jeff Ayars, Jeff Stormer, Jeffrey J.A. Fuller II, Jenn W., Jess Gleason,
Joey Wright, Jonathan Klick, Jonathan Siregar, Justin Scott, Keith Stanley, Kevin Reeves,
Kit Walsh, Laura Ely, Marcus Morrisey, Mark Walters, Matthew Young, Maureen Pisani,
Michael Duxbury, Peter Netzer, Randy S. McNally II, Ray Slakinski, Richard Gillingham,
Rob "Mr Mirage" Duke, Roger Edge, Scott Stormer, Scott Vondrasek, Sharon E. Jackson,
Son E. Lon, Sterling, Steve Pisani, Steve Wilson, Thade's Hammer, Tyke, Wayne Humfleet,
William Vaughn Wright, Xiomara Nittner

Contents

PART

1

Welcome to Agaptus!

WAR OF ASHES: FATE OF AGAPTUS presents a fantasy setting like you've never seen—at the same time both dark and humorous, wacky and gritty—with lots of story hooks, an extensive bestiary, and dangerous magic that rests on the whim of powerful but incompetent deities.

On the islands of Agaptus, the noble Elvorix, savage Vidaar, and disciplined Jaarl have warred for ages, but now all three face a threat from the gluttony of the endless Kuld—driven forward by advancing ice. The fickle gods have been angered and in punishment caused the sun to recede, glaciers to advance, and ashes to rain from the darkened skies.

You and your friends will collectively tell a tale set in the world of Agaptus. You'll make decisions for the characters as they move through the story, and the story changes as you make those choices. When someone tries something and you don't know for sure how it will turn out, it's time to roll the dice to see what happens next!

This book builds on the **FATE ACCELERATED EDITION** rules, a streamlined incarnation of the popular **FATE CORE SYSTEM**. We've expanded the rules by using miniatures, making equipment more interesting, creating powerful artifacts of the Ancients; adding ritual spellcasting, and providing step-by-step campaign and adventure creation.

In your hands rests the Fate of Agaptus!

The Four Factions

The Noble Elvorix

The Elvorix are a proud race, bordering on vain. They have a prestigious past and consider themselves to have been the pinnacle of civilization. Sadly, a drastic regime change led to the destruction of most of their records, followed by a long habit of discouraging invention and creativity. They are now unable to recreate the marvels of architecture, engineering, or art left by their ancestors.

Though they recovered from centuries of military rule and have rebuilt much, they now encourage blandness for a different reason—to remain unnoticed by a fickle god. Because they angered the Lord of the Sky, the red sun has dimmed and the northern realms grow too cold to inhabit.

The Savage Vidaar

The Vidaar descended from the same original stock as the Elvorix but represent the most aggressive fraction of the population. Centuries ago, they splintered from the Elvorix and left on warships in search of treasure among the islands, which was in truth an elaborate lie the Elvorix constructed to lure them away. When the Vidaar returned to the land of their origin, they had become a nation of raiders and pirates. And they were very, *very* resentful of having been tricked.

Though skilled in weapon-forging, ship-building, and brewing, they are prone to laziness and would rather steal from the Elvorix than tend their own crops (in those places that can still produce food).

The Disciplined Jaarl

The Jaarl are a different species, driven from their native land after it was destroyed in a cataclysmic volcanic eruption. The survivors conquered the island of Iradon and have gained a foothold on the still-inhabitable portions. They are considered a mutual enemy of the Elvorix and Vidaar.

They are more militarized and skilled in weapon-forging than the Vidaar, and more advanced than the Elvorix in engineering. While their numbers are small, they bolster their ranks by enlisting those they capture into forced labor. While conquering Agaptus to claim as their new home appears to be their prime objective, there is a small faction of the Jaarl who believe that a truce can be made. Above all else they value honor, order, and ruthlessness.

The Endless Kuld

All three races face the growing threat of the gluttonous Kuld, voracious creatures with insatiable appetites and very little discrimination between what does and doesn't count as food. Generally considered to be little more than a mindless horde, there are some however who have evolved past communicating merely by scent and crude art. They are still considered a tenuous ally at best, as even the more enlightened of their species can't promise to always control their ceaseless hunger.

The Kuld continue to migrate from areas now under ice, reclaiming the north as they move to warmer climates, away from the uninhabitable cold.

And it's growing ever colder.

What You'll Find in This Book

WAR OF ASHES: FATE OF AGAPTUS is organized in six parts:

❋ **Part 1** is this introduction, to get the reader oriented.

❋ **Part 2** describes the world of Agaptus, its history, the four factions in play, locations, adventure seeds, and notable figures.

❋ **Part 3** describes how to create a campaign and a group of heroes.

❋ **Part 4** provides the basic rules for play.

❋ **Part 5** discusses the gods, magic, and the wonders left by the Ancients.

❋ **Part 6** gives advice on running the game, planning and running adventures, and managing your campaign.

❋ **Part 7** contains useful appendices and reference materials.

Throughout the book, you'll see entries with special formatting. The ones of most immediate interest are *special terms* defined in the Glossary on page 343, and **aspects**, which are little bits of fiction that encapsulate an idea or theme and can be used to produce a mechanical effect. Aspects will be explained in *"Aspects and Fate Points"* on page 190.

> **Stunts** (page 198)
> Stunts are unique and distinctive tricks your character has that give them an extra benefit in narrow circumstances. Two characters can have the same rating in their approaches, but their stunts might have vastly different effects.

Aspects (page 190)
Aspects are phrases that describe some significant detail about a character. Aspects can cover a wide range of elements, such as personality traits, beliefs, relationships, issues and problems, or anything else that helps us know the character as a person rather than just a collection of stats.

Refresh (page 174)
Refresh is the number of fate points you get at the start of every game session to spend for your character. Your total replenishes to this number unless you ended the last session holding more than your original refresh.

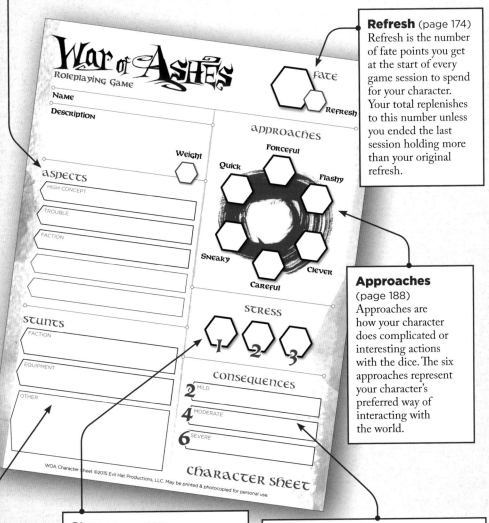

War of Ashes
Roleplaying Game

Name

Description

fate

Refresh

Weight

approaches

FORCEFUL

Quick

Flashy

aspects

HIGH CONCEPT

TROUBLE

FACTION

SNEAKY

CLEVER

CAREFUL

stunts

FACTION

STRESS

1 2 3

EQUIPMENT

consequences

2 MILD

OTHER

4 MODERATE

6 SEVERE

WOA Character Sheet ©2015 Evil Hat Productions, LLC. May be printed & photocopied for personal use.

character sheet

Approaches
(page 188)
Approaches are how your character does complicated or interesting actions with the dice. The six approaches represent your character's preferred way of interacting with the world.

Stress (page 231)
Stress is one of two options you have to stay in a conflict—it represents getting stymied, superficial injuries, and so on. You have three stress levels you can burn off to help keep you in a fight, and they reset at the end of a conflict, once you catch your breath.

Consequences (page 231)
Consequences are the other option you have to keep fighting, but have a more lasting impact. Taking a consequence puts a new aspect on your sheet describing your character's injuries. It takes time to recover from a consequence. Until then your character is vulnerable to complications or others wishing to take advantage of this new weakness.

The Gods side with the stronger.

—Elvorix proverb

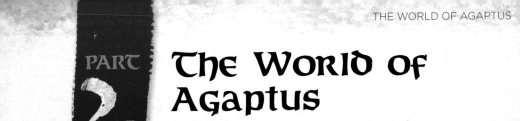

PART 2

The World of Agaptus

Your Humble Historian

What follows is a comprehensive study of the peoples and creatures of Agaptus compiled by Matia Bibulus ix Atronia co Agapta, daughter of Toranus, written 86AGC.

Three years ago, I was part of the civilian support staff for the allied army of General Orvas and Vidaarus the Ninetieth. When the Jaarl ambushed the armies, I was captured along with hundreds of others and marched off to serve the Jaarl as forced labor.

I spent almost two years as a captive until I escaped and returned to Agapta. I published the tale of my adventures in the book, "My Time Among the Enemy," which made the best-seller list for two weeks last summer and, I'm happy to report, was also accepted as my final thesis at Elvora Bibulus Academy.

My time among the Jaarl, along with my mixed heritage (being from the southern regions of Sentia, I have a few Vidaar among my ancestors), have given me some insight into the customs of our rivals for the control of Agaptus. I have also studied in detail the surviving notes of Kiptus Bibulus, detailing his experiments and observations of the Kuld. In light of the interest generated by my first book, I have been commissioned by the Academy to travel as far and wide as possible among the isles of Agaptus and to send my travel notes for publication.

The following is my research thus far.

Hey there readers! We've included notes just for you in boxes just like this one. For rules-specific chapters, turn to *"Playing The War of Ashes: Fate Of Agaptus"* on page 175.

The History of Agaptus

Thousands of years ago, gentle tribes inhabited the island of *Sentia*. Somewhere around 2350 BGC (Before the Great Catastrophe), a great drought parched the land, withering all the mosses and plants that fed the tribesfolk; the resulting famine nearly exterminated them.

The god of the sky, *Agaptus* himself, resolved to save his children and approached the survivors, bathed in a cloud of fire and light. Unfortunately this spectacular manifestation caused the frightened survivors to flee in panic. Terrified and blinded, most of them ran directly off a steep cliff and into a chasm, falling to their death. Only a few of the slower ones— infants, elders, physically disabled individuals, and a particularly sound sleeper named Sentius—were left. Feeling keenly guilty for having nearly eradicated his people, Agaptus bestowed upon Sentius his mighty sword.

Sentius, after some painful trial and error, discovered that swords can kill beasts such as ylark, and—thanks to Agaptus' burning presence—that ylark can be roasted and eaten. Starvation was at an end! Agaptus, pleased with himself, returned to the heavens; Sentius and the surviving tribesfolk began to build a civilization and eventually inhabited not only Sentia but the neighboring islands of Matriga and Iradon, as well as minor outlying islands, all forming the land of Agaptus.

These *Ancient Sentians* reached high levels of sophistication and created marvelous cities that still dot the landscape. But their expansion caused them to encounter the Kuld, a race at first seemingly harmless but which soon turned into a voracious, merciless enemy. To fight the Kuld, the Ancients created a warrior class that vanquished the Kuld in what is now called the Purging War.

Under the command of General Vidaarus, the warriors then immediately seized control of the kingdom from the traditional lineage of Scholar Kings. To consolidate their power, the military rulers destroyed every trace of writing, scholarship, and knowledge they could find; much Ancient wisdom was lost forever. In this way, they ruled for several hundred years.

At long last, a rogue scholar named Elvora Bibulus played on the greed and ambition of the ruler of the time, King Vidaarus the Thirty-First. Elvora cannily convinced Vidaarus of the existence of the fabulous

9

ISLE OF SENTIA

MURMADON

AGAPTA

Atronia

Gailus

Ilunus

Prolyus

ISLE OF IRADON

ISLE OF MATRIGA

Vilamr

ILARGIAN ISTHMUS

VIDAARA

N

KEY
● =Small City
○ =Large City
✳ =Capital
▬ =Road
☐ =Elvorix Territory
☐ =Vidaar Territory
☐ =Jaarl Territory

treasure island *Garigla*. King Vidaarus built a fleet and, taking the majority of his warriors with him—for fear perhaps that ambitious warlords left behind might carve up his kingdom—left in search of Garigla.

The downtrodden people left behind rose up under Elvora's leadership, toppled the few remaining military commanders, and reestablished the Ruling Council and the Scholar Kings. The newly liberated people called themselves the Elvorix in honor of their leader. This sequence of events is now called the "Great Deception."

Meanwhile, King Vidaarus and his descendants wandered the seas, from island to island in search of Garigla. After hundreds more years, these Vidaar as they now called themselves wandered back where they had started and realized they had been fooled. They established a foothold and started a protracted attempt to reconquer the land of Agaptus, but the Elvorix armies fought back.

Things changed again a century later when a terribly botched religious ceremony offended the god Agaptus, and he cursed the land. The sun dimmed, ashes rained from the sky, and the climate started cooling brutally as ice crept from the north. Soon after, the Kuld hordes, long thought banished, returned to fight for the shrinking areas of land that could support life.

Even worse, the mighty Jaarl fleet appeared and started conquering the eastern areas. Eventually, it would be discovered that their own island of Murmadon had been destroyed by their own fearsome god at about the same time Agaptus was forsaking his people.

Decades have elapsed since this *Great Catastrophe* and Elvorix, Vidaar, Jaarl, and Kuld fight on bitterly for the disappearing temperate lands.

Things to Know: The 30-Second Version

The Elvorix and the Vidaar are two subspecies of the Sentian species; Jaarl and Kuld are completely separate species.

Elvorix, Vidaar, and Jaarl refer to adult males as *bucks*, adult females as *does*, and their young as *fawns* or sometimes *buckies* for underage males.

The 30-Second Version Continued...

The technological level of the Agaptan factions resembles that of our Great Britain circa 900 A.D. Like Europeans during the early Middle Ages looking at Roman roads and aqueducts, the marvels of Ancient Sentians are beyond their ability to replicate.

Magic is granted by the gods to their priests, although a lot of it is really just trickery made to look like magic. Invoke the gods' names too much, and they may start paying you too much attention...

The Agaptan gods are meddlesome but inept. When they pay attention to the affairs of mortals even benevolently, their interference tends to cause inadvertent property damage. But they are also insecure and cause deliberate damage when they feel ignored by their flock.

Therefore, *Divine Interest* is a measure of the level of cosmic trouble one has attracted. When mortals attract the divine gaze of the gods, upheavals follow in their footsteps.

Through interference of the gods in events globally called the Great Catastrophe, the world's climate has been changing brutally for the past 86 years as an ice age is creeping up on formerly temperate areas.

War for land, power, or riches has long been a feature of Agaptan life; but since the Great Catastrophe and the steady advance of the ice, it has taken on a new urgency as more factions vie for more limited territory and resources.

While Agaptan factions fight for a bigger slice of the pie, the pie itself is shrinking.

Time Line of Sentia

* **Several thousand years BGC (Before the Great Catastrophe):** Tribes of Elvorix live in the mountains of the Atronian region in peace, subsisting on string-moss and river-berries.

* **2350 BGC:** A great famine afflicts the Elvorix. Concerned, the god Agaptus appears to his people in a grand display of fire and lightning, causing the inadvertent destruction of all but a few. The god gives his sword to survivor Sentius by way of apology. Sentius throws the sword in anger, accidentally slaying a ylark. The Elvorix tribes discover meat as an edible commodity.

  The Elvorix move from the mountain cliffs down to the plains of Teodor, founding their great city and building the mighty temple of Agaptus.

* **Around 1,200 BGC:** Eventually, the Elvorix meet the Kuld, leading shortly after to the Purging War. The hitherto peaceful if greedy Kuld discover that they can eat more than plant and lichen crops, and start devouring cattle and farmers.

✳ **987 BGC:** The great general Vidaarus the First leads the Sentian armies in what will be the final blow of the Purging War. Sending his troops both north and south, he drives the Kuld from the isles of Agaptus. He then takes control of the kingdom and burns all the records he can find, establishing a military rulership that will last for nearly 600 years.

✳ **c. 400 BGC:** The scholar Elvora Bibulus concocts the Great Deception (as it is known among the Elvorix) or the Great Betrayal (among the Vidaar), a scheme to fool Vidaarus the Thirty-First and most of his warriors into leaving in search of the island of Garigla, reputed to be overflowing with riches. As soon as they leave, Elvora Bibulus reestablishes a Ruling Council and a lineage of Scholar Kings; cities are rebuilt. This is the beginning of the Post-Deception Elvorix Restoration.

✳ **225 BGC:** The Marhn Troll Invasion. Although Elvorix armies had encountered these gigantic and savage creatures when hunting the Kuld during the Purging War, it's a surprise when the Marhn descend from the icy north to raid Elvorix lands. This leads to the re-militarization of the Elvorix for the first time since the Great Deception, and the Marhn are repelled within a few decades.

❋ **95 BGC:** The Vidaar land on the isle of Iradon after going around the world without finding Garigla, and blame the Elvorix for their deception. War between the Elvorix and the Vidaar rages for roughly a century.

❋ **The Great Catastrophe:** A botched ceremony in Agaptus' honor leads to the last recorded appearance of the god—and very angry. Between his wrath and the catastrophic eruption of the Murmadon volcano on Malios (home of the Jaarl), an incipient Ice Age begins. Chilled and hungry, the Kuld return to Sentia.

❋ **10 AGC:** The Jaarl first conquer the isle of Iradon, driving back both the Vidaar and Elvorix forces.

❋ **18 AGC:** The Pact of Prolyus is signed; the Elvorix and Vidaar agree to fight separately against the Kuld but jointly against the Jaarl.

❋ **83 AGC:** Orvas' Folly. A premature joint celebration of victory turns into a crushing defeat by the Jaarl and dissolves the alliance between Elvorix and Vidaar.

❋ **86 AGC:** The present.

The People of Agaptus

The following is this author's personal opinion of the greatest challenges that face our world.

For millennia the Elvorix have tried to avoid being singled out by powerful but dangerous deities; to stand out, whether because of merit, mistakes, or eccentricity, is to risk attracting the gods' interest, which can easily result in a lightning strike, inadvertent or intended. Creativity and daring come from the bottom of the social ladder or are carefully hidden under blandness—in a time of cataclysmal change when tradition is no longer a sure guide. In the wake of the Great Catastrophe, innovation may be the only chance to adapt.

The Vidaar officially hold science and education in contempt, and chief of all their "soft" Elvorix brethren; but secretly, the more modern-minded—or corrupted, as hard-liners would say—suspect that this attitude will cost them dearly by preventing them from learning and spreading knowledge fast enough to survive the war and impending ice age. The Elvorix and the Vidaar have lost the knowledge of how to match our ancestors' creations.

The Jaarl are somewhat better off because their catastrophe is recent, but they have nonetheless lost their homeland and its stores of knowledge. They are isolated in a foreign land, fighting a war on three fronts and determinedly preparing for a new one which we have yet to identify...

The Kuld used to be timid and harmless creatures living in balance with the tundra, but scarcity, a metabolism tuned to gorging, and the encroachment of settlers have combined to turn them into nigh-unstoppable eating machines. Their locust-like consumption of ever-scarcer resources and relative tolerance for the cold may grant them the dubious prize of being the last faction to go extinct in the coming decades.

During my travels, I met a fascinating group of individuals from three separate factions—Rustica Bibulus, an Elvorix scholar; Iva the Stubborn, a Jaarl scholar (and her fawn, Kuri); and Ulf Long-Teeth, a Vidaar Bondee. With the aid of transcriber Bura Bibulus Ven Proudheart, I present to you excerpts of my interview.

Rustica (Elvorix scholar): "We have lost so much since the Vidaarus killed the scholars. Engineering, mathematics, architecture, science."

Iva (Jaarl scholar): "Art, thaumaturgy, even knowledge of the gods themselves."

Rustica: "Not thaumaturgy of course, since thaumaturgy is just a myth based around the Ancient science of alchemical transformation."

Iva: "We know of works on thaumaturgy by many of the great Ancient writers."

Rustica: "Pure confabulation."

Ulf (Vidaar Bondee): "Stop, please."

Rustica: "In any event, much has been forgotten, with only tantalizing hints left. Ruins of buildings we can't reproduce from stone we can no longer effectively quarry and cut. References in the works we have preserved to others that we have lost. Finding one of those might contain the information we need to understand the Cataclysm, or even reverse it. Perhaps we could finally solve the mystery of the Kuld—where they came from, where they went when we thought we had killed them all, why they came back."

Iva: "Seems far-fetched to me. If the Ancients had known how to eradicate the Kuld they would have done so."

Rustica: "You can't know that! Perhaps the task was never completed."

Iva: "Are you suggesting that idiot Vidaarus—"

Rustica: "Vidaar-OS."

Iva: "—Vidaar-US killed everyone BEFORE finishing with the Kuld?"

Ulf: "Stop, please."

Iva: "So naturally when we found hints of a pre-Cataclysm library containing all eight volumes of Homerus—"

Rustica: "Ho-MAR-os! He lived before the linguistic shift!"

Iva: "Don't start! We found hints of a library containing all eight volumes. It seemed worth a look."

Rustica: "Only two volumes are known to have survived the great burning and the intervening years. To have all eight books—"

Iva: "Volumes. They were scrolls really, since even your fancy Ancients hadn't figured out book binding yet."

Ulf: "By the aromatic whey of Akka-Maas, *please stop!*"

(Here the two subjects fell to bickering.)

Ulf: "Me, I've never read a book in my life and couldn't if I tried. But the pay was good, it sounded like something I could brag about, and it must be said that for all their faults the Ancients could put a wicked edge on an axe."

From interview notes for the volume "The Explorers," by Matia Bibulus. Transcribed by Bura Bibulus Ven Proudheart, 88 AGC.

"I like to think that we Elvorix are the true descendants and rightful heirs to the Ancients. We honor them and their achievements by attempting to emulate them. We strive for a balanced society— one in which art, craft, philosophy, labor, theosophy, and politics all operate in concert. Given time we will equal and perhaps even surpass the levels of learning and creativity the Ancients achieved. Our refinement, social grace, and wisdom are the greatest of Sentia. These things must be preserved and even improved upon, if civilization is to survive."

—Rustica Bibulus, Elvorix scholar

From interview notes for the volume "The Explorers," by Matia Bibulus. Transcribed by Bura Bibulus Ven Proudheart, 88 AGC.

Elvorix Society

The Elvorix are headed by a ruling council and a scholar-king. This government structure was founded by Elvora Bibulus, the priest who fooled King Vidaarus the Thirty-First and his warriors into leaving for the fabled island of Garigla.

Local administration falls under the authority of a *Houselord*. In descending order of prestige and authority, the administrative units include the Royal House, Noble Houses, Warrior Houses, Mercantile Houses, and Common Houses. Houses are generally named for their leaders; for example, House Sigurod is the Warrior House led by General Sigurod Gladius.

The principal occupations among the population are priest, scholar, soldier, merchant, farmer, and laborer. Farmers tend to crops of river-berries and various mosses, especially string-moss, which is a staple food, and barley-moss, from which potent kogg is brewed. Ylark cattle is raised for its meat and dairy, its use as a beast of burden and for riding, and its value as a sacrifice to the gods.

Metals like iron, copper, lead, silver, and gold are mined and smelted, although Elvorix smiths have so far been unable to create anything as strong or durable as the steel of the weapons that the Jaarl brought from Murmadon. Elvorix craftsmen and builders are capable, but originality and creativity are discouraged for fear of attracting divine attention. Masons build with stone and brick, but are unable to reproduce the splendid feats of architecture of the Ancients.

Religion

Agaptus means well.

—*Elvorix saying*

Elvorix priests have the dangerous job of channeling divine power and conciliating the unpredictable gods. Given the deities' history of dangerous attention, the Elvorix try to pay just enough homage to the gods to keep them contented and placid, but not so much that the gods will want to visit in person. This means building them temples that show devotion, but not so nice that the gods will want to personally inhabit them.

Receiving divine benevolence can be as dangerous to the faithful as to their enemies. No one has forgotten the catastrophic Great Harvest of 225 BGC, when Atronia's blessing caused the Elvorix granaries to overflow with the bounties of the land. Alas, the ensuing dirkus infestation, which in turn attracted packs of runnigum, triggered the appearance of roaming Marhn trolls. Almost equally well-known is the Naval Tragedy of 36 BGC, when the favor of Ilunus caused powerful winds to push back a flotilla of Vidaar raiders from the coast of southern Sentia, but also wrecked the Elvorix fishing fleet, dashed against the rocks.

The Elvorix pantheon includes sixteen or seventeen deities, depending on how you count the siblings of Agaptus, Lord of the Sky. Many of the archives destroyed during the Vidaarian Dynasty might have shed some light on who does what; as it is, it's always delicate business to get involved with gods. They can be easily offended when you, for example, confuse the patron deity of streams and rivers with the god of hygiene. Only a few are remembered with any certainty by name.

Some Known Gods of the Elvorix Pantheon

Agaptus: *Ruler Of The Sky And Stars.*

Atronia: *Tender To The Soil And Its Bounties Of Grain And Moss.*

Gailus: *Ruler Of The Great Herds Of Ylark That Wander Free Across The Plains.*

Ilunus: *God Of The Sea And Waves.*

Kuldarus: *Ruler Of The Underworld.*

Prolyus: *God Of War And Conquest.*

For more information about the Elvorix gods, see *"The Nebulous Elvorix Pantheon"* on page 248.

Because Agaptus in particular tends to accidentally (when in a good mood) or intentionally (when offended) singe his devotees when he appears, priests of the Lord of the Sky shave or even burn part or all of their hair away to give the appearance that they receive divine favor. Other lesser deities may impart a variety of marks on their followers.

Some would consider Kuldarus the "forgotten" seventeenth god of the pantheon, but perhaps she is just omitted because of her "uncomely visage" or inauspicious nature. In truth, although a few scholars have made it their specialty to study her lore, it is difficult to obtain any material from oral tradition since most Elvorix prefer to avoid even saying her name, for fear of attracting her attention.

You're In The Army Now, Bucky: Elvorix Ranks

Spearbucks: Part-time, conscript levies usually raised by local Houselords among farmer, merchant, and laborer classes, equipped with spears. Along with Linebucks, they form the bulk of Elvorix forces.

Linebucks: The more enthusiastic and dedicated portion of part-time levies raised by local Houselords, equipped with short swords and round wooden buckler shields.

Greybucks: Experienced Linebucks formed into elite veteran units.

Wildbucks: Volunteer units of Vorix skirmishers. Small but brave and known for their pugnaciousness and hit-and-run tactics.

Savagebucks: Veteran elite units of Wildbucks.

Captains: Career veterans who have attracted their Houselord's attention and received a promotion. Not necessarily an enviable position, since the upper echelons of Elvorix society try to avoid calling individual attention.

Generals: The relatively rare senior officers who lead entire Elvorix armies. Those who reach this rank make efforts to look innocuous and just competent enough to get by. They also surround themselves with advisors, sycophants, priests, specialists, and other attendants in the hopes that if the Lord of the Sky singles out somebody, it will be some poor fool among their entourage.

Musicians: Musicians are often found among the staff of generals and other dignitaries as a means of distracting the gods' attention. They also provide the cadence for marching units.

Standard Bearers: Standard bearers also serve as lightning rods to distract divine attention, but they are essential to coordinate and regroup units on the battlefield, and serve as signal corps.

Priests: The battle clergy serve as support, distraction, last-resort weapon, and moral inspiration for Elvorix forces. Most of their magic consists of convincing the troops that the gods bless their endeavors while avoiding actual divine attention. They are masters at interpreting anything as an omen.

Ylark Handlers: Ylark are used on the battlefield as cavalry, beasts of burden, living weapons, and sacrifice to Agaptus. Linebucks tend to the poor beasts until those selected as sacrifice are set on fire by the battle priests and sent stampeding towards enemy lines in rage and agony.

People

The Elvorix are hardy, warm-blooded, fur-bearing, bipedal, placental mammals; like their cousins the Vidaar (but unlike the Jaarl or Kuld) they are equipped with opposable thumbs and four fingers.

With a gestation period of about five months, the does rarely bear more than one fawn at a time, giving birth to live young, whom they will nurse for three to six months. Metabolically, they are efficient omnivores who can gain sustenance from food of low energetic value, making them relatively resistant to starvation.

Their average life span is about sixty years but under good conditions can reach several decades more. Although Elvorix lineages are able to cross-breed (this author is one such example of mixed Elvorix and Vidaar blood), they have developed some distinctive characteristics. Overall Elvorix population is estimated at fourteen million.

Atronians: Elvorix from the southern regions of Sentia represent the oldest lineages in the land. Some of the more common fur colors include the "Atronian blue," which isn't blue really but a cool grey, typically quite soft and thick in texture, and a white or white-grey blend. These pale tones contribute to some of the difficulty in proving intermixing with the nearby Vidaar, who also tend towards pale fur.

Highborn: Elvorix whose blood lines have remained "pure" since the Great Deception and the departure of Elvora Bibulus and his warriors nearly 900 years ago refer to themselves as "Highborn." They tend towards auburn colorings, ringstraked with lighter tans and whites. Other Highborn varieties include a darker chestnut color, and ruddier earthen tones. Those who sport such colors often claim to trace their lineage to Sentius himself, regardless of the state of their family tree. Conversely, those with impeccable ancestry but unfashionable coloring may help nature along with some discreetly purchased fur dye.

Northerners: The Elvorix from the northern regions, toward the cities of Syradon and Tsoria that have fallen to the gluttonous Kuld. Their fur tends to more mottled and marbled coloring, blends of browns, black, and greys, which are considered unattractive by Noble Elvorix. They often form the rank and file of the military front lines since they have lost their homelands, trade, and heritage.

Vorix: The diminutive and often belittled strain of Sentians of very short stature. Born from every known rank in society at a rate of about one in ten live births, they do not breed true. They are, in general, more prone to arthritis, asthma, and heart failure, but tend to show bravery and resourcefulness. Because they suffer from disdain, derision, and abuse due their size, most of them tend to forsake their House and congregate in loose but loyal Vorix Clans.

"The Elvorix are weak, disorganized, and impractical. They're also smug and self-satisfied about it. They act like there's nothing better in the world than spending hour after hour talking about some dull, obscure topic, and then bragging to everyone afterwards that they did. Always going on about 'the Ancients' this and 'the gods' that. They spend so much time learning how to read and write that they barely know which end of a spear to point."
—Ulf Long-Teeth, Vidaar Bondee

From interview notes for the volume "The Explorers," by Matia Bibulus. Transcribed by Bura Bibulus Ven Proudheart, 88 AGC.

Names

Most Elvorix use the following naming convention:
[Title] [Personal name] [Occupation name] ix [City of origin] co [Adopted city of residence]

Children's occupation name is simply "Parvulus"; upon reaching adulthood, a doe or buck picks a profession and takes a new occupation name to indicate it.

Highborn Elvorix make more of a fuss about these conventions and favor fashionable names ending in -us or -a. Northerners tend to use harsher names with more consonants. Commoners usually go by their given name only, and sometimes add a nickname or "son of" or "daughter of" a parent to help distinguish them from other Elvorix with similar names, or connect themselves to a well-known parent's reputation.

Vorix clan members are the exception; they have more attachment to clan than profession or House, reflected in their names:
[Title] [Personal name] [Clan name]

However, they are often called only by their personal names except in formal circumstances.

Sample Names
Occupation names: Aedituus (priest), Agrius (farmer), Bibulus (scholar), Gladius (soldier), Nummus (merchant), Parvulus (child), Usus (laborer).

Personal names: Aart, Aguros, Atronia, Baseros, Biblius, Bluum, Brojan, Brutilus, Caperna, Elani, Elantrix, Elvora, Elwo, Evrard, Ficca, Flautul, Garigla, Gicca, Ggorll, Hlarn, Homarus, Huudos, Hyllva, Ilunas, Kalamus, Killim, Kiptus, Kiriko, Kkahl, Lilia, Lukkus, Maladros, Matia, Mauro, Mearios, Monru, Naril, Nyllo, Orvas, Pallo, Rogus, Seadros, Semela, Sentius, Sigurod, Tera, Tomlin, Toranus, Torvus, Ven, Wiccar, Yladuur.

Vorix Clan Names: Arrowflight, Deathsong, Proudheart, Quickstrike, Shadowstep, Two-Blades.

Individuals of Note
Lord Maladros Bibulus ix Agapta co Agapta: *Scholar King of Agapta, Lord of the Elvorix*.

Seadros Bibulus ix Atronius: *Scribe to Lord Maladros*.

Homarus, son of Rogus: *Painter to Lord Maladros*.

General Sigurod Gladius: *General of the Northern Provincial Garrison*.

For more details on individuals of note, see *"Gamemaster Characters"* on page 99.

Discretion as the Better Part of Valor?

"Wear too big a hat, put too many fancy titles before your name, and soon enough, the Lord of the Sky is going to notice you, and quite frankly, nobody needs that."

—Elvorix proverb

Something one must understand about Sentia: blandness is cultivated among Elvorix political and religious leaders in order to avoid Agaptus' attention, so mavericks and eccentrics are more common among the lower classes (to wit, the Wildbucks), and the leaders exemplify golden mediocrity. But the truly ambitious and crafty seem entirely innocuous; they are the advisors, clerks, assistants, and paper-pushers.

The lowly among the Elvorix are not necessarily in tune with the Highborn, especially those from areas where there has been a lot of mingling with returning Vidaar in the last 200 years. When you're already unimportant and overlooked, you can afford a little more independence and eccentricity.

"Viewing Elvorix society is like looking at a reflection of our own, but through a distorted mirror. Clearly at one point the Elvorix had a society and a level of learning similar to what we Jaarl had before the Cataclysm. But it was destroyed, not by some outside catastrophe, but by their own short-sightedness and greed. Now they spend their time digging through the rubble of their former glory and pretending to be heirs to a lost civilization, when really in their own way they have fallen as far into barbarism and ignorance as their Vidaar cousins."
—Iva the Stubborn, Jaarl scholar

From interview notes for the volume "The Explorers," by Matia Bibulus. Transcribed by Bura Bibulus Ven Proudheart, 88 AGC.

Places

In the Cities

Agapta, the capital of the Elvorix Empire, is still full of marvels, though every year they fall deeper into disrepair. Other important cities still in Elvorix control include Atronia in the southern part of the Isle of Sentia, threatened by the Vidaar; and Prolyus on the Lycian Isthmus in the southeast, pinched between Vidaar and Jaarl forces. Cities of importance are generally named for a patron deity and boast a major temple to that god.

Elvorix cities are a mixture of grandiose, unequaled building feats of the Ancients, classic Post-Deception Restoration architecture, and partly repaired war damage from the recent years of conflict.

What you can find there:

Official buildings of the Administratum, the anonymous bureaucracy that makes the wheels of Agapta turn round.

Schools, academies, and libraries dedicated to preserving and restoring the fragments of knowledge saved from the destruction wrought under Vidaarian Dynasty rule.

Major temples to the patron deity, such as the Temple of Agaptus in Agapta.

Shops, merchant houses, workshops, markets, counting houses, warehouses, and other centers of trade and business.

Harbors and river-based or sea-based ship traffic.

Wonders of Ancient engineering like aqueducts, sewers, roads, bridges, and public buildings—when they still stand. They work marvelously until the day they collapse.

Mansions and palaces of the Highborn.

Dwellings of the common city folk.

Derelict tenements and slums where refugees from war-torn areas hide, at the periphery of cities.

Market day in the city. So many ways to get lost, noticed, rich, cheated, beaten up, or meet that special someone...

Things that can happen:

What's All This, Then? It's all too easy to get in trouble with the Town Watch. A shriek is heard in streets—"My coin purse!"—and now the town guards are looking to you; Captain Tera Gladius has just lost a thief in the streets that looks like one of the heroes.

What Is It About Sewers? There are rumors of strange goings-on under the streets, odd noises and unexplained disappearances at night. You hear there is a monster hidden in the sewer tunnels, with its cherished treasure. The question is whether the monster and the treasure are what you think.

I Want to Be Just Like You! The heroes stumble onto an orphan, a refugee from one of the war-torn areas, and the urchin develops hero-worship for one or more of them (perhaps for the wrong reasons). But now there is a whole band of such urchins, and the heroes' new fan has pledged to find them all a new home…

Milk Run. Ylark milk has become a recent fad among sophisticated city dwellers, and it's selling like mad today. Pavia Nummus has hired the heroes to fetch more barrels from the ice house where the ylark milk was stored last night and bring to her stand in the busy marketplace. The barrels must reach her before her current supplies run out—and intact, please! Don't let a competitor steal them.

We've listed some story seeds in the forms of aspects in the *"Things that can happen"* section after each setting location. Aspects are explained more in *"Aspects and Fate Points"* on page 190.

Some of the story seeds are more detailed and fleshed; others are sketches or outlines you can adapt to your own story when you need to improvise a plot complication.

Elvora Bibulus Academy

The legendary Elvora Bibulus founded a school in Agaptus on the grounds of the Agaptan academy that had been burned by Vidaarus the First so many centuries earlier. In fact, he founded such academies throughout the land, but the one in Agapta is the most influential. A diploma from the Elvora Bibulus Academy guarantees a long and uneventful career in the middle ranks of the Administratum.

To excel academically, one must embrace conformity and stick close to the norm; students are reprimanded for doing anything too "noticeable" or "interesting," which would run the risk of attracting divine attention.

Those who go against the grain may, for example, be sent away on long research expeditions…

What you can find there:

Amphitheaters filled with students coached to learn by rote the basics of administration, bureaucracy, literature, history, geography, arithmetic, architecture, divination, herbalism, and theology.

Entire walls of scroll cabinets, filled with rolls of brittle documents identified by colored tassels.

Copying rooms where one elderly scholar reads a text and groups of students transcribe the dictation.

Cubicles where artists-in-residence illustrate and illuminate particularly valuable scrolls, copying as exactly as possible an older manuscript.

The vaults deep underground where the rarest and most valuable original scrolls are kept hidden.

Copies of the latest bestsellers, such as Nyllo Bibulus ix Atronia co Agapta's *They Came From the Deeps: The Jaarl Invasion and What It Means To You*, and Tera Bibulus' *Compendium of Agaptan Gods: Their Roles and History in Sentia and Its Surrounding Provinces*.

Things that can happen:

A Contract Is A Contract, And The Rules Are The Rules. Buried among the paperwork in the Academy's library is a prestigious marriage contract. A few years ago, Old King Baseros and General Vidaarus the Ninetieth had agreed to unite their families through a marriage alliance shortly before the disaster now called Orvas' Folly; unfortunately, a lot of the principals died at the battle or since then. Nevertheless, after much arguing, scholars have reached a consensus of sorts: this was a sacred oath and the contract must be honored, which means finding marriageable candidates of each family line and getting them blissfully united. If not, the school will legally change hands to General Vidaarus, who is coincidentally looking for space to build an elaborate obstacle course for new recruits.

It's My Own Design. One of the scholars, Marinax Bibulus, has taken the duty to preserve and reconstruct archives far too much to heart; by cross-referencing several sources and filling in the blanks, Marinax has produced actual original thought and even invention… The heroes are hired to keep watch on him while he finishes his current project without letting any catastrophes unfold, then whisk him away to a less prominent location with fewer bystanders.

Oh, That Old Thing? Who knows what marvels of Ancient knowledge have yet to be rediscovered among the dusty scrolls curated by fusty old Nilf Bibulus the Elder? The recipe for an indelible dye or a super glue, the detailed map of a lost city, the schematics for a better type of ship, the secrets to celestial mechanics…

Heretical Knowledge. A long-lost, rediscovered manuscript gives the names and domains of the entire Elvorix pantheon. There are many surprises, and every sect is likely to cry heresy. On the plus side, the manuscript also provides the locations of temples long-forgotten where daring heroes might seek divine help.

Temple of Agaptus

The temple of Agaptus was badly damaged at the onset of the Great
Catastrophe, and to this day no one has had the courage to rebuild it.
The god left in a decidedly bad mood, and nobody wants to attract his
attention, so the priesthood is dragging its collective feet about it. Damned
if one does, damned if one doesn't: if Agaptus is not satisfied with the
result, things will get ugly, but if he's pleased, he might decide to visit
more often. So the thing to do, it was decided, is to look busy and make a
convincing show of working on the repairs—without finishing. Eventually,
Agaptus may figure it out...

Until then, the half-ruined temple is used for devotions and rituals. Like
all Elvorix temples, it is decorated in garish, eye-stabbing colors and
bathed in fumes of putrid incense to make sure Agaptus doesn't feel like
visiting too often. As a result, no one but the clergy feels much like visiting
either.

What you can find there:
Untidy piles of stone, timbers, bricks, pitch, and other building materials, slowly degraded by the elements.

Detour signs, scaffolding, pulleys, and all the signs of a major construction site—well-worn and discolored by time.

Barricaded, rickety wings of the temple, barely standing.

Foul-smelling fumes, discordant singing, hideous murals depicting scenes of Elvorix history.

A priesthood where success is based on attracting as little attention as possible and appearing mediocre and forgettable.

The secret passion of a few intellectuals for knowledge and books, disguised as blandness.

Things that can happen:
Still Working On It! The priesthood of Agaptus must find a way to prolong the rebuilding of the temple without angering the god any further. Guess who the task gets delegated to? The heroes must find a solution; will they sabotage the rebuilding and risk getting caught? Will they go questing for rare or even nonexistent materials in the perilous lands of Agaptus?

Uh, Skip A Bit, Brother... One of the younger clerics and member of the royal family is showing dangerous religious zeal for the cult of Agaptus: Sibili Bibulus ix Agapta wants to propitiate the god and gain divine forgiveness for the events of the Great Catastrophe. Barring this, Sibili claims, ice will eventually cover all of Sentia—and unfortunately, people are beginning to listen. *Someone* has to babysit this troublemaker and make sure nothing interesting happens.

I'm Averting My Eyes, O Lord! Agaptus appears to the unlucky heroes and gives them a message they must carry very exactly; alas, it came out a little garbled through the mask the god was wearing to avoid smelling the foul incense. Why them? How do they fulfill his divine will? Or is it some other god posing as Agaptus, out to recruit a new following?

Divine Conciliation. Misfiled in the temple archives is a very nice BGC-era scroll that details a ritual for appeasing the wrath of Agaptus. That's good, right?

Out in the Country

In addition to interview transcriptions I also cite the "descriptions" of a seemingly non-aggressive Kuld being studied at the Bibulus Academy. Referred to as "Mossback" by scholars here, the creature has learned to understand Elvorish. Its replies are listed as descriptions of the smells it emitted when asked questions about the various races.

Burned paper/dust/wine/grass. Breath of an infant. Broken stone.
—"Mossback," Kuld research subject, describing the Elvorix.

From interview notes for the volume "The Explorers," by Matia Bibulus. Transcribed by Bura Bibulus Ven Proudheart, 88 AGC.

Small Town

Examples of small Elvorix towns vary from the coastal town of Sorilyia, the frontier town of Snareham; to Gowanna, proudly resisting invasion on the Lycian Peninsula; and sadly, to the cities of Syradon and Tsoria in the north, both now fallen to the Kuld.

These towns are well-built, if not equal to the marvels of the Ancients, as comfortable and sensible as they can be given the decades of warfare, the rapid cooling of the climate, and the whims of meddlesome deities. They are typically surrounded by farms where mosses and berries are cultivated and ylark are raised. Coastal towns will also boast small fishing fleets and a modest harbor.

What you can find there:

Fortifications, more or less well-tended depending on how frequent invasions are in the region.

City hall, with its large but quiet administrative bureaucracy.

The Town Watch building, with space for mustering, ylark stables, watch towers, and barracks.

Shops, usually with the owners' living quarters in the back or on the upper floors.

A central plaza, park, or assembly area for speeches.

Market day once or twice a week.

Fire brigade hall, situated midway between the town center and the temple.

A small local temple set well away to the outside edge of town, far from anything valuable.

The estates of one or more Houselords, depending on how important the town is and how quiet or dangerous the surroundings are.

Things that can happen:

Congratulations on Your Wedding Day! Thanks to an arranged marriage between two Houses, agreed upon over a decade ago, one of the heroes gets blessed, lured, or roped (depending on who you ask) into matrimony. Surely nothing bad could happen on such an auspicious day,! Will the hero manage to escape this fate without creating disaster between the Houses and alienating the entire clan? Will the hero unexpectedly fall in love with the spouse-to-be?

The Seven Savagebucks. A village of farmers hires the heroes to combat Vidaar bandits who have threatened to return after the string-moss harvest to steal their crops.

Recovery Mission. The Shimmering Stone of Gailus, which tells where the wild ylark herds will migrate this year, must be recovered from Bluemossford, a village that fell to the Kuld some time ago. Once they had eaten everything they could swallow, the blubbers probably moved on so the trip should be relatively safe, right? Did we mention that this is really, really important?

Frontier Village

Out in the cold, on the edge of ever-advancing tundra, the inhabitants are more hardened but also take their responsibilities seriously. If they have refused to move to warmer climes and safer towns, it's because something keeps them here: ties to their ancestral lands or their community, duty to protect the rest of Agaptus from invaders, or love for family members or friends who refuse to leave.

Life used to be decent here, but now it's harsh and only the stubborn and the brave make it. The growing season is very short and grows shorter every year, so spring and summer mean a few months of back-breaking work and vigilance. The long winter months are spent teaching the fawns, crafting goods that will be needed next harvest, repairing weapons and equipment, and telling stories.

Paradoxically, winter can also be the best time to visit friends in neighboring villages; although snow covers the roads, in fair weather skis, snowshoes, sleds, and ylark-pulled sleighs make for quicker travel. But beware storms and avalanches in the high mountain passes.

What you can find there:
Rudimentary accommodations by Elvorix standards, but well-insulated.

Caches of food and equipment in caves or underground warehouses.

Rugged, stoic inhabitants.

Small but vigilant militia and scout units watching for enemy advances and ready to bring the alarm to neighboring villages.

Fire-tower and bell, used to send warnings.

Things that can happen:
Winter Games. The village holds annual games and neighbors come from all over the region to compete in cooking, singing, story-telling, wrestling, archery, sled races, and ylark fights.

Fire! When you live so close to the edge of destitution, a fire is even deadlier than usual. The village resources are devastated and the survivors will face starvation. Only the heroes can help the surviving villagers. Will they bring food back? Get help from distant hamlets? Organize the refugees to move to a new spot?

Night Hauntings. Strange lights are sometimes seen and noises heard at night around the village. Is it enemy scout activity, an illicit romance between a villager and a Vidaar from across the lines, or something more mysterious?

Blessing the Newborn. The village is too small to have its own priest. Upon discovering that one of the heroes is one, the villagers are insistent that the fawn who was just born last night should receive a proper blessing.

Ylark Farm

Elvorix use the mighty ylark for their milk and meat, as beasts of burden and riding animals, and as fiery sacrifices to Agaptus, Lord of the Sky. The portions of the countryside that still have a temperate enough climate to support agriculture are dotted with ylark farms. Naturally, in recent decades farmers have tried to develop hardier breeds that can withstand colder conditions. The closer to a disputed border such farms are, the more heavily they are defended by the local militia or levies, since Vidaar make heavy use of ylark meat and dairy products and Kuld are fond of devouring the beasts whole.

What you can find there:

Pasture land, often enclosed by low walls of piled up stones to prevent the cattle from straying too far.

Stables to keep the ylark at night in summer and pretty much all the time in winter.

Fodder storage.

Piles of ylark manure, collected to trade to neighboring farmers for forage.

Farm house and other farm buildings arranged to provide modest defense in case of attack.

A bell tower to ring for alarm or to call in the animals.

Things that can happen:
Cattle Drive. The farm was raided by the Kuld while the ylark were out on the pasture; now the surviving Elvorix must round up the cattle and drive it to some refuge such as a neighboring farm or town, or some caves that can offer shelter during the cold months, before winter sets in.

Border Traffic. Someone in the village is stealing ylark milk to trade across the border into Vidaar-occupied territory. Even though they were conquered, the people on the other side are still family—how could the thief refuse to help them?

Prize Animal. The farm has been breeding a particularly excellent or useful type of ylark, one that is amazingly frugal and resistant to cold and expected to make the fortune of the House. But according to the local priest, the animal also bears markings that designate it as a necessary sacrifice to Agaptus—nay, one that it would be *dangerous* to refuse to the god. Now everyone wants the beast!

Rural Shrine

Small shrines to Agaptus or one of the other gods can be found dotting the landscape in the most unexpected places, usually some place that was struck by ill fortune at some point, leaving the inhabitants eager to propitiate the deities and avert further bad luck. Some are old enough to go back to the Ancient themselves, other may have cropped up in recent years. They are lavishly tended when the locals feel the need to appease the gods, modestly when all they want to avoid divine notice, but never completely abandoned as long as there are still Elvorix living or passing nearby.

What you can find there:
Piles of stones forming an altar, in various states of repair.

Signs of burning, lightning strikes, avalanche, flooding, and other disasters.

Offerings to the god the shrine honors.

Pilgrims furtively offering devotions, then hurrying away.

Things that can happen:

Sacrifice—Or Else. Things go from bad to worse for the traveling heroes, disaster follows calamity, until they come to an untended roadside altar. Will restoring the altar to its former glory appease the god? Will the god continue to pay attention to the heroes?

Wrong God! Wrong God! Sacrifices were made, but unfortunately, the wrong god was invoked. The angry deity left some mark of displeasure, which must now be correctly interpreted and the right sacrifice must be made to avoid further anger.

But I Need It! Someone left an offering to the gods at a roadside shrine and it is *exactly* what the heroes badly need right now. A moral dilemma, to be sure.

"Pray to one if needful, but donate to all alike."

—*Elvorix proverb*

The Savage Vidaar

"The Vidaar are the true rulers of Sentia, by reason of our strength, our martial skill, and our loyalty to our king and clans. We don't spend our time endlessly debating and discussing and planning—Vidaar are doers! Others may brag about their achievements, but we travelled the world in our ancestral ships for centuries before returning home. During that time we learned what is important and what is dross. Loyalty, bravery, a strong arm, and a trusted shield-mate—these are the things that matter. Reading, writing, figuring, and—most worthless of all—the ability to talk for hours about nothing—these things only make you weak."
—Ulf Long-Teeth, Vidaar Bondee

From interview notes for the volume "The Explorers," by Matia Bibulus. Transcribed by Bura Bibulus Ven Proudheart, 88 AGC.

Vidaar Society

Vidaar leadership is martial and authoritarian, based on a leader's ability to impose one's will on others. At the top is the king, General Vidaarus the Ninety-First, and his most trusted retainers; first among these are the Dowodik, generals who command entire armies. They in turn command lower-level chieftains, all the way down to the lowest Bondee. However, this chain of command is frequently disrupted as ascendant leaders challenge their superiors for position, or when the king decides to pit one Dowodik against another rather than allow them to get too ambitious.

Vidaar rally around clans that are named for things that sound impressive. The most important and powerful are Chieftain Clans, whose armies are commanded by a Dowodik. Below them are Skeppare Clans, who supply troops headed by a Styrsik commander and oversee the common clans, usually named for weapons, tools, or other things that hurt: Axe Clan, Shield Clan, Anvil Clan, Vise Clan, Hammer Clan, etc.

The Vidaar have no written records and in fact no writing system; any building and crafting traditions they have were laboriously reconstructed, first for ship-building and sailing, then later for the land-bound skills they needed when they returned to Matriga and Sentia. They are still quite clumsy compared to the Elvorix. To further slow the march of progress, the contempt they hold for "Bookworms" makes any efforts to imitate Elvorix techniques a cause of derision among Vidaar society.

Buildings are constructed primarily of wood, mud, and thatch; masonry is very rare and often not successful. However, security is a primary consideration and Vidaar settlements, from small war camps to their largest cities, are always remarkably defensible. Vidaar builders use the terrain to conceal and protect the dwellings, so villages are often hidden in caves, perched on hills with unimpeded view of the surroundings, or nestled against strong cliffs.

Food-growing is a necessary chore, kogg-brewing is an honored tradition, and ylark are raised for their dairy and meat. Whenever they can, Vidaar love raiding Elvorix supplies, but that's not enough. In conquered areas where Vidaar and Elvorix have mixed rather thoroughly, there is a little more interest and skill brought to food-growing, and some instances of very, very discreet trade with Elvorix populations, especially with more rural Atronian villages.

Vidaar weapon-crafting, however, is nothing to sneeze at. While they are no match for Jaarl steel, they can make good swords and axes that keep an edge as well as any Elvorix weapon. However, lazier or more inept smiths will invariably do shoddy work.

The art of ship-building has been maintained and even improved since landing on Iradon in 95 BGC. Vidaar mastery of the seas gave them an advantage over their Elvorix and Kuld foes, although the arrival of the Jaarl about 75 years ago dented that superiority. But the Vidaar have many more ships and sailors than the Jaarl at the moment, and they plan on keeping that edge.

Trade amongst the Vidaar is lively; fishing villages smoke their meat and deliver it to the armies, while cloth, an ever-needed commodity in these frigid times, comes from the central Matrigan villages. Such cloth is made from processed natural fibers, like hair-tree bark, cheapest and flimsiest; silk-moss, finer and much prized by persons of stature; or ylark wool, coarse but warm.

Religion

The Vidaar recognize only one god, which they call Akka-Maas—a corruption of Agaptus. Why all the other gods were abandoned, no one is quite sure; the Vidaar keep no written records and the fidelity of their oral traditions is tenuous. Mentioning any god but Akka-Maas the Only God is considered blasphemy, which tends to cut short any historical research.

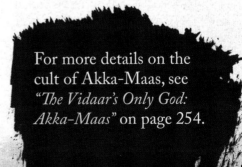

Acolytes perform divinations using *tyromancy*, the art of reading the future by examining ylark cheese. The pungent cheese doubles as a holy weapon when the catapults of Akka-Maas lob it across enemy lines.

Ceremonies involve dancing (bordering on gyrating, this author must frankly note) to rhythmic music; as a result, priests of Akka-Maas tend to dress lightly. This has given the rise to unsavory speculations among the polytheist Elvorix, usually represented by the myth of exotic, promiscuous, scantily clad priestesses. The Vidaar may be as wary of Akka-Maas as the Elvorix are of Agaptus and other gods, but becoming a priest is a sign of great bravery and therefore much admired—often from a safe distance.

There are indeed many does among the clergy, and the "High Priest" is in fact a priestess—the title is not gendered.

For more details on the cult of Akka-Maas, see *"The Vidaar's Only God: Akka-Maas"* on page 254.

We Want You As A New Recruit: Vidaar Ranks

Bondee: The most common type of Vidaar troop, armed with axe and rectangular wooden shield. Each Vidaar ship carries a complement of Bondee.

Fyrdee: The Fyrdee are used as occupying forces when the Vidaar intend to stay. They are equipped with long spears that are too unwieldy for use aboard ships.

Ceoree: Skirmisher troops used as scouts and diversion; even among Vidaar forces they have a reputation for being ornery and unruly. Equipped with a variety of melee weapons.

Ulfryee: Berserker troops, used as deadly but undisciplined shock troops in melee. Equipped with heavy two-handed melee weapons.

Lunghshyld: The shieldwall troops *par excellence*, Lunghshyld are equipped with axes and heavy, oversized rectangular wooden shields. Their advance is slower than the Bondee, but almost inexorable.

Nhilde Trolls: These gigantic creatures, easily twice as tall as any Sentian and enormously strong, are used as shock troops by the Vidaar. They are armed with massive stone hammers or poleaxes.

Udvlag: The battle priests of Akka-Maas who use arcane magic and divination based on pestilential ylark cheese to influence the tide of battle and rouse the spirits of Vidaar warriors.

Totember: The carrier of the Vidaar commanders' and clans' battle standards, around whom the warriors rally in combat.

Tromik: The Tromik play a musical instrument (or wield it as a weapon, according to mood), to send messages to other units, provide cadence for marching forces, or entertain officers.

Styrsik: Experienced and savage battle commanders who lead Vidaar troops. Unfortunately an unpopular promotion, as it requires spending more time explaining what you need done and yelling at troops, and less time engaging the enemy in glorious hand-to-hand battle.

Dowodik: The higher, the fewer. Requires even more talking and less fighting than the job of Styrsik, and excelling at it may result in making King Vidaarus suspicious of you, so this honor is avoided as far as possible.

People

Physiologically, the Vidaar are very similar to the Elvorix, though they exhibit a prominently jutting lower jaw. Because of their centuries-long isolation, they suffered from in-breeding by the time they returned to Iradon, but the last two centuries of cross-breeding with Elvorix have vastly increased diversity as well as population (now estimated at ten million). This author must note that she herself is of mixed blood, and can attest that inbreeding among the Vidaar is now a historical footnote, perhaps exaggerated by the less informed or more nationalistic among our scholars.

Ghost-Furs: These albino Vidaar exhibit pale white fur with a faint yellowish hue, accompanied by blood-red eyes. This trait appears to breed true; those albinos who breed with others of the same coloration have strictly albino children. However, Ghost-Furs can be born to regularly colored parents, though they tend to appear more often in certain bloodlines. Priests of Akka-Maas consider Ghost-Furs to be holy or chosen.

Sea-Leggers: These traditionalist Vidaar are proud seafarers and show a measure of disdain for land-lubbers. For them, a Vidaar's place is on the high seas, pursuing a Jaarl galley, attacking an Elvorix coastal city, or invading a new island to kill its monsters and pillage its treasures. They spend most of their life on an ancestral Vidaar ship, carrying on this fine tradition, though even the most old-fashioned now think of one port or another as "home" when they get maudlin.

Half-Breeds: Like their counterparts in Agaptus, half-Elvorix Sentians bear traits from both ancestries, though the jutting jaw is a feature that always seems to pass down if there is any significant amount of Vidaar blood in either parent. The infusion of new Elvorix blood and varying exposure to Elvorix culture seem to leave these Sentians less impulsive and aggressive, more centered on their local community, and more willing to learn from thinking and experimentation rather than from the hard knocks and traditions of their chiefs. Many Vidaar now can claim at least one recent Elvorix ancestor, but generally forget to mention it. Half-Breeds who either can't or won't hide their mixed heritage tend to be given the most obnoxious chores and the roughest treatment.

Late-Comers: Not all the Vidaar ships arrived together; some showed up generations after the landing on Iradon of 95 BGC. Those who arrived later often maintain a culture somewhat distinct from the bulk of Vidaar society, and are referred to as Late-Comers, though they have a multitude of names for themselves, often based on the name of their flagship or Styrsik at landfall. For example, the Kruakans are those who claimed that their ancestors, led by Styrsik Kruaka, got delayed on the fourth Island-That-Wasn't-Garigla when they fought a rear-guard action against the giant killer birds that inhabited the island, allowing the rest of the fleet to leave. The Vyggorans arrived on the ancestor ship Vyggori after clearing a group of Islands-That-Weren't-Garigla far to the south-southwest of Matriga and brought back a number of strange customs, weird drinks, and strange musical instruments. Late-Comer clans are usually very tight-knit and don't easily share details of their customs with other Vidaar, but are only loosely allied with other Late-Comer clans.

"Lovely it is, when the winds are churning up the waves on the great sea, to gaze from the prow on the great efforts of someone else which you can then proceed to plunder."

—*Captain Venks "Ghostie" of the Black Raiders*

"Uncouth, undisciplined, and warlike. They build little and spend most of their time fighting, getting drunk, fighting, bragging about getting drunk, fighting, and stealing so that they can afford to get drunk. Also, they fight a lot. Really there is little to say about them because there is so little to their society that it barely needs to be mentioned at all. Everything you need to know about them can be summed up in the fact that they worship their silly god using a particularly repugnant sort of cheese and consider books to be useful primarily for starting fires."—Iva the Stubborn, Jaarl scholar

From interview notes for the volume "The Explorers," by Matia Bibulus. Transcribed by Bura Bibulus Ven Proudheart, 88 AGC.

Names

The Vidaar are pretty simple and consistent in their naming practices. They like a name that sounds fierce and is not too complicated to remember. Noteworthy individuals may earn a nickname, or if there are too many Vaads to keep them straight, one might be known as Vaad of the Green Raiders, another as Vaad son of Krula, and a third as Vaad the Ugly. A prestigious clan name may also be mentioned; clans are usually named for things that are scary or painful.
[Title] [Personal Name] [Possible Nickname] [Possible Clan Name]

Sample Names
Personal Names: Aenwubba, Blagaard, Forlad, Gholas, Gubba, Kraka, Krula, Nhilde, Offrus, Ragnhild, Sverra, Tahrynn, Ulryg, Vaad, Vaett, Valeran, Vendela, Venks, Vidaarus, Vigdis, Villd, Volo, Vulgg, Ylwa.

Clan Names: Black Raiders, Death Singers, Piercing Lances, Red Hammers, Skull Crushers, Wave Riders, White Wights.

Individuals of Note

General Vidaarus: *Ninety-First King of the Vidaar*.

Dowodik Aenwubba: *Chieftain of the Rabble Clans and their Fleet of Raiders*.

Ragnhild the Fair: *High Priest of Akka-Maas*.

Ulryg of the Death Singers: *Moody Albino Warrior*.

For more details on individuals of note, see *"Gamemaster Characters"* on

Hot iron and old leather. Alcohol and vomit. Horrible, cheesy stench—nearly overpowering. Blood.—"Mossback," Kuld research subject, describing the Vidaar.

From interview notes for the volume "The Explorers," by Matia Bibulus. Transcribed by Bura Bibulus Ven Proudheart, 88 AGC.

Places

Cities

Examples of great cities include Vidaara, the capital, perhaps the only major city actually built by the Vidaar rather than just occupied, and cities captured from the Elvorix, such as Ilunus. Most large Vidaar cities lie on the island of Matriga, the more fertile and temperate part of the territory they control.

A city captured and settled by the Vidaar is reinforced and turned into a fortress. A city *built* by the Vidaar is an ugly thing indeed, but its position is easy to defend with a handful of Fyrdee; its moats are steep, and its walls and approaches bristle with spikes and defenses. For example, Vidaara is seated onto a very narrow platform of rock above the turbulent White Sea. All noteworthy Vidaar settlements are located on the coast or up a navigable river.

What you can find there:

City garrison and its quarters.

Well-defended harbor and its raider fleet.

Luxury quarters for important individuals such as clan heads and Dowodiks.

Dwellings of conquered Elvorix and mixed-blood population.

Shops and markets offering limited goods and food.

Warehouses and caches of goods brought back by Vidaar raids.

Ancient and Elvorix structures falling into disrepair because they are not part of the defenses, or even mined for rock.

Things that can happen:

Kogg Festival! It's the celebrated Koggtoberfest in the city! There will be many libations in honor of Akka-Maas, pungent cheeses will be read or consumed, and the day will end with glorious fireworks (assuming they haven't been lost or tampered with). If the city does not burn down, tomorrow is known as Hangover Day.

You're in the Wrong Neighborhood, Bucko. It's easy enough for Vidaar to get into fights on the best of days, but things get downright volatile if a Half-Breed wanders into a more traditional neighborhood or a Sea-Legger questions the valor of a Late-Comer's ancestors.

Harbor in the Storm. A terrible storm, complete with sleet, high winds, and freak lightning, is raking the region. The seas are dangerously choppy and the harbor is the only refuge, but now even that harbor is a danger as the ships are being smashed together. Can the heroes make it to safety? Can they save other ships from being smashed to splinters? Can they rescue drowning sailors?

Hall of the Warrior King

Built by, and dedicated to, General Vidaarus the Eighty-Third, who began the re-conquest of Sentia nearly two hundred years ago and founded the imaginatively named city of Vidaara. This drafty but impressive, unwelcoming but well-defended building still serves as the King's palace. Its location atop a hill overlooking both the city and the surroundings makes it impossible for an army to seize it by surprise.

What you can find there:
The Throne Room, lavishly and garishly decorated, with a large carved chair atop an imposing dais, and benches along the sides for dignitaries to sit on.

The armory, kept under guard, which serves both to display the weapons of the Royal Clan and to arm the guards in case of attack.

Large, busy kitchens with huge ovens in which whole ylarks are roasted for royal feasts.

The Royal Clan members' private apartments, all with their own secret defenses since attrition among potential heirs is both frequent and brutal.

The Treasure Room, where the nicest, shiniest pieces pillaged by Vidaar Kings over the centuries are kept safe for private viewing by the King.

Things that can happen:
Secret Assassination Plot. Chieftains and courtiers are always trying to eliminate rivals, real and imagined. When single combat is not a practical option, an accidental fall from a high window will serve. The heroes may be targets, hirelings, or scapegoats.

A Royal Pain in the Butt. The heroes are assigned to guard, protect, serve, and otherwise fetch and carry for one of the king's currently favorite fawns. Naturally, not everyone wants the little twerp in good health but if anything happens, the heroes will be blamed.

The King's Feast! A huge banquet is being prepared in the Hall of the Warrior King—perhaps for a holy day, a victory, a wedding, or the anniversary of the King's Naming Day—and the castle is all abuzz. The kitchens are a battlefield and the chamberlain is desperately trying to organize seating so that fights won't break out too early in the event— there is a time and place for this, after all. Any Fyrdee or Bondee worth his moss is trying to get on duty because that's where the action will be.

Rural Settlements

Traditional Vidaar villages are usually very small but very well-suited for defense, while larger Vidaar towns are often formed around conquered Elvorix settlements. The populace includes numerous mixed-blood and Elvorix commoners, who often want nothing to do with either Vidaar *or* Elvorix authorities. The more traditional or war-minded tend to join the Vidaar army as Ceoree skirmishers. The more independent or entrepreneurial-minded make a brisk business as smugglers, bandits, or even spies.

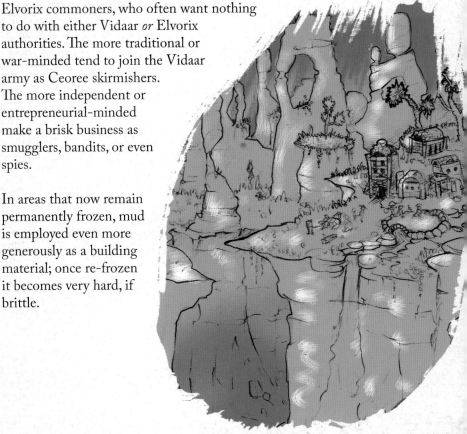

In areas that now remain permanently frozen, mud is employed even more generously as a building material; once re-frozen it becomes very hard, if brittle.

What you can find there:

Half-camouflaged huts of wood, mud, and thatch.

Small plots of land tended in common.

Mixed-blood children who have learned to run away at the sight of strangers.

Underground caches of food hidden from the local lord at harvest time or of goods smuggled across the border.

Traps and snares around the village to catch predators, thieves, and unwanted visitors.

Things that can happen:

Underground Economy. Because of the combination of rough climate, state of warfare, and snooping tax collectors sent by the local lords, most villages have sizeable underground hidey-holes for both people and goods. These are particularly loved by smugglers and black-marketeers of all stripes, who enthusiastically but inexpertly add connections via networks of unstable tunnels. If anyone is helping Elvorix families reunite or trading without paying duty fees, there will be tunnels involved.

Multicultural Diapers. Just like on the Elvorix side of the shifting border, questions of ancestry are not always treated in the same way by common folks and by lords. Many families are divided, many traditions are shared; it's a toss-up whether anyone you talk to will be an Elvorix hater or ally. When an Elvorix baby is found abandoned, what is to become of it?

It's Just the Local Custom... Is it me, or are a lot of people disappearing in this village, especially when both moons are up in the sky? Why do the villagers frequently cast a pebble over their left shoulder when a newcomer walks into town? And what's that weird music they play?

Shyldhal

The Vidaar are no great architects and builders, so when they settle somewhere they reserve their best for the important buildings. In the case of the Vidaar, the most vital building is often considered to be the kogg brewery, but the Shyldhal where the Fyrdee soldiers will be garrisoned also garners some importance. It's got all that a warrior needs: armory, watch tower, comfortable quarters for the Styrsik, a forge nearby to take care of the weapons, armor and shields, and a kogg brewery just around the corner.

However, the Vidaar often find building to be a tedious task, and will lament that all the best spots seem to be occupied. A smart Styrsik founding a new Vidaar settlement will go for efficiency, using any not-too-ruined Elvorix stone buildings left after conquering a village that's in the right spot, maybe even using conscripted Bookworm labor. The add-ons are typically built of wood, mud, and thatch, because rocks are heavy and prove difficult to nail or stick together. A good coat of paint is often regarded as a better improvement on shoddy workmanship than using sturdier materials.

What you can find there:

Vidaar warriors training, sleeping, resting, playing games of chance, and arguing. The Shyldhal might be garrisoned with ten to twenty Bondee, ten to twenty Fyrdee, six to ten Lunghshyld, and two to six Ceoree.

Administrative quarters for the Styrsik's ill-used war staff: a Totember, a Tromik, and a Bondee or two as the Styrsik's personal assistants.

Udvlag may be reporting, but probably has separate quarters in a ramshackle temple nearby.

Styrsik's quarters, tended by a Bondee as punishment for dereliction of duty or maybe by Elvorix prisoners.

Armory supplied with axes, spears, swords, shields, armor, etc.

Bondee doing laundry as punishment detail.

On-going repairs for leaky thatched roofs and damaged walls.

Things that can happen:

It's a Trap! The bulk of the garrison is out, meeting an attack by the enemy, but now a second army is in sight! The useless cowards who were left behind must defend the settlement or answer to Styrsik Grummold…

Put Your Money Where Your Big Fat Mouth Is. A group of ill-disciplined warriors get into a stupid bet about whose unit is the best, and must now sneak out to settle their differences properly.

Revenge! The conquered Elvorix, who seemed so thoroughly broken, infiltrate the Shyldhal in an effort to seize the armory and recapture the town.

Basement Treasure. Unbeknownst to the Vidaar conquerors, the Elvorix had built a nice cache under the building. Maybe it contains precious books filled with ancient lore preserved at great risk; food supplies for emergencies, which a clever Bondee might trade bit by bit on the black market; or a half-finished invention by the local quirky genius, which Elvorix authorities would have disapproved of as way too likely to attract divine attention.

Don't Trouble Yourself on My Account. Dowodik Aenwubba, moving his six banners to go open new frontier areas, decides to stop by and temporarily take over the Shyldhal. He runs everyone ragged with demands, commandeers Styrsik Rinnick Blackshield's quarters, garrisoning his best troops there, and billets other units with Elvorix peasants—ruining the comfy routine that the locals had settled in. Will the visiting troops notice how friendly the garrison has become with the Elvorix villagers?

Stinky War Games. The garrison must train with live ammunitions when Udvlag Toronav the Pungent talks Styrsik Ulma of the Hammer Clan into conducting cheese artillery training.

Forge

Whenever possible, the Vidaar village forge is built by reusing stone masonry left by the Ancients or contemporary Elvorix. If they really *must*, the Vidaar will make an effort at piling stones themselves or perhaps using Elvorix labor. Even the laziest of builders must admit that a forge made of wood and mud will have technical difficulties. It's often the only spot in town that is truly warm, what with the climate growing steadily colder.

What you can find there:
Blacksmith and a small number of hard-working assistants.

Rhythmic sound of iron being pounded into shape.

Local bucks' gossip circle, shooting the breeze as they watch the blacksmith work and warming their bones for a spell.

Half-finished or partly-repaired weapons and tools.

Stockpiles of fuel, mostly wood but coal whenever possible.

Ingots of iron and old metal bits waiting to be smelted.

Piles of pig iron just outside, a waste product.

Things that can happen:
Rumor Has It. The forge is a great place to hear all sort of rumors, as good as any tavern and you don't pass out drunk before being rolled for your money. You can even get your battle axe sharpened!

Short On Supplies. The forge is low on ore, fuel, or other key supplies, and unless someone brings in a new load, there's no way the smith can repair the damage from the latest battle. To make matters worse, Ceoree scouts say the enemy is regrouping in the hills and preparing a new strike...

What Do You Mean, It Was Picked Up Already? Dowodik Thrumm's weapon—a family heirloom—was being repaired at the forge; when someone came to take delivery this morning, one of the blacksmith's assistants packed the weapon and cheerfully sent it home to its owner. Alas, the *real* courier is here now, asking where the weapon is.

Hey, I Got An Idea... A smart alec—perhaps the Vidaar equivalent of a Bookworm, or an Elvorix or Jaarl prisoner—figures out that if the temperature gets hot enough, the pig iron can be melted to make an even better grade of metal. This is valuable experimental technology, difficult to reproduce, but it could make the difference in the war! The heroes may be the ones to protect—or steal—this secret. They may even decide that no faction should receive such a tremendous advantage...

Kogg Brewery

Kogg is a potent alcohol brewed from barley-moss. It's not fancy, it's not delicate, and it's not hard to make, so if you can find Vidaar, you can find kogg. Its brewing requires large metal vats, wooden casks, a good strong fire, a master-brewer and some half-competent assistants, plus time. The kogg brewery is what makes a town a town and not just a village.

What you can find there:

Stores of barley-moss in various stages of preparation.

Rows of wooden casks sorted by age, which a true master-brewer can guess by the color and bulging of the staves alone.

Huge vats heating over the fire pit, sending pungent steam over the entire area.

Customers returning small empty casks to trade them for full ones.

Another gossip circle enjoying the warmth and the occasional taste of a new batch of kogg.

"With a good mate, a sharp axe, and a barrel of kogg I can lay waste to all before me!"

—*Brewmaster Vild the Hammered*

Things that can happen:

The House Special. Vidaar come from all over to sample the wares from *this* brewery. Voora's House Special is unbeatable, so she charges a little more for it, but that means a lot of not-so-friendly competition from other breweries in neighboring villages. Finally, they decide to join forces to open a rival brewery right here in town, down the street from Voora, and put her out of business by selling below cost.

The Latest Batch Seems Different... A wily entrepreneur carrying a strange artifact of the Ancients. A suspicious Styrsik looking for smugglers. A worried smuggler hiding the artifact behind the brewery's vats. A new batch of kogg with unexpected effects...

Special Tax! Styrsik Bruddor the Greedy strolls into town with a brick of Bondee, and announces that as a "special tax," he is requisitioning thirty barrels of kogg. This would mean almost the entire winter reserve!

Thank Akka-Maas It's Pay Day. When the Bondee get their army pay, it's fun times at the brewery. And by fun times, we mean all hell breaks loose.

Shrine of Akka-Maas

Can you, reader, call to mind those impressive temples that both dwarf the visitors and send their souls soaring with majestic grandeur? This isn't one of those. For one thing, as the Vidaar proverb says, "Akka-Maas cannot fit inside any building made by buck or doe." There is an outdoor altar with crude representations of Akka-Maas such as a statue, carving, or painting, and a fire pit. The building nearby is not a temple, but the Udvlag and acolytes' workshop and living quarters.

This building is a little local ramshackle affair put together under the direction of an Udvlag, raised as far up as possible without collapsing under its own weight—which, for Vidaar construction methods, means a few usable floors and a dangerously unstable belfry. The Udvlag and acolytes have embellished it as much as they could by painting sacred glyphs and whatever else appealed to them at the time. It's not like there are frequent visits anyway—the place smells of noxious fermented cheese.

What you can find there:

Crudely decorated altar to Akka-Maas, where a flame burns and is never allowed to go out.

Sleeping quarters of the priesthood.

Regalia, sacred implements, religious insignia, drums, musical instruments, and paraphernalia.

Cheese-making workshop.

Cheese reserves.

Things that can happen:

Cheesed Off. There is no more ylark milk to make the sacred cheese! The last deliveries never made it to the shrine. What is going on?

You Mean It Worked? An acolyte (preferably one of the heroes) has been using tyromancy just the way they should be, i.e., faking it. But the acolyte is seeing unlikely success: every prediction has come true. Now they're getting a little too famous for Udvlag Roggia's taste...

Look Out, She's Gonna Blow! The deadly vapors from potent, aged cheese wheels can reach dangerous concentrations. When that happens, one spark and up it goes! A poorly ventilated cheese reserve can become powerfully explosive.

You Mean You Can't Hear That? When in the vicinity of the outdoor altar to Akka-Maas, one of the heroes can distinctly hear a voice addressing them. No one else seems to hear this.

"The Vidaar are our shameful secret, buried in the past for generations but now returned to haunt us. They represent the very worst in Sentian society—willful ignorance, anti-intellectualism, contempt for the benefits of education and study. They are everything that brought about the downfall of the Ancients, sealed in the amphorae of their ancestral ships and left to ferment for centuries before washing back up on our shores. That their culture and outlook have changed so little is stark testament to the danger they pose to all that we have rebuilt during their absence."—Rustica Bibulus, Elvorix scholar

From interview notes for the volume "The Explorers," by Matia Bibulus. Transcribed by Bura Bibulus Ven Proudheart, 88 AGC.

Nhilde Troll Breeding Grounds

At some point in their quest for the island of Garigla, the Vidaar discovered a race they could not merely conquer. The savage trolls on the Fifty-fifth Island that Wasn't Garigla were enormous creatures, twice as high as any Vidaar warrior and strong in proportion. At the time the Vidaar left prudently, since there was nothing on that island they really wanted. Two hundred years later, King Vidaar the Umpteenth sent Captain Nhilde with ten ships and a crew of rascals to rediscover that island and bring back trolls as their secret weapon in an effort to lurch out of the stalemate they had reached with the Elvorix. The voyage cost six ships, ten years, and the lives of many Vidaar sailors, but eventually Nhilde returned with a dangerous cargo of trolls.

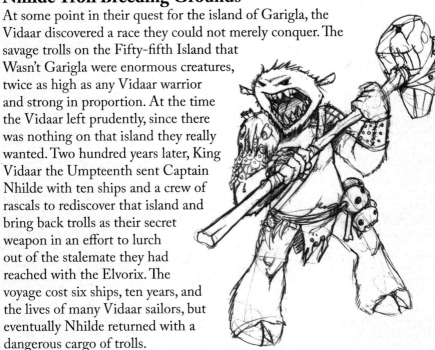

The so-called Nhilde trolls refused to breed and nearly died off in captivity, however, until the Vidaar learned to keep them on isolated islands where the trolls live wild and free. And breed. It's very dangerous business to "harvest" young Nhilde; the Vidaar cautiously trade with their parents for food, and conscript the young trolls into special units which they keep apart from the rest of the army, give large weapons to, and point at the enemy.

What you can find there:

Small landing where the Vidaar boats tie down.

Traces of the last "harvesting" expedition to visit and fail.

Bone yard full of mismatched animal fragments.

Wailing Nhilde cubs.

Steaming piles of troll dung.

Troll fights or troll smooching, sometimes difficult to tell apart.

Things that can happen:

Be Very, Very Quiet... The heroes have been given the plum assignment of bringing food to the island and trading it for young Nhilde. Maybe the heroes are Vidaar, or even better, are from another faction and doubly trespassing.

Precious Cargo From Hell. The heroes must prevent the Vidaar minders from returning from the island with viable Nhilde reinforcements. At all costs!

What's THAT Doing Here? Oops, this was the wrong island to land on. Who knew there were Nhilde here?

Ancestral Ship

The mighty Vidaar ships are the same ones they took to the sea in search of the fabled island of Garigla hundreds of years ago, rebuilt over and over—in the words of the scholar Seadros Bibulus, "They had been repaired, rebuilt, patched, and expanded into hulking monstrosities of barnacles and pitch." For the more traditional Vidaar, a ship is the true home—a hated, smelly, cramped, uncomfortable home, but home nonetheless. Land is just a period of looting and resting between sea expeditions.

Fleets of Vidaar raiders carry troops, ambush Elvorix and Jaarl vessels, pillage coastal towns, ferry troublesome cargoes of Nhilde trolls, and occasionally visit yet another island in the dejected hope that maybe there is such a place as Garigla after all.

Ancestral ships are often a collection of vessels secured together for added capacity and stability, which can be detached if circumstances call for greater speed or more points of attack.

What you can find there:
The Styrsik's cabin where the best loot is kept, along with whatever maps may have been stolen from Elvorix or Jaarl captains.

Fierce-looking carved prow figure.

Masts, spars, sails, a tangle of lines, the crow's nest, and lots of other places to climb to or from.

Rowing benches, along with the big oars that are kept shipped when not in use.

The small arms locker, filled with boarding axes, swords, cutlasses, and other implements of mayhem.

Hammocks, rolled and stowed when not in use, or slung below-deck and filled with snoring Bondee.

Stores of canvas, coils of rope, preserved string-moss, slabs of ylark jerky, wheels of ylark cheese, and barrels of kogg and water, all stowed in the hold.

Things that can happen:
Clear For Action! Nothing is dearer to a true Vidaar's ears than the call to prepare for good old piracy. Except perhaps the words "Treasure ship!"

Land Ahoy! Hey, was that island there before? I'm pretty sure it wasn't. We should explore it, it might be Garigla!

Our Only Hope. Vidaar are used to holding mastery of the seas; the puny Elvorix boats are no match for the Vidaar armada. But even though they are severely outnumbered, the Jaarl are a tougher nut to crack. Now unless the valiant ship *Gruagh* can escape the war galleys' pursuit, there will be no one to warn the city of Lughhyl of the impending Jaarl attack...

Rustica: "The biggest difference between the Elvorix and the Vidaar is their comparative intelligence. It is true that we are similar in appearance, but one need only compare the mighty works of the Sentian Empire, or even the more modest works of today's Elvorix, with the squalid nature of Vidaar towns—which are barely more advanced than Kuld dwellings—to know that this is so."

Ulf: "Bah! The biggest difference between the Vidaar and the Elvorix is one of character! It is we who spent generations at sea! It is we who were chosen by the God of the Sky! It is we who were given the ability to divine through the holy cheese! These so-called great works of theirs exist only as crutches to support them in their weakness. We need them not!"

Iva: "They're really not that different."

Rustica: "What?"

Ulf: "What?"

Matia: "What?"

Kuri (Iva's fawn, who sat on her lap for the interview): "HEE!"

Iva: "They look the same. They act the same. Other than the fact that one smells like a midden and one smells like a sewer they smell the same. One bunch brought on the Great Catastrophe and the other sailed around for 300 years due to blind greed and bad maps so there isn't much to tell them apart in terms of intelligence. One group worships a bunch of petty, useless, false deities while the other worships a single petty, useless, false deity, which amounts to nothing more than a larger helping of the same thing. Neither of them can make a half-decent dinner, let alone a half-decent sword. The only thing that differentiates them is their excuses about why they aren't the same."

(Silence)

Ulf: "Well, there is one other way that we are the same, 'tis true."

Rustica: "We're all grateful we aren't Jaarl."

Kuri: "HEE!"

From interview notes for the volume "The Explorers," by Matia Bibulus. Transcribed by Bura Bibulus Ven Proudheart, 88 AGC.

The Disciplined Jaarl

"What sets us apart from the Weaklings and Broke-Backs is that we are a disciplined people. While the Elvorix waste time trying to one-up one another's dullness and the Vidaar waste time hitting one another over the head with heavy objects, we Jaarl are focused and goal-oriented. As individuals and as a society we understand what is needed and what part we each must play in order to succeed as individuals, groups, and a society. Our goal is to establish a new homeland for ourselves here in Sentia. This is uppermost in the minds of every Jaarl, and it is because of this sense of purpose and focus that we have succeeded in establishing a foothold—one that we will continue to expand."—Iva the Stubborn, Jaarl scholar

From interview notes for the volume "The Explorers," by Matia Bibulus. Transcribed by Bura Bibulus Ven Proudheart, 88 AGC.

Jaarl Society

The Jaarl (pronounced with a "y" as opposed to a hard "j"), were more advanced than the Elvorix and Vidaar in terms of architecture, engineering, technology, and warfare, comparable to the Ancient Sentians before the Purge Wars. And yet they never showed themselves for all this time, hidden from view in their black stone cities on the Island Elvorix called Malios, until the Great Catastrophe and the eruption of the Murmadon volcano. Why?

Clearly, the enemy the Jaarl had armed against was elsewhere. Was it the Kuld? Or is someone else coming? Is that why the Jaarl are so focused on building and arming a new homeland here? Either way, the Jaarl intend on being ready for that fight.

In their native land of Murmadon, they used the phenomenal heat of an active volcano to forge steel far superior to anything the Elvorix and the Vidaar produce. Since the Great Catastrophe and the eruption of Mount Murmadon sent them scrambling for a new homeland, even the most capable smiths have been unable to forge new swords equal to the ones they brought from the island. Nevertheless, they can still create weapons and armor that easily match those of Sentians, but they carry them in shame. Called *volcanium*, the Jaarl steel shines with a coppery, ruddy hue and cannot be melted by the hottest Sentian forges. Objects made of Jaarl steel, and particularly swords, are treasured and passed on from generation to generation.

Their buildings and ships are also superior to current Sentian works, but the *Weaklings* and *Broke-Backs* (as the Jaarl would refer to as Elvorix and Vidaar, respectively) each outnumber the Jaarl by ten or twenty to one. Jaarl farming and craft techniques are solid, but utilitarian; so far, they have shown little interest for anything frivolous like art or even comfort. One exception is music; they quite like it, especially martial music of course.

It would also surprise many Sentians to learn that the Jaarl have a sense of humor—dry, understated, dark humor, and you don't want to be the butt of the joke. However, honor and loyalty are paramount, and a Jaarl failing to carry out duties can expect to be ostracized; in the military, failure is often expected to be redeemed by ritual suicide.

The Jaarl are a nation of laws. Political power is controlled by the five major guilds— Military, Arcane, Preservers, Providers, and Builders—each with its internal cabals. Each community elects representatives who in turn elect sixty-four senators to form the legislative body, the Jaarl Senate, and these elect three Executors who lead the nation. Most top-level decisions require only a simple majority among the three Executors, but some require unanimous agreement. Laws are written clearly and prescriptively; when legislators write laws that offer loopholes and are difficult to interpret, they can be impeached and sanctioned, even executed, for incompetence. Jaarl legists pleading a case to a court are encouraged to be brief and to the point; impatient Adjudicators occasionally have a wordy legist whipped or stripped of credentials as an example to others.

Current Jaarl population numbers are estimated at a few hundred thousand, anywhere from 400,000 to one million.

Use of Captive Labor:
The discussion of forced labor is a sensitive matter for this author, as she was captured at the battle now remembered as Orvas' Folly and held by the Jaarl for two years. Though not harmed physically, the emotional scars from the experience will never fade.

A few decades ago, when the Jaarl started struggling to fight off the sheer number of the Vidaar and Elvorix armies united under the Pact of Prolyus, they reconsidered their policy towards prisoners of war and captured populations. Simple extermination shifted to capture and forced labor. Sentian prisoners are used for hard labor on clearing and building projects, as beasts of burden, and even as menial servants in private households. This freed up the Jaarl workforce for more skilled tasks.

Although these captives are not deliberately ill-treated and usually given sufficient if meager rations, Jaarl discipline is merciless. Any prisoner caught fomenting revolt, stealing, fighting back, or otherwise causing trouble is executed swiftly and brutally, and the body is left on public display for weeks as a reminder to the rest.

For a more detailed account of this author's time with the Jaarl, the reader can refer to the book "My Time Among the Enemy," published under imprint of the Elvora Bibulus Academy Press.

To read this excerpt, check out page 135 in WAR OF ASHES: SHIELDWALL.

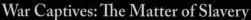

War Captives: The Matter of Slavery
As you read this, you may be thinking, "But slavery is not funny!" We agree with you, it's not funny at all. Remember when we said the world of Agaptus was both grim and whimsical? The Jaarl's use of prisoners as labor is grim.

To put this in context, we're using the concept the way it was known to a lot of ancient civilizations in our history: war captives used as forced labor, not sentient cattle that are bought and sold. Along with the death and dismemberment you'll find throughout the book, it's part of the grimness of the setting.

We're not encouraging players to be the "bad guys", the group could play through the taking down of a brutal institution. But maybe the subject matter isn't your cup of tea. If you don't want slavery in your game, that's okay; employ your right to customize the game to suit the players. Prisoners of war can be changed to Jaarl criminals serving out a sentence, or as punishment for dishonoring their Jaarl heritage.

Religion—of Sorts

The Jaarl proudly deny the existence of any Sentian gods, and explain away even the most pointed divine occurrences as natural coincidences. Yet they are no strangers to the sacred and the arcane: on every battlefield they bring a chunk of dark porous rock, a remnant from the volcano of Murmadon. These rock fragments store formidable energy that Jaarl war priests, called Popio, use to create what Sentians would call magical effects.

The Jaarl protect these stones at any cost, and their retaliation was so terrifying the only time Elvorix adversaries captured one that nobody has ever tried again. The more of these rock chunks are gathered in one place, the stronger and farther-reaching the effects. It's very rare for the individual Jaarl to retain such a relic, since even a sliver of the rock will be claimed by the authorities and jealously guarded.

Even young Jaarl born after the Great Catastrophe are not told what exactly is the nature of these volcanic rocks. Was the mountain magical in the days where the Jaarl still lived on Murmadon? Did they meddle with things too powerful for them and somehow precipitate the volcano's eruption?

All Jaarl, as well as Sentian and Kuld priests, can sense the presence of Murmadon rock when they get within arm's reach. In addition, some Jaarl are more attuned to it and can detect it over greater distances (see *"Faction Stunts"* on page 170). For more details on the Murmadon rock and the Jaarl's troubled relationship with the gods, see *"The Jaarl's Scorned God: Murmadon"* on page 255.

We Are Legion—Jaarl Ranks
Redemption must be earned,
and a shamed warrior does not complain.
—*Jaarl proverb*

Roccio: The youngest and most common type of soldier in the Jaarl forces. They fight in close formation, equipped with a rectangular shield made of wood and leather with metal facing, and a sword inherited from a parent, usually the Roccio's father. They do not use the shieldwall tactic of the Sentians and are more mobile, using instead a series of well-rehearsed maneuvers, making use of their heavy shields to offer maximum protection.

Valani: If a Roccio proves worthy and the family holds a *corduu*, or second sword also made of Jaarl steel, in time the youngster will be presented with it and become a Valani. The shield is abandoned and the new Valani must learn to fight as a skirmisher with two swords instead, a style that requires much more mobility and alertness.

Cospico: When a Roccio survives battle but his Jaarl sword does not—broken or lost—he is disgraced. He has few choices: Cospico, Rigenti, or mustered out. If brave enough to choose to become Cospico, he is given a heavy double-bladed polearm called a *skirra* and banished to the frontier. He becomes a monster-hunter, fighting savage beasts, trolls, and Kuld.

Rigenti: Jaarl that have served well as Roccio but who lack family connections or a Jaarl sword can choose to become Rigenti. Like the Roccio, they fight in formation with a heavy shield but wield pilums. Though none doubts their bravery, this rank lacks the prestige of sword-wielders, and the Rigenti units are treated as somewhat more expendable.

Commandi: Officers, or Commandi, are selected among the worthiest and most experienced Roccio and Valani, after grueling testing, to lead warbands.

Rettori: Generals, or Rettori, are chosen among Commandi based on years of service, on the assumptions that if they have made it that long, they know their stuff. They have a much better grasp of strategy and tactics than their Sentian counterparts.

Segino: The Segino has proven his worth and been tasked with carrying the Sacred Rock in battle. Not only does he serve as the equivalent of a standard bearer, but the value of the Sacred Rock to the Jaarl is much more than symbolic; the Segino is expected to die protecting it. Because of the delicate nature of magic, he may also simply die carrying it.

Tambio: The Tambio corps are musicians that provide cadence for marches and signals for units to maneuver, change formation, rally, execute an attack sequence, etc.

Popio: The equivalent of a war priest, the Popio draws on the power of the Sacred Rock carried by the Segino to perform arcane rituals in battle and inspire the troops.

Ilk Master: It took decades for the Jaarl to finally release what could be their doomsday weapon. Only a few years ago, they hatched the desiccated eggs of creatures nearly as voracious and unstoppable as the Kuld themselves, the Ilk. These creatures only obey the Ilk-Master, always a decorated veteran, who uses arcane means to control the swarm. For more information about the ilk, see their entry in *"Beasts of Agaptus"* on page 118.

People

Jaarl bucks are roughly the same height as the average Sentian—except for the diminutive Vorix—but they are much bulkier and heavier; a Jaarl easily weighs twice as much as an Elvorix or Vidaar buck. Jaarl does tend to be a bit taller but less massive. Jaarl bucks' voices are deep and gravelly; does' voices are higher-pitched, but still quite low. Jaarl hands have only three fingers, not four like Sentians, plus an opposable thumb.

Fur patterns are more uniform than among Sentians, with rarer occurrence of stripes, rings, or mottling. The most common coloration among bucks is a dull, dark brown fur, almost black when not in full daylight. Does' fur tends to grays and muted browns. Another common color is chestnut brown with darker patches across the arms, legs, and face. The rarest is jet black and is mostly seen in individuals occupying leadership positions; Jaarl fur darkens with age, and fawns' coats are typically blond or pale grey.

Like Sentians and unlike the Kuld, Jaarl are warm-blooded and nurse their young. Unlike Sentians, however, they are egg-laying mammals; instead of giving birth to live young, does carry one egg at a time internally for about two months, then lay the egg and incubate it in a pouch for another month. During incubation, the doe is almost entirely inactive and loses much of her body fat.

After the egg hatches, the doe will lactate and nurse her young for at least four months and up to eight in the case of fragile or sickly fawns. During this period, the doe requires enormous amounts of food to regain her body mass and provide nutrients for her young.

Civilian Jaarl society folds itself around the reproductive cycle, as a high birth rate and infant survival rate are deemed necessary to establish a new homeland. It's routine for a doe to bring her fawn everywhere with her, whether she is an architect, a grocer, or a scribe. When this would be dangerous to the fawn or would interfere with tasks, does arrange to put fawn rearing duties in common and trade time so that a few does may care for many fawns.

The fawns begin schooling at the age of two, and start apprenticeship of a career or trade by age ten. A Jaarl is considered adult after undergoing a challenge at the age of sixteen.

The Jaarl come from warm jungle climes and the bosom of an active volcano, so they have trouble adapting to the colder weather that now prevails; their body temperature is a little lower than Sentians. The houses of older Jaarl are often kept very warm, with fires blazing even in the midst of summer. By contrast, in order to toughen them up and get them ready to conquer the new land, Jaarl youth are trained to endure the weather with only the lightest of clothing and sleep in unheated rooms.

The Jaarl tongue is much harsher and more guttural than even the Vidaar language. It contains certain sounds that Sentians are barely able to reproduce, including tongue clicks, throaty rasps, glottal stops, and very low rumbles that extend into the subsonic range.

Although she has yet to convince the academic community, this author suspects that the Jaarl benefit from an additional sense that allows them to feel the presence of Sacred Rock from Murmadon, as well as some other arcane forces. This suspicion is based on covert observation of Jaarl individuals' reaction in the presence of the substance. It has also been reported in earlier texts that contact with Sacred Rock can cause fits and seizures in Vidaar and Elvorix priests.

"The Jaarl are flawed in ways opposite those of the Vidaar. Clearly they are an advanced people, capable of great feats of science, architecture, and learning. And yet their society benefits little from any of these. There seems to be no happiness or enjoyment in their lives. Save perhaps for the enjoyment of music, they cultivate little of refinement, pleasure, or aesthetic appeal within their society. Rather they seem always to be impatient. Like the ant-people of ancient legend they are disciplined and skilled, but with little independent thought. Now that their ant-hill has been kicked over they are capable only of mindless aggression."
—Rustica Bibulus, Elvorix scholar

From interview notes for the volume "The Explorers," by Matia Bibulus. Transcribed by Bura Bibulus Ven Proudheart, 88 AGC.

Guilds

Although Jaarl society knew divisions of class, lineage, and politics before the Great Catastrophe, nowadays the by-word is unity. What's left of the mighty Jaarl must see each other as kin in order to build a new home and thrive on these shores. Those who remember old ideals or bear grudges do well to keep these to themselves. Some sub-cultures are still faintly visible, remnants of the disparate refugees fleeing from Murmadon's lava-covered slopes, but all are encouraged to overlook these differences.

Therefore, Jaarl guilds are based on occupation and inclination, and much more fluid than the old bloodline-based groups, since anyone can join. Leaving can be a more delicate issue, generating disdain or suspicion.

Military: The ranks of military might on land or at sea are almost all that the outside world sees of the Jaarl. The Military secures territory for the new homeland and protects it from all other would-be occupants. This is the only group where bucks hold the majority, because of the difficulties of combining military discipline with the Jaarl doe's gestation cycle. It's also the one place where ties of lineage remain the strongest, as swords forged in the heat of Mount Murmadon are irreplaceable and passed only from parent to child, usually father to son.

Arcane: The mysterious individuals who deny all gods but seem to worship chunks of stone are part of the Arcane. In addition to the Popio, who wield applied if unstable power in battle, the Intellego work on more theoretical aspects, trying to create specific effects and decrease unpredictability. The Virian use arcane abilities to act as champions, bodyguards, protectors, mediators, advisors, and adjudicators.

Builders: Those who plan the new homeland and construct its infrastructure are the Builders. They create public works and edifices (Deviso plan and Paveo build), but also plan entire institutions for the future (Scriptio), modifying existing ones as needed.

Preservers: The Preservers are tasked with collecting, organizing, and protecting even the slightest bit of knowledge or culture from Murmadon. Like Elvorix scholars, they seek the wisdom of their ancestors in all manners of science, but they also seek to connect the fragments, rebuild the parts that have been lost, and are equally interested in reconstructing centuries-old gossip as sea charts. They have lost so much, now every bit is precious.

Providers: The Jaarl who dedicate themselves to sustaining normalcy and make the cogs of society turn, such as farmers, crafters, teachers, civil servants, jurists, and merchants, are all part of the Providers. It's the most diverse guild and with time, as Jaarl society reestablishes itself, will probably split into several guilds.

Names

Jaarl personal names are a feast of alternating vowels and hard consonants; sibilants and fricatives are rarer. Distinctive nicknames are common, usually given in admiration. Jaarl names generally take the form: [Title] [Personal Name] [Possible Nickname]

Clan names are very rare since most were lost after the Great Catastrophe; only the oldest Jaarl will still refer to them, and usually only in secret to another elder.

Sample Names
Personal Names: Agirix, Arabaldo, Arduino, Asdrubale, Azzone, Bodo, Burlanda, Ezzo, Ghinga, Harrie, Hgglar, Illinani, Jusipio, Khugg, Lele, Meloria, Morenus, Mortox, Nofri, Rigarda, Rocco, Rolius, Tedaldo, Tenghi, Tybal, Ugolina.

Individuals of Note
Adalgisa: *Senior Executor of the Jaarl Nation.*

Rettori Agirix: *Commander of the 1st Company, Legion of the Red Morning.*

Gualterutia: *Head Planner of Karthak.*

Rocca: *Venerable Master of the Viridian Order.*

For more details on individuals of note, see *"Gamemaster Characters"* on page 99.

"I can't understand them. They are skilled warriors, but they take no joy from fighting. They don't raid. Their wine is weak. The only thing they seem truly to love is that music of theirs, and even that seems overly complicated and bloodless. They seem to be clever in their own way, and yet they claim that there are no gods when clearly Akka-Maas is real. They do have some pretty nice swords though, and that I can appreciate."—Ulf Long-teeth, Vidaar Bondee

From interview notes for the volume "The Explorers," by Matia Bibulus. Transcribed by Bura Bibulus Ven Proudheart, 88 AGC.

Places

City of Karthak

When the city of Gailus in the north of Iradon was captured from the Elvorix, it was left in ruins. The Jaarl then rebuilt a new model city just south of it, clearing a large area to take advantage of a defensible hill and using limestone from a local quarry for the masonry and pavement works. The new city, which Sentians still refer to as Gailus but the Jaarl call Karthak, is still under construction but already boasts formidable defenses; using prisoner labor, the Jaarl are raising a perimeter wall higher than has been seen in Agaptus since the days of the Ancients.

What you can find there:
New roads, new buildings, new everything—shiny, sharp, and perfectly aligned.

Large numbers of Elvorix and Vidaar prisoners used as forced labor in the construction of buildings and public works.

Straight, smooth, and wide roads and large plazas paved in minutely adjusted limestone blocks.

Large numbers of Jaarl does and fawns everywhere, easily outnumbering bucks.

Half-finished marvels of architecture and engineering.

Cleverly built bathing establishments fed from natural hot springs, where Jaarl can relax in a sauna room, get a massage, soak in icy or scalding water, or get their fur groomed.

Pillory, gallows, and spikes where the justice system exhibits those who have been found guilty.

Playgrounds with climbing bars, swings, slides, wading pools, ball courts, and other amusements for fawns.

Schools for fawns aged two to ten, with disciplined youngsters receiving moral, mental, and physical training.

Elvorix shantytowns outside the city walls in the ruins of Old Gailus. Those who live there are not war prisoners but the occupied population, with default status as forced labor.

"Domesticated" Elvorix, descended not from local stock but from Elvorix fishermen who tried exploring Murmadon centuries ago, were captured, and never released.

Things that can happen:
Ambassadorial Delegation. Despite the state of hostilities, a truce has been worked between the Jaarl and the Elvorix, and a small ambassadorial delegation of Weaklings has been allowed in the city. Will the talks lead to a lasting armistice, an agreement against the Kuld, betrayal, or renewed hostilities?

We Said No Witnesses! A Jaarl fawn overhears the details of a rebellion plot among the captives.

Culture Shock. "Domesticated" and "feral" Elvorix captives come to terms with cultural differences and torn loyalties. How long can they put aside their differences and find common purpose?

Murmadolunagh
The most prominent building in Karthak is the Murmadolunagh, the equivalent of a temple in the middle of the city where the Arcane have their headquarters. It looks like a great cone with a broken top, emulating the volcano symbol the Jaarl use as their coat-of arms. In the center of the cone is a great porous Sacred Rock that is constantly alight with black flame, the largest known remnant piece of Murmadon rock.

Under the guidance of the best Intellego scholars, research conducted at Murmadolunagh examines the properties of the Sacred Rock and attempts to understand what caused the eruption of Mount Murmadon; some insist that overuse of the volcano's arcane properties precipitated the catastrophe and Jaarl hubris must be curbed.

Rumors among Elvorix and Vidaar captives whisper that the complex also houses the Virian Academy, which trains gifted youngsters in magic. Virian candidates are chosen from those who are most sensitive to the Sacred Rock and its powers.

Although the scholar Matia Bibulus would not have complete information on this, the Virian Academy trains those gifted youngsters to hone their Sixth Sense and use it to serve their homeland. If you think Jedi Academy, you're not far off.

What you can find there:
Murmadon Stone beacon.

Intellego research laboratories and library.

Virian Academy, training hopeful recruits.

An elite unit of Roccio guarding the perimeter of the complex.

Tapestries, wall hangings, murals, and mosaics depicting arcane symbols on a massive scale, in black, dark reds, purples, and indigo.

Floors of lustrous black stone.

Things that can happen:
Guardians of the Future. Because of the recent population boom, the ratio of young Virian recruits to adult Virian masters is eight to one, which makes things a bit chaotic by Jaarl standards...

Atonement? I've Got Your Atonement Right Here... Thulan, a prominent Intellego scholar, has come up with a research project to "safely" replicate the events that led to the volcano's eruption under controlled conditions. What could possibly go wrong?

Research Accident. Although everything is *fine, stop asking*, you just can't get into the Intellego's laboratories in the lower levels right now. Heavy stone doors have been shut and barred, and elite Valani who look like they mean business are guarding all the exits with both swords at the ready. But your friend/ally/loved one is now stuck in the underground labs!

Preserver Insula

The Preservers are very concerned with saving any snippets they can of the way things used to be before the Great Catastrophe. They have libraries to preserve ancient manuscripts and copy them, but they also treasure the aging members of the population, who still remember Murmadon in its glory, even if dimly.

Jaarl elders are not overlooked or forgotten, nor allowed to simply while away their waning years in retirement; they are fussed over, pampered, and relentlessly questioned about anything at all they can remember from their earliest days. They live in housing complexes that include all the facilities for interviews and document preservation. There are also greenhouses, coaxing plants from the warmer climes of their lost island, and small museums displaying objects from their Murmadon that are broken but can't be discarded.

A Jaarl's fur darkens with age; the halls of the Preserver buildings are haunted by frail, shriveled Jaarl shadows.

What you can find there:

Library and workshop dedicated to stabilizing, conserving, and copying old documents, from lofty books of great tacticians to menus of long-past banquets.

Scriptorium with comfortable seats, writing desks, and shelves containing notes from countless interviews with those who remember anything of the old ways.

Small apartments for pensioners, each connected to the central heating system with steam pipes.

Stooped, elderly Jaarl walking the grounds, bundled up to keep warm.

More aging Jaarl gathered in the overheated solarium, attended by Preserver fawn apprentices.

Small greenhouse filled with tropical plants.

Memorium, a small museum containing a jumble of objects from the old homeland such as damaged weapons, finely-made but chipped clay dishes, jewelry, and broken common-day items.

Things that can happen:

One Last Mission. Some elderly Jaarl feel bored with this comfortable but constricting retirement. They have some unfinished business out there in the world and nothing will prevent them from escaping to attend to it—not age, old injuries, nor dedicated nursing aides.

Keepers of Old Secrets. Perhaps not all memories should be revived. Some of the pensioners here remember dangerous things they try to keep buried. But the Preservers are determined to pierce the veil... while someone is picking off the last of those who know too much.

Secret Master. This old Jaarl remembers the way things were—the venerable blood lines now blurred, the hierarchies tumbled, the power and honor that belonged to the powerful few. None of this egalitarian nonsense! From the shadows of an innocuous insula, the Secret Master has converted Preservers to this cause and is reaching out to rebuild old Jaarl glory.

Provider Granary

To secure their food and other consumable resources from attack, the Jaarl build great granaries in which they store grains, berries, mosses, and other edibles, as well as fabric, furs, wax, lamp oil, even building materials. The Providers operate these immense warehouses and associated market places in orderly fashion.

Each granary—sturdily constructed by the Builders to meet Provider requirements—includes rows of neatly built stalls from which goods can be sold or distributed. Unlike Elvorix and Vidaar merchants, who often live in the same building where they have their shops, Jaarl artisans and merchants close shop at night and go home; no one is allowed to remain on the premises after hours except the posted guards.

What you can find there:

Tall shelving filled with barrels, bundles, boxes, bottles, and baskets of goods in well-ordered rows.

Thick walls of stone, brick, and mortar, pierced with a few small window openings.

Elevated foundation raising the floor well above ground level to prevent flooding and make it harder for vermin to get in.

Inclined stone ramp out front, leading to the only door for each storage unit—too small to let carts through. Everything delivered to or shipped from the granary has to be loaded or unloaded by hand, counted, and verified by watchful Providers.

Watch posts for the Rigenti guards protecting the storehouse.

Central courtyard with rows of merchant booths, built of stone and brick.

Torch holders and lamps to provide additional light.

Heavy locks on every door.

Dead quiet during the off-hours, with only the guards' footsteps echoing through.

Things that can happen:

Market Day. The granary is bustling with activity: artisans show off their wares, merchants deal out goods, customers look for a good deal, porters and laborers move crates, functionaries check inventory or collect taxes, and fawn apprentices used as messengers hurry about. This is the perfect backdrop for covert meetings, chases, thefts, and mistaken deliveries.

Under Siege! A ferocious Kuld force threatens to overrun the town, and the granary is one of the best fortified locations—as well as the choicest target for the hungry blue mob. But it's about more than surviving the attack: if the Kuld break into the granary, starvation will follow. Can the citizens defend the supplies? Should they consider allying with neighboring Sentians for defense?

The Great Heist. It's incredibly risky, and the punishment would be brutal if they got caught. But this band of ne'er-do-wells, con artists, and burglars are the best at what they do, and they are determined to rob the best-guarded place in the city.

Military Outpost

Even in the smallest, most rugged camps on the least disputed border, the Jaarl maintain impeccable military discipline and rigorous training. The camps are perfectly laid out, the tents in meticulous order, the defenses carefully organized, the routine of guard shifts precisely observed, the youngest Roccio knowing exactly what to do and when to do it.

The tents are not the ragged affairs found in Vidaar camps but good solid cloth, all exactly made to the same dimensions and set up prim and proper. Furniture such as tables, benches, cots, and chairs either folds or can be taken apart so that camp can be broken and everything packed in ylark-drawn wagons in record time. Ylark are a relatively recent addition to Jaarl military material but the much vaster distances in Agaptus, compared to their relatively compact territorial footprint in the former homeland of Murmadon, makes beasts of burden a welcome addition to the supply line.

In an amazing display of precision and skill, Jaarl soldiers exercise at sunrise and sunset, standing in perfect rows and columns to form a square on the training grounds under the watchful eye of an officer. Using their swords, they perform a series of complex movements and poses or *kata*. They move as one, following the rhythm of the leading officer, using their entire bodies. This training goes a long way to explain the smooth perfection of Jaarl maneuvers in even the most chaotic battles.

What you can find there:

Precisely ordered and delineated camp areas for each unit, the command staff, and support personnel.

Quarter-master's supply depot, frequently including a complement of Sentian captives for menial work.

Well-kept training field.

Watchposts on hills, in trees, or in portable wooden watchtowers.

Camp perimeter defenses.

Alert sentinels, regularly relieved by the next shift.

Things that can happen:

Ilk on the Loose! The ilk pens have burst open and the deadly critters are free. Was it an accident, did someone mess up the construction of the pens, did a saboteur slip in to free them, or is the Ilk-Master losing control of the creatures? The explanation will probably have to wait until the carnage is stopped... (See *"Beasts of Agaptus"* on page 118 for details on the ilk.)

Area 51. The Jaarl Military and Arcane are conducting joint experiments on this site and others, carefully accumulating precise quantities of Murmadon volcano rock and observing the effects. Naturally, it's all very hush-hush, which only makes it more tempting to find out what's *really* going on.

Chain of Command. In a most unusual quandary among the elite soldiers of the Jaarl officer corps, the camp Commandi has been acting strangely in the last few days. After nonsensical and even dangerous orders have been issued, which would leave the camp vulnerable to attack, the veteran Valani who serve as non-commissioned officers must decide what to do.

Builder Project

This is a new great construction work such as a new fortress, town, major road, bridge, dam, or forward watch position; alternately, it may be the site of a mine, a stone quarry (the Jaarl particularly prize black stone), or a naval yard. Some day it will be a proud testament to the Jaarl's dedication to build a new homeland, but right now it's an organized disaster with Jaarl running like ants across its face.

What you can find there:

Jaarl Builders planning and directing the work or providing the skilled labor.

Crafters of diverse trades: stone-cutters, masons, architects, carpenters, and so forth, many accompanied by fawn apprentices.

Well-tended huts in neat rows where workers are housed and Builder offices are located.

Locked sheds where the tools are kept when not in use.

Lines of workers at meal time, waiting for their food allotments of pepper-moss soup and sweet-berry bread.

Elvorix and Vidaar prisoners from different origins, used for back-breaking unskilled labor.

Stern and pitiless but not wantonly cruel Jaarl guards.

Small, bare prisoner dormitories that are frequently inspected.

Open area with spikes, where the bodies of the last batch of troublemakers are still displayed, rotting.

Things that can happen:

Secrets of Jaarl Engineering. The Jaarl must protect, and Elvorix spies must steal, any little bit of useful knowledge that could provide an edge in the war.

This Wasn't Supposed to Be Here... The Builder work has uncovered an Ancient site. The Builders were going to keep smashing through it—after all, what could the locals' ancestors have had that would matter?—but its location is problematic and the plans have to be adjusted. While construction has stopped, some prisoners figured out that there was something... interesting down there. Meanwhile, the Arcane figured out the same and sent investigators.

Bridge on the River Kwai. If the works are completed, they may provide the Jaarl with a significant tactical advantage, a turning point in the conflict. Some prisoners are willing to fight, and even die, to prevent that.

Attica! Yeah, prisoner escape is costly and very rarely works, but periodically someone has to try, especially among the Broke-Backs. What will it be this time? Tunnels, hiding among loads of stone, swimming across the fjord, ambush, open revolt?

War Galley

In many ways galleys are the marine version of a Jaarl military fortress. The number of ships in the fleet is much smaller than what the Vidaar can muster; the Jaarl galleys are powerful, well-built, and eminently sea-worthy. They feature several advances on their counterparts, such as extremely stable hulls, armored sides protecting the crew, and often a portable altar carrying a Sacred Stone.

Triremes feature elevated forecastle and quarterdeck, multiple superposed rowing decks, and a ramming prow spike; while turtleships exhibit multiple elevated, enclosed, and covered decks, double ramming prow spikes, and upper deck firing ports. Troop transports are simpler but sturdy affairs where the Roccio and Rigenti's shields are lashed to the sides to keep them out of the way and provide supplemental armor, with only one small area of the aft deck covered and enclosed.

> *Boiling sea water. Sweat. Decay.*—"Mossback," Kuld research subject, describing the Jaarl.
>
> *From interview notes for the volume "The Explorers," by Matia Bibulus. Transcribed by Bura Bibulus Ven Proudheart, 88 AGC.*

What you can find there:

Large crew complements making do with the cramped quarters thanks to draconian discipline.

Cargo of military gear.

Rows of angled rowing benches.

Well-stowed coils of rope, lashed barrels, and neatly bundled spars.

Open altar for the Sacred Stone.

Commandi's cabin, spartan and utilitarian but well-appointed.

Things that can happen:

The Voyage Home. For the first time in decades, ships have been sent to not only examine the coast of Lost Murmadon, but venture on what is left of it as well as neighboring islands. Their mission is to see if any more Sacred Stones can be retrieved either from the still-smoking volcano or from the rocks that were ejected for leagues around. Everyone's Sixth Sense is tingling with the proximity...

Wrath of the Sea God. Ilunus, worshiped by cautious Elvorix fishermen as the god of the seas and waves, takes exception to the Jaarl's militant atheism. That, or bad luck, or the Sacred Stone is acting up, take your pick. The ship is tossed by a monstrous storm, turned back every time it comes within sight of the home port, repeatedly beached on small islands inhabited only by ferocious predators.

Night Attack. A small fleet of war galleys is sailing down along the Larcian Isthmus to the east, while your lone galley, faster and lighter, has been given the mission to sail on the west side—under the noses of Vidaar raiders—to the narrowest point of the isthmus. There, your task is to attack well-fortified Vidaar positions and isolate them so that the fleet can take the entire isthmus at once! You must take the Vidaar town and control its artillery, an array of large catapults able to lob heavy rocks, barrels of incendiary oil, and humiliatingly dangerous ylark cheese.

The Endless Kuld

Winter air. Lichen and rock. Wood smoke. Raw meat.
—"Mossback," Kuld research subject, descibing the Kuld.

From interview notes for the volume "The Explorers," by Matia Bibulus.
Transcribed by Bura Bibulus Ven Proudheart, 88 AGC.

Kuld Society?

According to Elvorix scholars studying Ancient Sentian records of the
First War, also known as the Purging War—the one after which the Kuld
were first thought extinct and in which General Vidaar acquired the
leverage to seize the crown of Agaptus—the Kuld were originally harmless
nomadic tribes of two to three hundred that lived off the tundras of the
north. They would feed on grass, bark, shrubs, insects, and carcasses; in
winter, foraging bands would occasionally isolate and hunt the weakest of
the wild ylark herds. They seemed to have reached a balance with what the
land could bear.

Things changed when Sentian settlers started building farms just south of
the high plains where the Kuld lived. At first the Kuld seemed timid and
harmless, but eventually they realized that the well-fed domesticated ylark
and tended fields made a wonderful source of food. Conditioned by both
evolution and habit to gorge when a feast is available in order to survive
the lean season, the Kuld ate and ate, overrunning the settlers.

In response, the Sentians marshaled armies and marched against these
invaders from the north, who seemed to be mere brutes incapable of
speech or understanding. At first the Kuld were massacred without
resistance; but the scent of all the dead meat only attracted more hordes.
The Kuld kept coming and their sheer numbers were enough to stymie the
Sentians.

Naturally endowed with a high birth rate, short maturing cycle, and long
life span, the Kuld numbers had previously been kept in check by the
scarcity of food, but no more. They could replenish their numbers much
faster than the Sentians—who, it turned out, were also tasty delicacies.

After years of war, the Kuld were seemingly eradicated from Sentia;
General Vidaarus' armies scoured the icelands to locate any remaining
Kuld nests. It's only then that Sentian scholars realized that the creatures
had a culture, writing system, religion, social structure, and so forth. But by
then Vidaarus had declared himself king and decreed the destruction of all

scholarly work and writings, so that knowledge of the Kuld was lost again until sparse manuscripts were rediscovered by Elvorix scholars centuries later.

Following the Great Catastrophe, areas that were previously treeless tundra were covered under ice sheets. The Kuld, who had gradually repopulated their territory, started moving south—coming in contact with Elvorix, Vidaar, and Jaarl forces already vying for reduced resources.

Religion

Most of what is known of the Kuld religion was tentatively decoded from their etched stone writings or learned from battlefield observers. They worship what they call the Source, as near as anyone can translate—the origin of all life and all food, which vomited the Kuld out of its depth at the dawn of creation. Nothing found so far actively supports the Elvorix myth that links the Kuld to the forgotten goddess Kuldarus.

The Source is not a personified deity, but a force of nature; according to their recent writings, it appears the Kuld believe that the Great Catastrophe—the "great upheaval"—is what happened when the Source ate something unpleasant and vomited the glaciers over the former lands of the Kuld. No mention has been found so far of the fact that the sun looks redder and smaller.

Kuld society is a sort of caste system where the oldest individuals are the most respected and form the priesthood. Individuals who have reached an advanced age also display greater digestive ability, allowing them to consume a greater range of substances, including some still toxic to younger Kuld.

The Kuld's religious ceremonies consist of one or more shaman regurgitating into a great bowl that is placed on top of a sacred pillar etched and carved with glyphs. The scents from the vomit are used to share instruction with other Kuld on the Source and enlighten them on different edible substances.

For more details on Kuldarus, see *"Kuldarus: Ruler of the Underworld"* on page 253; for the Source, see *"The Kuld's All-Powerful Source"* on page 255.

The Kuld Hordes

Kuld: The nameless, short, fat, and blue rank-and-file of Kuld forces.

Shuda: Kuld who have an ability—whether natural or developed is unknown—to project their acidic vomit and use it as a weapon in battle. They must gorge to the point of near-bursting before they can perform this feat, and often rupture explosively when they are killed.

Ur-Kuld: Smarter Kuld who manage to pick up the weapons and armor of fallen opponents and use them without disemboweling themselves.

Goola: Veteran Kuld whose hide is now greatly toughened with age and scarring. Goola are identified by their distinctive scars from one battle to the next and are typically several times as old as any Sentian.

Marhn: The huge creatures the Kuld use as their shock forces.

Guldul Rider: The strange Kuld cavalry are mounted on relatively slow but unpredictable snail-like creatures that leave a caustic ooze and bite savagely.

Augurst: The most revered among the Kuld, they are battle-priests, elders, and leaders. They are followed by attendants that carry huge bowls in which the Augurst vomits; the regurgitations are used to interpret the will of the Source and perform rituals.

"The Kuld are sufficiently numerous and dangerous to make alliance with the Elvorix and/or Vidaar an attractive option from time to time. We avoid them when we can—the lands they occupy are poor, and would make a desolate homeland in any event. We will have to fight them eventually, but we can use them to our advantage until then. Let the Broke-Backs and the Weaklings fight them—that only means that there will be less of all of them to fight *us*."
—Iva the Stubborn, Jaarl scholar

From interview notes for the volume "The Explorers," by Matia Bibulus. Transcribed by Bura Bibulus Ven Proudheart, 88 AGC.

People

The Kuld are voracious creatures capable of eating and digesting just about anything but metal and rock. It all goes into their insatiable gullets. Armor, helms, and even weapons can be stored in a vestigial cavity to be regurgitated later and hurled back at the enemy.

They have a language, a writing system, a caste system, rudimentary tools, and a religion, but no one has been able to make significant progress in communicating with them. While Elvorix scholars can partly decipher their etchings and glyphs, most attempts at communication with live Kuld have resulted in partial or complete consumption of said scholars.

Kuld biology remains poorly understood. They do not appear to be mammalian; they have blueish skin, no fur, and like the Jaarl have only three fingers plus an opposable thumb on each hand. Their keenest sense is smell, and they can pick up the scent of food from miles away. They are capable of regurgitating partially eaten food to use the resulting smell for communication with other Kuld; to create etchings, carvings, and tattoos using their acidic stomach juices; or as projectile weapon against foes.

Male and female Kuld are distinguishable only by slight variations in hide coloration in and around the eyes, elbows, knees, and navel; females often have slightly reddened flesh and males are more ashen in complexion. Based on cautious observation of a Kuld nest over the course of two years, one Elvorix scholar claimed that individual Kuld shifted from male to female, then back to male again over the course of her study.

Female Kuld can bear four or five spawn in a single pregnancy, with an apparent gestation period of no more than two months. Infant Kuld are born with a thick, viscous coating of extremely toxic mucus, possibly needed to prevent its parents from immediately consuming their offspring. Well-fed infants progress to adolescence in about a month, and well-fed adolescents reach adulthood in an additional two months.

Despite their rapid maturation, Kuld can show great longevity, with some documented to be well over 200 years old, as recognized by their particular battle scars and glyph tattoos.

Wandering Kuld

The following is presented by this author in the interest of completeness, but has been vehemently disputed by most scholars. However, this author must insist that her careful research supports the veracity of this unexpected phenomenon.

Sometimes a Kuld will suddenly stop eating, or will look quizzically at their own vomit or freeze mid-scratch. A look of bewilderment will pass over their normally placid faces. Some say it is a bad bit of gas, others that Kuldarus has taken her eye off them for just a moment. Regardless of the reason, these Kuld will leave the others behind and walk towards the warm lands. Often once reaching civilization they are mistaken for their voracious cousins. Sometimes, however, they are noticed to be, well, not exactly smart, but… different somehow.

These rare "Wandering Kuld" make attempts at communicating with civilized beings, sometimes going as far as learning rudimentary speech. They may behave in ways that appear friendly, even loyal to those they manage to communicate with. If they are recognized as Wanderers by their own kind, they may be ostracized or devoured.

Kuld Player Characters?

As a faction, the Kuld are difficult to mix with any of the others since they tend to, well, eat everyone else. Nevertheless, they are sentient and playable, but they communicate through scent and their mysterious writing, which in a mixed party creates another hurdle.

The "Wandering Kuld" phenomenon is the way to go for people who wish to include Kuld player characters among a group of non-Kuld PCs. Alternately, your entire group may consist of Kuld.

We recommend you read the section *"Creating the Heroes"* on page 148 before you decide whether to treat them as player characters, antagonists, or both.

If you choose the default option to have Kuld as non-player characters, use the stat blocks provided in the *"Beasts of Agaptus"* section on page 109; if you prefer to use them as player characters, use the same rules as for other player characters and the information provided here to, ahem, flesh them out.

"Where did they come from, and how did they survive? We thought them wiped out after the Purging War—where have they been for the last thousand years? What do they want? Why have they returned? There are so many things about the Kuld that we do not know and so few that we know for certain. Learning the answers may mean the difference between defeat and victory, and hence between extinction and survival. Getting the answers without being devoured does, however, pose quite a technical challenge."
—Rustica Bibulus, Elvorix scholar

From interview notes for the volume "The Explorers," by Matia Bibulus. Transcribed by Bura Bibulus Ven Proudheart, 88 AGC.

Names

The Kuld don't really have names as we know them, since they communicate through scent. Any names as we know them—as far as we can reconstruct from the glyphs deciphered to date—have been given to notable Kuld leaders and Marhn by their Elvorix, Vidaar, or Jaarl opponents, often based on a characteristic sound they make or a recognizable physical characteristic (or smell, which they may emit intentionally or as a result of their diet). Among themselves, they use name-equivalents that are descriptive, at least in writing.

Given Names: Aaaagrrblah, Aargh, Ack, AhhhWuun, Blubbous, Clubfoot, Dank Cave, Goola, Grrsnikt, Grunt, HnnHnn, Kagaar, Maaahaunn, Mossback, Old White-Scar, River-Berries, Shambla, Waaanoooo, Ylark Sweat.

Scent-Names: Brood-Bearer, Flatulent Hero, Horde-Leader, Inspiring Perfume, Meal-Finder, Old Odoriferous Retcher, Powerful Pungency, Rock-Eater, Source-Scented.

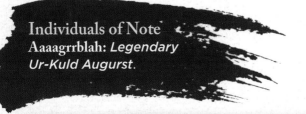

Individuals of Note
Aaaagrrblah: *Legendary Ur-Kuld Augurst.*

"I'll take my place in the shieldwall against any foe who takes the field, but the Kuld…. There seems to be no end to them. It's easy enough to kill one or two, but there are never just one or two. Not only do they eat almost anything, they eat almost everything— including the wounded if they have an opportunity. I've seen my share of fighting, and dying, but nothing is as horrible as the screams of your injured comrades as they get pulled apart like joints of ylark and stuffed into those greedy, rubbery mouths."
—Ulf Long-teeth, Vidaar Bondee

From interview notes for the volume "The Explorers," by Matia Bibulus. Transcribed by Bura Bibulus Ven Proudheart, 88 AGC.

Places

Kuld-Overrun Village

This used to be a mountain village, but the Kuld hordes descending from the north scared away or ate everything and everyone that used to live here. The Kuld settled in since food was plentiful and the place was suitable to carve burrows, but the climate continued to cool. Soon, the horde will be on the move again, looking for a new place to eat and nest.

What you can find there:

Tundra, largely stripped of vegetation.

Nearby snow fields and advancing glaciers.

Ruins of former settlements, stripped bare of all but rock and metal elements.

Graffiti etchings of Kuld glyphs on rock facings, ice walls, and stone ruins.

Sacred pedestal carved and etched with glyphs, topped with a flat slab. On the slab usually sits a large bowl filled with the recent contents of an Augurst's stomach.

Burrows or caves the Kuld use as dwellings, either natural or carved.

Spawning grounds in a larger burrow.

Kuld artisans crafting bowls, jewelry, and rudimentary tools.

Guldul pens in a separate burrow.

Marhn herd wandering around on the tundra.

Things that can happen:

Smelling Ceremony. A horde of Kuld, especially young ones, are gathered around a carved pillar and showing reverence as a gnarly old Augurst is lifting a large bowl filled with smelly bits.

Glyph-Carving. Kuld sages trace glyphs in a rock face using stomach acids. Though unappetizing to non-Kuld, the task requires great precision over several passes. Younger Kuld assist and learn the process. Professor Marinus Bibulus of the North Sentia Academy of Sciences is convinced that some of the glyphs carved here indicate the location of a lost Ancient metropolis the Kuld have stumbled on. Can a group of explorers return with the secret—and without attracting the Kuld hordes back with them?

Assembling the Horde! The scent of food is on the wind and other hordes of Kuld are converging; the venerable Augurst is vomiting forth commands, and the exodus will begin soon. It's too bad the heroes' hometown lies straight in their path…

"The Kuld are unable to live in society, and have no need because they are sufficient unto themselves. They must be either beasts or gods."

—Calpurnus Bibulus ix Agapta co Agapta

Gamemaster Characters

Here are thumbnails of a few people this author has met in her travels, who have gained notoriety or infamy in the Sentian lands.

The character and creature descriptions are accompanied by summary boxes providing some key details so you can add them to your adventures. You'll notice that most don't have approaches. That's because we use the Fractal Adventure method with its own approaches; minor non-player characters (NPCs) just add a few stunts to customize each scene. See *"Creating Adventures"* on page 288 for how this works!

Elvorix

Lord Maladros Bibulus ix Agapta co Agapta

The Elvorix ruler is fair of face, with rich auburn fur and splendid bearing. His mind is keen and he is known as a capable scholar; his writings are noted for their extensive bibliographies. He shows the same attention to detail in his rulership as in his research. He keeps informed of everything, but he shows great deliberation in reaching decisions and even more in demanding their implementation. This author speaks from limited observation, of course, as she has only been in the king's presence on two occasions, both at a distance.

LORD MALADROS

High Concept: *Scholar King of Agapta, Lord of the Elvorix.*
Trouble: *We Must Not Be Hasty.*
Other Aspects: *Patron of the Arts, Attention to Detail.*
Skilled (+2) at: Research, protocol, art appreciation.
Bad (-2) at: Making decisions.

"The wise prince knows that the attention of the gods is attracted as often by good works as by evil."

—Lord Maladros Bibulus ix Agapta co Agapta, *"Treatise on Rulership"*

Seadros Bibulus ix Atronius

The well-known author of *A Comprehensive Summary to the History and Geography of the Glorious Elvorix Nation and Some of Its Barbaric Neighbors*, Seadros is a more popular than rigorous scholar who holds both the prestigious position of Scribe to Lord Maladros and the Marinus Nummus Chair of Literature at the Elvora Bibulus Academy. This author is unable to understand why Seadros' writings are not routinely filed in the fiction section of the library.

SEADROS BIBULUS

High Concept: *Scribe to Lord Maladros.*
Trouble: *We Must Not Hold It Against Them, They're Not As Civilized As We Are.*
Other Aspects: *My Graduate Students Will Take Care of It.*
Skilled (+2) at: Etiquette, hobnobbing, getting grants, managing grad students.
Bad (-2) at: Making friends, pretending to be humble.

Homarus, son of Rogus

Homarus is the most celebrated artist of his generation, walking the thin line between technical excellence and obedience to the classic canon. The elderly painter's work, which has been so remarkably consistent throughout his long career, has started recently to depart from his more typical style in ways that some critics have praised and others have blamed on age. He is rumored to be working on a large mural that he allows no one to see, but promises will be his masterwork.

HOMARUS

High Concept: *Painter to Lord Maladros.*
Trouble: *Itching to Break New Artistic Ground.*
Other Aspects: *It's Not Ready Yet!*
Skilled (+2) at: Art, pretending to be inoffensive, flattering his subjects.
Bad (-2) at: Business, athletic pursuits.

General Sigurod Gladius

In charge of the area in the most dire position against the Kuld, General Sigurod Gladius has shown limited strategic ability against the enemy, but immense skill in retaining his position. He seems to have a knack for surrounding himself with people with the right abilities—even when that ability consists of falling on one's own sword to save the general's reputation. Metaphorically speaking… mostly.

SIGUROD GLADIUS

High Concept: *General of the Northeastern Provincial Garrison.*
Trouble: *It's Not My Fault, It's These Idiots.*
Other Aspects: *Good Eye for Personnel Selection, Skilled Bureaucrat.*
Skilled (+2) at: Golden mediocrity, passing the buck, wielding a sword.
Bad (-2) at: Strategy, seizing the moment.

Laetitia Bibulus ix Gailus

This infamous scholar was evicted from the Elvora Bibulus Academy and stripped of her credentials for falsifying research over a decade ago. While she has formulated innovative and daring theories, she has also shown herself to be willing to go to unethical lengths in support of her ideas. Her current whereabouts are unknown, but she is rumored to be sponsored by a fringe religious and political organization dedicated to Prolyus, Elvorix god of war, in order to conduct illegal archaeological research.

LAETITIA BIBULUS

High Concept: *Rogue Elvorix Scholar.*
Trouble: *I'll Show Them All!*
Other Aspects: *Sponsored by the Seal of Prolyus.*
Skilled (+2) at: Finding obscure information, enduring discomfort.
Bad (-2) at: Taking criticism, patience.

Matia Bibulus ix Atronia co Agapta, daughter of Toranus

Your humble historian. Of modest origins, she has often been sneered at by better-born scholars, as much for her mixed ancestry as for her iconoclastic ideas. To earn her keep while studying at Elvora Bibulus Academy, she worked as part of the civilian support staff for General Orvas' army and was captured by the Jaarl. She escaped nearly two years later and published her story, earning a certain amount of fame. Her notoriety made other scholars nervous; she was commissioned by the Academy to travel as far away as possible and send her travel notes for publication.

High Concept: *Well-Traveled Elvorix Scholar.*
Trouble: *Never Satisfied With the Easy Path*
Other Aspects: *Ex-Jaarl Captive*, *Commoner and Proud of It.*
Skilled (+2) at: Exploring, understanding new cultures, making friends, adapting to change.
Bad (-2) at: Enduring boredom, conforming to convention.

Vidaar

General Vidaarus

The ninety-first Vidaarian king is a burly, aging buck with booming laughter and a seemingly limitless love of partying. He is also a canny politician who manages to keep his throne by maneuvering his potential rivals into fighting one another rather than setting their sights on him. The list of these potential rivals includes the Dowodiks, the High Priest, and Vidaarus' own brood of maladjusted children.

VIDAARUS
High Concept: *Ninety-First King of the Vidaar.*
Trouble: *Ruthless Schemer.*
Other Aspects: *Jolly Patriarch Demeanor*, *Healthy Paranoia.*
Skilled (+2) at: Warfare, politics, manipulation, feasting.
Bad (-2) at: Parenting, trusting.

Dowodik Aenwubba

Despite his old war wounds, the Dowodik of the East remains a force to contend with. He manages to keep both the Jaarl and Elvorix forces at bay, although he has mostly maneuvered to remain out of direct armed clashes with the Kuld. His enemies say he's been afraid of them since the mighty Goola ate his leg; his faithful claim he's got a cunning plan.

AENWUBBA
High Concept: *Chieftain of the Rabble Clan and its Fleet of Raiders*.
Trouble: *Lost a Leg to a Goola*.
Other Aspects: *Dowodik of the East*.
Skilled (+2) at: Surviving, warfare, sailing, keeping the troops in line.
Bad (-2) at: Learning new tricks, making allies.

Ragnhild the Fair

The High Priest of Akka-Maas is not pleased with the way the War of Ashes is going. She sometimes feels she could do a much better job if the Vidaar nation was a theocracy, but wily old King Vidaarus has been able to keep her focused on the infighting among her own ranks.

RAGNHILD
High Concept: *High Priest of Akka-Maas*.
Trouble: *Do Not Question Me!*
Other Aspects: *It Doesn't Mean What You Think It Means, The One God Is Watching*.
Skilled (+2) at: Tyromancy, artillery, dancing, putting on a good show, keeping her position.
Bad (-2) at: Ecumenism, sharing power.

Ulryg of the Death Singers

This tall, gaunt Vidaar warrior with an oversized sword is rumored to sometimes show up on the battlefield, slaying enemies left and right with the might of many bucks; but he always disappears after the fray. Witnesses claim to have heard him brag that he wields the original Sword of Sentius. However, these witnesses tend to come to a bad end shortly after.

ULRYG
High Concept: *Moody Albino Warrior.*
Trouble: *Pawn of the Gods.*
Other Aspects: *"It's the Sword of Sentius Himself!"*
Skilled (+2) at: Killing things with a big sword, brooding, getting in trouble.
Bad (-2) at: Keeping his troops alive.

Captain Volo Troll-Axe

The greedy captain is an ally of rogue scholar Laetitia Bibulus, at least as long as she brings him profit. He and his crew of miscreants can be found looting Ancient ruins, in between bouts of piracy near the coast of Sentia.

VOLO TROLL-AXE
High Concept: *Vidaar Captain for Hire.*
Trouble: *Is This Thing Valuable?*
Other Aspects: *Captain of the Skyhammer.*
Skilled (+2) at: Commanding his crew, battle, sailing, looting.
Bad (-2) at: Book knowledge, resisting temptation, being trustworthy.

Jaarl

Executor Adalgisa

The three Executors elected by the Jaarl senate lead the nation, and Executor Adalgisa is currently the senior of the three. She comes from the Provider Guild and can call on favors from just about anyone. Her mastery of the art of deal-brokering has served her well in her political career. Her dedication to the creation of the new Jaarl homeland is unswerving and she shows nothing but disdain for Sentians.

ADALGISA

High Concept: *Senior Executor of the Jaarl Nation.*
Trouble: *The Jaarl Must Prevail at Any Cost.*
Other Aspects: *They Owe Me a Favor, Skilled Mediator.*
Skilled (+2) at: Negotiating, politics, finding resources, having a Plan B, remembering friends.
Bad (-2) at: Relaxing, accepting help with no strings attached.

Rettori Agirix

Perhaps the most prestigious general in the nation, Agirix commands the devotion of the Legion of the Red Morning thanks to a series of decisive victories over the Elvorix and Vidaar since the dissolution of the Pact of Prolyus. He was responsible for the strategy that lured General Orvas' armies into celebrating victory prematurely, and allowed the Jaarl to slaughter them. But Agirix was hard-hit when both his offspring were killed in recent months, one reportedly fallen against the Kuld and the other crushed in the collapse of a construction site.

AGIRIX

High Concept: *Commander of the 1st Company, Legion of the Red Morning.*
Trouble: *Where Is the Heir Who Will Carry My Sword?*
Other Aspects: *Savvy Strategist, Duty is My Honor.*
Skilled (+2) at: Warfare, discipline, commanding the respect of his troops.
Bad (-2) at: The mushy sentimental stuff.

Head Planner Gualterutia

The Head Planner of the new city of Karthak is an up-and-coming leader in the Planner Guild, a member of the far-seeing and theory-minded Scriptio. She shows total confidence in her own judgment of what's best for the nation. She feels that the current political structure, devised after the Murmadon refugees landed on Iradon, was hasty; until the new homeland is secure and the vermin have been removed, the Builder Guild should be in charge without having to waste so much time courting votes from the other guilds. She plans to get elected to the senate and introduce a bill to delegate all executive authority to the Builders.

> ### GUALTERUTIA
> High Concept: *Head Planner of Karthak*.
> Trouble: *It's for the Greater Good*.
> Other Aspects: *The Builders Need to Be in Charge, Influent Member of the Scriptio*.
> **Skilled (+2) at:** Figuring things out, politics, planning, swaying opinions, making herself indispensable.
> **Bad (-2) at:** Taking no for an answer, military tactics.

Venerable Master Rocca

The undisputed master of the Virian Order for over fifty years, Rocca is still fit and spry but she's not the Jaarl she used to be. While her arcane powers are impressive, her strength is waning. But she commands the loyalty of the generations of Virian adepts she has trained and her word remains unchallenged. She is rarely seen outside of Murmadolunagh anymore.

> ### ROCCA
> High Concept: *Venerable Master of the Virian Order*.
> Trouble: *Frail With Age*.
> Other Aspects: *Attuned to the Sacred Rock, All Jaarl Are My Children*.
> **Skilled (+2) at:** Using arcane powers, knowing obscure lore, commanding respect, teaching.
> **Bad (-2) at:** Recovering from damage, enduring cold weather.

Kuld
Mossback

Found wandering alone in the tundra by Boegert Aedituus the Mellow, a priest of Atronia, this Kuld seemed quite harmless and even eager to interact with non-Kuld. He was brought back to the Bibulus Academy and affectionately named "Mossback" in reference to the mossy growth between his shoulders, which suggests he is quite old. He appears to be able to find the direction of North thanks to this lichen. Over time he learned to understand, but not speak, Elvorish. As far as the scholars can tell, he is quite content to stay in his (extremely secured) quarters, save for the occasional (military-supervised) stroll outside to sniff the air and eat whatever happens to be laying about (*no Sentians!*).

MOSSBACK

High Concept: *Wandering Kuld*

Trouble: *Captive—Er, Research Subject—at Bibulus Academy*

Other Aspects: *Built-In Compass, Just Wants to be Friends*.

Skilled (+2) at: Communicating through scents and glyphs, orienteering, hiding small objects.

Bad (-2) at: Etiquette, playing with pets without eating them.

"Day 206. At last a breakthrough! I have finally learned the reason for Mossback's frequent regurgitation—he has been learning to write Elvorix! Each day I have been sharing with him excerpts from the same book I used to teach my own fawns to read; today Mossback etched the words "walk" and "food" into the stone tile. I predict that we will need to increase our budget for flooring."

—From the journal of Boegert Aedituus the Mellow, Elvorix scholar

Beasts of Agaptus

The information provided in this chapter has been pulled from numerous well-authenticated sources, from Utari Bibulus' "On the Creatures of Sentia and Surrounding Isles" to Marien Bibulus' "Field Guide to Iradon Carnivores." Where possible, incomplete or obsolete information has been supplemented from personal observations and interviews with the most reliable Vidaar captains and sailors this author could find.

Matia: "Shall we continue where we left off yesterday? You had been following the ancient map to the ruins of a library."

Rustica: "Yes, well we realized that there were some mistakes on our copy of the map."

Iva: "One little copying error, and she'll never let me forget it."

Rustica: "'Upside down' is not a little copying error. Now hush. The entire area was a woody marshland. Cold, wet, and dismal."

Iva: "I kept fishing Kuri out of mud puddles and picking brambles out of his fur."

Kuri: "HEE!"

Rustica: "Then one of the hills moved. It turns out we had spent several days hiking on, over, and around a svampfode. It looked just like a hill, with trees, bushes, even pools of stagnant water."

Iva: "It was lying on top of the entrance to the library. We needed to move it."

Ulf: "A simple matter! Here at last was a creature worthy of my talents. I charged, found a suitable location near the top, and began plunging my spear into it to get its attention.

Rustica: "It was like everything on the hill was suddenly trying to kill us. Packs of kanids came baying out of the brush, and the air was thick with uhyre and ilk."

Ulf: "Aye! It was glorious! After weeks of nothing but walking and listening to these two argue, to hear the blood sing in my veins, to feel the axe in my hands once again!"

Rustica: "While we were dealing with all this the svampfode got to its feet and started lumbering off!"

Ulf: "I, Ulf Long-teeth, alone against a creature of legend!"

Iva: "An uhyre almost bit Kuri's head off."

Rustica: "And the kanids ruined my best pair of boots."

Ulf: "And all the while the svampfode travelled on, league after league."

Iva: "We decided to rescue—I mean, retrieve—Ulf. The library had been there for a thousand years, what difference could a couple of days make?"

Rustica: "So of course while we were gone the Kuld moved in."

From interview notes for the volume "The Explorers," by Matia Bibulus. Transcribed by Bura Bibulus Ven Proudheart, 88 AGC.

Stat blocks for these creatures are presented here for the sake of easy reference. For a full explanation of their meaning, read on to *"Playing The War of Ashes: Fate of Agaptus"* on page 175.

Most of the time, beasts will be like minions or groups of minions. (See *"Characters and Creatures"* on page 302).

However, depending on how formidable the creature is you may use different stats for it.

» If the creature is a standard specimen of its species, use the stats below.

» If the creature is a particularly dangerous, tough, canny, or otherwise harder to kill, add the stress boxes in parenthesis (where applicable).

» If the creature is a named character or main adversary, for instance Urbash the Marhn Overlord, use the stats below as a guideline for making them a full character sheet.

Dirkus: Depending on whether you are talking to a farmer, builder, merchant, or city-dweller, the dirkus is a welcome addition to the menu, a pest, a fur-bearing source of revenue, or a cute pet. Dirkus are found in heavily vegetated areas where they feed on giant fungus trees, keeping them from becoming too large. Sadly, their habitat has been shrinking steadily for the better part of a century; some now venture into the open to reach villages and gnaw on wooden buildings. Nevertheless, they are very soft and make charming cooing sounds, and are often adopted as pets.

DIRKUS

Weight: 0 (Smaller than a Sentian; it takes a small swarm to get a weight of 1.)
High Concept: *Cute Little Vermin*.
Trouble: *Gnaw, Gnaw, Gnaw*.
Other Aspects: *Soft Plushy Fur*.
Skilled (+2) at: Gnawing, scurrying, ganging up.
Bad (-2) at: Climbing, obeying commands.

STRESS
Individual: None (An overcome action will defeat them.)
Swarm: ○○

Fedtik: These sizable creatures bear the cold fairly well and thus are becoming more common in areas where they used to be unknown. They graze tundra grasses and shrubs, and during mating season they fight in brutal but cheerful competitions that trample the barely-thawed plains. Both males and females bear horns which fall off in summer and grow back a little larger every year. The cubs do not start bearing horns until their second year.

They are generally friendly and unafraid of Sentians, and on occasion have seemed to confuse one for a young fedtik. It can be very difficult to evade the parental affection of a fedtik without making it angry. Fortunately, they possess at least enough intelligence to flee in terror at the approach of the Kuld.

Fedtik

Weight: 2 (Bigger than a Sentian.)
High Concept: *Tundra-Dwelling Yahoo.*
Trouble: *Horribly Friendly.*
Other Aspects: *Those Arms Are STRONG!*
Skilled (+2) at: Roughhousing, sprinting, parenting.
Bad (-2) at: Inter-species communication.

STRESS
○○

Flalhund: In the northern parts of Sentia, flalhund are kept as pets and used to guard cattle, dwellings, and farms. They are prized for their friendliness, their ruggedness, but especially for their ability to detect the approach of the Kuld early on. When all the flalhund disappear, villagers grab their most precious and portable possessions and start running.

Flalhund are rather inexpensive to keep because they are omnivorous and will eat any table leavings. They make good companions for fawns and are friendly and obedient, and even proactive in anticipating command, but not all that finely attuned to proper time and place.

FLALHUND

Weight: 0 (Smaller than a Sentian; it takes a small swarm to get a weight of 1.)
High Concept: *A Sentian's Best Friend*.
Trouble: *Overly Literal In Obeying Commands*.
Other Aspects: *The Kuld Are Coming! The Kuld Are Coming!*
Skilled (+2) at: Guarding, tracking, playing, running.
Bad (-2) at: Standing up to the Kuld.

STRESS
Individual: None (An overcome action will defeat them.)
Swarm: ○ ○

Foadstor (Agapta's Paw): The enormous foadstor are very rare, although they live thousands of years. Their movements and metabolism are so slow that they are sometimes confused for strange terrain formations. Foadstor are herbivores; they position themselves over their target and slurp up the vegetation with their tentacles.

Because of their size and relatively benign behavior, they are generally not attacked; when they are spotted, they are prodded away from the paths of villages and cities. Some Sentians worship their droppings, which are also very rare. This is not as peculiar as it sounds: some clever Elvorix farmers lure foadstor to wild areas they wish to convert to crop-growing, and let the foadstor do the brush clearing. The droppings are a bonus—rich in nutrients and relatively free from unpleasant smells, they make superlative fertilizer for the newly cleared plots.

Kuld try to gnaw on foadstor now and again, but so far have not taken to adding them to their regular "menu."

FOADSTOR (AGAPTA'S PAW)

Weight: 8 (Big as a castle.)
High Concept: *Giant Forest-Clearing Machine.*
Trouble: *Slow, Slow, Slooooowwww.*
Other Aspects: *Doesn't Care What It Steps On.*
Skilled (+2) at: Eating vegetation. (A foadstor grazes one full zone at a time.)
Bad (-2) at: Moving fast.

STRESS
OOOO(OO), +1 mild consequence, +1 moderate consequence
Special: A Foadstor may invoke the aspect *Giant Forest-Clearing Machine* for effect to reduce the damage of any attack to one stress (even if the attack was lethal).
Special: A Foadstor may invoke the aspect *Doesn't Care What It Steps On* for effect when using the attack action to affect everyone in an adjacent zone (but not its own). The Foadstor rolls only once for the attack, but everyone in the zone defends individually.

Gamba: Crustaceans distantly related to the ilk, used by Jaarl as battle mounts. They are favored when cavalry units need to be transported by sea over long distances because, like ilk, their dried eggs can be kept for long periods of dormancy then rehydrated and hatched once their destination is reached. Unlike ilk, they do not swarm and in fact do not like each other all that much, so gamba cavalry units are never kept in tight formation for very long or they start fighting among themselves. To prevent them from seeing other gamba and becoming agitated, the Jaarl usually keep their eyes covered with goggles that limit their peripheral vision and keep the units in dispersed formation.

The goggles are also useful to prevent the gamba from being distracted or blinded by excess light. They have excellent low-light vision. They are kept in the southern areas conquered by the Jaarl as they do not fare well in freezing conditions.

GAMBA
Weight: 2 (Bigger than a Sentian.)
High Concept: *Crustacean Juggernaut.*
Trouble: *Not So Good With the Cold.*
Other Aspects: *Low-Light Vision.*
Skilled (+2) at: Shrugging off damage, moving quickly.
Bad (-2) at: Navigating in bright light, getting along with other gamba.

STRESS
○○(○○), +1 mild consequence

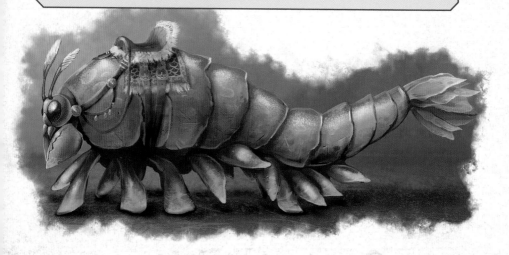

Gromal: Gromal are omnivores found primarily in mountainous areas. Their dexterous paws and flexible spines allow them to keep their footing and reach impressive speeds in rough terrain and steep inclines. Some rural communities reportedly use them as mounts. Their spiky tails should be avoided as the spines are venomous; the gromal use their tail to swat at anyone or anything that irritates them.

They primarily feed on small scurrying animals but in a pinch they will snack on an insect hive as an easy source of protein.

GROMAL
Weight: 2 (Bigger than a Sentian.)
High Concept: *Agile Mountain-Side Dweller*.
Trouble: *Not Too Patient*.
Other Aspects: *Smarter Than You Think*, *Venomous Spines*.
Skilled (+2) at: Running up and down slopes, enduring cold conditions.
Bad (-2) at: Long-distance running.

STRESS
○○(○), +1 mild consequence

Grotte: Grotte are predators who use aggressive mimicry to disguise themselves as rock formations and even caves, waiting for prey to enter their maw in search of shelter. They don't typically seek confrontation, but they are well-armored against it. Dispatching a grotte is a difficult task because they are so tough and so very, very patient; to make matters worse, they are not nearly as slow as one might expect for something that poses as a rock.

GROTTE

Weight: 6 (Big as a town hall.)
High Concept: *This Cave Has Teeth?*
Trouble: *Once You See It, You Can't Miss It.*
Other Aspects: *Huge Rock-Like Claws.*
Skilled (+2) at: Pretending to be a cave, eating creatures that walk into its maw. (A grotte lying in wait constitutes an entire zone.)
Bad (-2) at: Maneuvering in tight confines.

STRESS

○○○○(○○○), +1 mild consequence
Special: A Grotte may invoke the aspect *This Cave Has Teeth?* when using the attack action to affect everyone in its zone. The Grotte rolls only once for the attack, but everyone in the zone defends individually.

Guldul: A giant snail used as a battle mount by some Kuld. It sports numerous large teeth and armored skin like broken glass, which secretes a viscous ooze that burns the skin and bleaches fur. Only the voracious Kuld have managed to domesticate them, probably because the gulgul are inedible even to them.

They generally move very slowly but are known for their unexpected bursts of speed; Elvorix scholars theorize that the caustic mucus trail they secrete becomes so slick that they just slide along until the slime has spread thin.

GULDUL
Weight: 2 (Bigger than a Sentian.)
High Concept: *Tough, Toothed Giant Snail*.
Trouble: *Slow Creeping Death*.
Other Aspects: *Caustic Slime*.
Skilled (+2) at: Sudden burst of speed, biting.
Bad (-2) at: Chasing, maneuvering.

STRESS
○○(○), +1 mild consequence

Ilk: The ilk are crustacean-like creatures that move as a crawling swarm of locusts, antennae twitching and wings clicking in the air. A swarm of ilk can strip an area of life almost as efficiently as the Kuld themselves; unlike the Kuld, however, they only seem to care for live prey. The Jaarl Ilk-Masters have some control over them, and jealously guard the secret of this mastery.

Ilk

Weight: 0 (Smaller than a Sentian; it takes a small swarm to get a weight of 1.)
High Concept: *Unstoppable Carnivorous Swarm.*
Trouble: *Bloodlust.*
Other Aspects: *The Eggs Will Keep Forever!*
Skilled (+2) at: Swarming, biting, flying.
Bad (-2) at: Everything else.

STRESS
Individual: None (An overcome action will defeat them.)
Swarm: ○ ○ (○)

"Ilk-masters are always easy to identify. They have an otherworldly calm about them, as though nothing, no matter how terrible, can disturb or upset them. They also have nicknames like 'One-Foot,' 'Scarface,' and 'Armless.'" —Iva, Jaarl scholar

From interview notes for the volume "The Explorers," by Matia Bibulus. Transcribed by Bura Bibulus Ven Proudheart, 88 AGC.

Jormund: An amphibious denizen of seasonal wetland areas in the Sentian lowlands, a hungry jormund can mean trouble for the unwary traveler. The jormund is known for its eerie song; whether the song is used to communicate with other jormund or to attract or confuse potential prey is not certain.

What some enterprising luthiers have discovered, however, is that if you can get past a jormond's tough defenses and venomous fangs, its ribcage makes excellent musical instruments with a very pure sound. Additionally, if the tough hide has not been too badly damaged during the acquisition of the ribcage and if the artisan doesn't lose a few fingers on its sharp scales while preparing it, the hide makes an excellent skin for the instrument.

JORMUND
Weight: 1 (Sentian-sized.)
High Concept: *Four-Legged Amphibian Swamp Worm.*
Trouble: *Can't Get Too Far Away From Water.*
Other Aspects: *Eerie Song.*
Skilled (+2) at: Singing, biting, swimming.
Bad (-2) at: Everything else.

STRESS

Kanid: A wild carnivore of the southern, more temperate areas of Sentia and Matriga, the kanid live in packs, stalking herds of large herbivores such as wild ylark and culling out the weaker creatures. Because of their pack mentality, kanid have also been domesticated by both Elvorix and Vidaar villagers and can make excellent pets, fiercely protective of their adopted "pack." Elvorix farmers use them to herd domestic ylark, and Vidaar use them to hunt.

KANID
Weight: 0 (Smaller than a Sentian; it takes a small swarm to get a weight of 1.)
High Concept: *Stealthy Pack Hunter.*
Trouble: *Pack Mentality.*
Other Aspects: *Fast Sprinter.*
Skilled (+2) at: Ganging up, hunting, running.
Bad (-2) at: Fighting determined opposition.

STRESS
Individual: None (An overcome action will defeat them.)
Swarm: ○○(○), +1 mild consequence

Kreob (Howler): A sea mollusk of southern Sentia that makes a howling noise by blowing air through its chitinous shell. Kreob colonies dwell in the shallow near-shore areas and bury their eggs in clutches on sandy beaches in the intertidal zone. The howling sound is intended to warn intruders away from their nest and territory.

KREOB

Weight: 0 (Smaller than a Sentian; it takes a small swarm to get a weight of 1.)

High Concept: *Howler Crab.*

Trouble: *The Eggs—They're Always in Trouble!*

Other Aspects: *Nasty Sharp Pointy Spikes.*

Skilled (+2) at: Digging in the sand, pinching, swarming.

Bad (-2) at: Anything upland.

STRESS

Individual: None (An overcome action will defeat them.)

Swarm: ○ ○

The Kuld

The Kuld are discussed in their own chapter as a possible player faction, but they are likely to figure as antagonists as well in most campaigns.

The smaller, young Kuld form the bulk of a Kuld horde.

KULD

Weight: 0 (Smaller than a Sentian; it takes a small swarm to get a weight of 1.)
High Concept: *Blubberous Eating Machine*.
Trouble: *You Can't Have Just One*.
Other Aspects: *Tough Little Buggers*.
Skilled (+2) at: Smelling food, eating, ganging up.
Bad (-2) at: Communicating with non-Kuld.

STRESS

Individual: None (An overcome action will defeat them.)
Swarm: O(O)

SHUDA

Weight: 1 (Sentian-sized.)
High Concept: *Projectile-Vomiting Walking Artillery*.
Trouble: *Need to Gorge to Near-Death*.
Other Aspects: *Explosive Death Throes*.
Skilled (+2) at: Gorging, projectile vomiting.
Bad (-2) at: Everything else.

STRESS

O, +1 mild consequence (*About to Burst*)
Special: Shuda vomit attacks may be used against targets in its zone or an adjacent zone. A Shuda may invoke the aspect *Projectile-Vomiting Walking Artillery* when using the attack action to affect everyone in its zone or an adjacent zone. The Shuda rolls only once for the attack, but everyone in the zone defends individually.
Special: If a Shuda has the consequence *About to Burst*, after a successful attack against it, anyone may invoke that aspect for effect to immediately make an attack on everyone in the zone and one random adjacent zone, including themselves if they are close! The Shuda rolls one attack roll for this and everyone affected defends individually.

Ur-Kuld

Weight: 1 (Sentian-sized.)
High Concept: *Smarter, Weapon-Using Kuld.*
Trouble: *Not All That Dexterous.*
Other Aspects: *Scary As All Heck.*
Skilled (+2) at: Smelling food, eating, ganging up, using weapons.
Bad (-2) at: Everything else.

STRESS
○○

See "Creating the Heroes" on page 148 for details on how to play a Kuld as a player character.

GOOLA

Weight: 2 (Bigger than a Sentian.)

High Concept: *Legendary Ur-Kuld Leader.*

Trouble: *This Make Goola HUN-GRY!*

Other Aspects: *Stone-Hard Hide.*

Skilled (+2) at: Smelling food, eating, deflecting hits.

Bad (-2) at: Everything else.

STRESS

○○○(○), +1 mild consequence, +1 moderate consequence

MARHN

Weight: 4 (Big as a small hut.)

High Concept: *Kuld's Larger, Tougher Cousin.*

Trouble: *Smart As A Rock.*

Other Aspects: *Inspiring Sight for Kuld Eyes.*

Skilled (+2) at: Hitting things, survival in mountain terrain.

Bad (-2) at: Anything that requires smarts.

STRESS

○○○(○○), +1 mild consequence, +1 moderate consequence

Special: A Marhn may invoke the aspect *Kuld's Larger, Tougher Cousin* when using the attack action to make its attack lethal. For more information about lethal attacks, see *"Lethal Attacks"* on page 235.

AUGURST
Weight: 1 (Sentian-sized.)
High Concept: *Kuld Battle-Shaman*.
Trouble: *Need to Vomit to Reload*.
Other Aspects: *Pungent Bowl of Vomit*.
Skilled (+2) at: Stinking, vomiting, performing rituals.
Bad (-2) at: Everything else.

STRESS
○○(○○), +1 mild consequence, +1 moderate consequence
Special: For more information on performing rituals, see *"Magic"* on page 262.

Morgala: Morgala feed on the insect colonies that dwell in the tops of sweet-moss and sticky-fungus. They locate their food by scent and sound. Then they use their large, heavy feet to crush the protective needles and bramble around the prize, their small but nimble and well-protected hand-paws to pull the branches down, and their long flexible snout to suck up the insect colonies. They also use the large claws on their feet to peel off the bark at the base of large umbrella trees in search of succulent honey termites.

Morgala are fairly harmless but if terrified or cornered they can do a good deal of damage.

MORGALA
Weight: 1 (Sentian-sized.)
High Concept: *Armored Bipedal Anteater*.
Trouble: *Tiny Little Arms*.
Other Aspects: *Big Stompy Clawed Feet*.
Skilled (+2) at: Sniffing, stomping, sprinting.
Bad (-2) at: Stand-up fights.

STRESS
○

Mundicus: Mundicus are grazers from tundra zones, feeding on the short and hardy vegetation. As their former home has become iced over and southern regions are becoming more tundra-like, they have been migrating south. They are tough and bear the cold stoically; under that thick scaly armor is a layer of felt-like fur that serves as insulation. Their beady eyes have a limited field of vision, protected in the recesses under the frontal armor, so they navigate primarily by sound. They are able to feel approaching Kuld and other enemies through vibrations in the ground, which their sensitive feet detect.

Mundicus are relatively harmless except for the occasional stampede. Because they are amazingly hard to injure, weaponsmiths covet their insulated, cushioned, scaly plates to fashion into armor. However, since they tend to be found in the same regions as the Kuld or further north, hunting is limited and risky.

Mundicus

Weight: 2 (Bigger than a Sentian.)
High Concept: *Cold-Resistant Tundra Grazer*.
Trouble: *Limited Vision*.
Other Aspects: *Thick Armor-Like Hide*.
Skilled (+2) at: Withstanding cold conditions, charging, detecting vibrations.
Bad (-2) at: Seeing.

STRESS
OO(O)

Nhilde "trolls" are also discussed earlier in *"We Want You As A New Recruit: Vidaar Ranks"* on page 46.

Nhilde Trolls

The Nhilde trolls are at least twice as tall as the average Sentian, and four or five times as massive and powerful. They sport sloping brows, widely spaced dark eyes, and prominent ears; their receding chins hide large toothy jaws. They are covered in coarse fur ranging from almost white all the way to dark russet browns and slate greys. Nhilde have hands with opposable thumbs and four fingers like Sentians, and are able to use weapons, tools, and pieces of armor; but their powerful legs end in hooves similar to a ylark's instead of feet.

NHILDE TROLL
Weight: 4 (Big as a small hut.)
High Concept: *Giant Creature of Destruction*.
Trouble: *Dim-Witted*.
Other Aspects: *Big-Ass Axe*.
Skilled (+2) at: Bashing things, lifting things.
Bad (-2) at: Strategy, living in captivity.

STRESS
○○○(○○), +1 mild consequence, +1 moderate consequence
Special: A Nhilde troll may invoke the *Giant Creature of Destruction* when using the attack action to make its attack lethal. For more information about lethal attacks, see *"Lethal Attacks"* on page 235.

Runnigum: Spirited carnivores whose natural range is found in hilly, temperate regions of southern Sentia and Matriga. Runnigum feed on small prey, which they catch thanks to their speed. Some sub-species have also adapted to the colder temperatures in central Sentia. Their long tail is used to chase away importunate insects.

With patience and prudence, young runnigum can be domesticated; once grown they are used by both Elvorix and Vidaar as beasts of burden and mounts. However, they are not for the complacent or timid.

RUNNIGUM
Weight: 2 (Bigger than a Sentian.)
High Concept: *Swift Carnivorous Riding Beast*.
Trouble: *Irritable*.
Other Aspects: *Skilled Hunter*.
Skilled (+2) at: Biting, sprinting.
Bad (-2) at: Getting used to change.

STRESS
○○(○), +1 mild consequence

Saladont: Saladonts are found in rocky areas and in abandoned buildings, where their long legs and spiked feet allow for easy scrambling over difficult terrain. Saladonts feed on live prey, though usually small vermin-like creatures. While they are normally curious and unaggressive, they can become fiercely protective when their nest is threatened. Their long tail ends in a sharp scythe-like horn blade that can slash at enemies up to three or four paces away.

SALADONT
Weight: 2 (Bigger than a Sentian.)
High Concept: *Chitinous, Leggy Rock-Nester.*
Trouble: *Competes With Sentients for Building Reclamation.*
Other Aspects: *Scythe-Like Tail.*
Skilled (+2) at: Scurrying, scouting, protecting the nest.
Bad (-2) at: Moving in spongy terrain.

STRESS
○○(○○)
Special: Because of their *Scythe-Like Tail* a Saladont can attack enemies in their zone or in an adjacent zone.

Skikt: Found in forested areas, skikt dwell in the tops of the tallest fungus trees. Their spindly but strong legs allow them to climb and jump with agility in the canopy. Despite their size and apparent bulk, they are mostly fur and hollow bones and thus quite light. In spite of their great agility, skikt often spend entire days seemingly without moving, sunning themselves. They have become rarer since the climate started cooling. They feed primarily on the soft mosses that wrap the treetops.

Their most startling feature, however, is their ability to learn Sentian and even Jaarl speech patterns, and suddenly repeat them. Although most scholars conclude that the skikt are not intelligent and are simply repeating sounds at random, if with excellent memory, some assert that the skikt are in fact wise beyond understanding and are delivering messages from the gods themselves. There are many tales of brave would-be heroes hearing a skikt's presumed gibberish, only to understand later that this was actually an astute augury.

SKIKT

Weight: 1 (Sentian-sized.)
High Concept: *Tree-Dwelling Oracle*.
Trouble: *Spouts Gibberish*.
Other Aspects: *Jumps and Climbs Swiftly*.
Skilled (+2) at: Jumping, climbing, mimicking sounds, uttering cryptic pronouncements.
Bad (-2) at: Everything else.

STRESS
O(O), +1 mild consequence

Skjeggy: Skjeggy are related to mundicus, but they are omnivores. They have traded some of the thick protective armor for speed and agility, allowing them to hunt small and medium prey if need be. When they feel threatened by something large or fierce, skjeggy will take the initiative and charge.

More versatile than mundicus, skjeggy are found in groups of two to twelve individuals in tundra, taiga, and ice field areas as well as in boreal forest zones. They are smart and adaptable.

Skjeggy
Weight: 2 (Bigger than a Sentian.)
High Concept: *King of the Ice Lands*.
Trouble: *Doesn't Like to Be Challenged*.
Other Aspects: *Easy Learner*.
Skilled (+2) at: Working with the herd, charging, maneuvering.
Bad (-2) at: Resisting a perceived challenge.

STRESS
○○○(○), +1 mild consequence

Svampfode: The hulking svampfode is a denizen of forested wetland areas. Svampfode use defensive mimicry to blend in with the landscape and attract entire colonies of insects, small predators, lichens, mosses, etc., which seek shelter into the svampfode's hide. Svampfode are more ambulatory ecosystems than predator or prey, absorbing their nutrients directly from all the life forms that live in their skin.

They live for centuries, though exactly how long is not certain; in fact, no one has ever found a svampfode who died of natural death, although this may be because their body gets reabsorbed by the ecosystem.

Although they are not typically aggressive, they are sometimes found fiercely guarding an area and preventing larger life forms from entering it. Some Elvorix scholars have gone as far as to suggest these svampfode may be guarding Ancient sites.

SVAMPFODE

Weight: 4 (Big as a small hut.)
High Concept: *Shambling Ecosystem.*
Trouble: *Slow to React.*
Other Aspects: *Guardian of Forgotten Places.*
Skilled (+2) at: Guarding its chosen spot, forming an ecosystem.
Bad (-2) at: Moving fast.

STRESS
OOOO(OOOO), +1 mild consequence, +1 moderate consequence

Uhyre: A nasty form of small but aggressive flying predator, uhyre attack their prey by biting its head off. Their primary sensory organs seem to be the long wings that also serve as ears, picking up sound vibrations. The uhyre emit a high-pitched sound and use echolocation to identify their prey (and its head) with uncanny accuracy. Their numerous rows of sharp teeth allow them to bite the head of smaller creatures clean off; for larger prey, the uhyre may simply opt to start digesting the head in place until their victim dies from its wounds. This makes them exceptionally dangerous for their size.

UHYRE
Weight: 1 (Smaller than a Sentian.)
High Concept: *Flying Headbiter*.
Trouble: *Ears as Wings*.
Other Aspects: *Hunts by Sonar*.
Skilled (+2) at: Flying, biting heads off, swarming, echolocation.
Bad (-2) at: Everything else.

STRESS
○(○○), +1 mild consequence
Special: When they succed with style on an attack, uhyre can invoke the aspect *Flying Headbiter* for effect to attach themselves to a victim's head, causing one point of stress per round that they remained attached.

Ylark: Pronounced both as *lark* and *yuh-lark*, depending on the region, these herbivores are used for dairy production, beasts of burden, and cattle. In the case of the Elvorix, they are also used as cavalry, divine sacrifice, and shock weapons when set on fire and sent galloping towards the enemy. Wild ylark can still be found in low plains of southern and eastern Sentia, but the bulk of ylark population is represented by the domesticated variety.

Ylark

Weight: 2 (Bigger than a Sentian.)
High Concept: *Large Tough Beast of Burden.*
Trouble: *Favorite Flaming Sacrifice to Agaptus.*
Other Aspects: *Galloping Terror.*
Skilled (+2) at: Carrying or pulling burdens, charging, obeying.
Bad (-2) at: Changing its mind.

STRESS
○○(○○), +1 mild consequence

The War of Ashes

The War of Ashes is a bitter and blind conflict between Elvorix, Vidaar, Jaarl, and Kuld for the shrinking area of temperate lands on the islands of Sentia, Iradon, and Matriga. The rain of ashes and the cooling rays of a feeble sun may be marks of divine fury, but the carnage in the lands of Agaptus has a more immediate source: the war between the factions, and especially the Kuld. To make matters worse, there are reports of additional factions making forays into the disputed territory, strange creatures unnamed in the patchy records preserved by Elvorix scholars though dimly remembered in Vidaar legends.

In this author's opinion, the cooling of the climate and the rains of ashes are likely to continue on for decades barring further divine intervention. The areas of arable land and food production will continue to shrink even as new enemies appear in the struggle for control of these resources. Although this author has encountered staunch opposition from academic circles to her conclusions, they must be reiterated here before it is too late. In order to allow the greatest survival with the least bloodshed, this author recommends:

1. Learning more about the motivations and capabilities of known antagonists.

2. Identifying and evaluating any signs of mass arrival of new antagonists.

3. Forging a new and stronger alliance between Elvorix and Vidaar as soon as possible, and exploring possibilities of compromise with the Jaarl.

4. Exploring further south for more temperate lands that might provide a food base for the lean decades ahead. This will entail clearing them of ferocious beasts and the possibility of encountering other sentient factions and potential rivals for resources.

5. Trying to reestablish good standing with angry deities and petitioning them for reprieve.

It is my hope that the research I have detailed thus far in this publication
will lead to a greater understanding of the history of this land, its
inhabitants, and what lies ahead.

Matia Bibulus
:x Atronia co Agaptus

PART 3

Campaign and Character Creation

Getting Started

What Do We Need?

While WAR OF ASHES: FATE OF AGAPTUS takes elements of the *Fate* engine, it is a stand-alone game that also supports full-fledged use of miniatures and more detailed combat scenarios.

Here's what you'll need in order to play:

> **Three to five people.** One of you will be the *gamemaster*, or GM for short, the others *players*. We'll talk about what those mean in a little bit.

> *Fate Dice™*, at least four, preferably four per person. These are a special kind of six-sided dice that are marked on two sides with a plus symbol ⊞, two sides with a minus symbol ⊟, and two sides are blank ■. You can get these dice from many hobby and game stores, often under their original name—Fudge dice. We call them Fate dice in this book, but you can call them whatever you like. You can find Fate Dice™ for sale at *evilhat.com*.

> If you don't want to use Fate or Fudge dice, you don't have to—any set of regular six-sided dice will work. If you're using regular dice, read 5 or 6 as ⊞, 1 or 2 as ⊟, and 3 or 4 as ■.

> The *Deck of Fate* is an alternative to Fate dice. It's a deck of cards that mimics the probability of Fate dice, and it's designed to be used in the same way Fate dice are. The Deck of Fate is also available from Evil Hat.

> **Character sheets**, one for each player. You can copy the blank one at the end of this book or download it from *evilhat.com*.

War of ASHES

Roleplaying Game

Name

Description

Weight

ASPECTS

HIGH CONCEPT

TROUBLE

Quic

Index cards, **sticky notes**, or similar slips of paper.

Tokens for fate points. These can be Campaign Coins' Fate Tokens (see *"Inspirations and Resources"* on page 333), poker chips, beads, pennies, or anything similar. Get a handful—about 30 or 40.

Something to draw maps on, like poster paper, a whiteboard, or an erasable mat.

War of Ashes miniatures. Miniatures are used in conjunction with maps to create vivid and exciting visual support for action and conflict. ZombieSmith provides a line of 35mm-scale miniatures which can be used to play with this game, but you can also use tokens or markers, as long as those are easily identified as individual characters.

You can find War of Ashes miniatures for sale at *zombiesmith.com*.

Next, let's talk about how to use WAR OF ASHES: FATE OF AGAPTUS.

SO HOW DO WE DO It?

First you need to figure out what kind of story you're going to tell. Read the setting information in the *The World of Agaptus* chapter to learn about the world of Agaptus and the War of Ashes and think about what sounds interesting to you. Then refer to the sections below to decide on the *premise*, *scale*, and *big issues* affecting the story. What are some important *faces and places* to interact with?

Next, it's time to choose who will be the players, and who will be the gamemaster. Of the people around the table, all but one are referred to as players. Each player takes on the role of one *player character* (or PC) in the story, and puts themselves in their character's shoes to make the decisions that their character would make. The remaining person is called the gamemaster or GM.

The GM's job is to present challenges to the players and to portray all the characters that aren't controlled by the players (non-player characters or NPCs).

The GM has many responsibilities, such as presenting the conflict to the players, controlling NPCs, and helping everyone apply the rules to the situation in the game. Let's talk about the first of the GM's jobs: to help the group build *campaigns*.

A campaign is a series of games you play with the same characters, where the story builds on what happened in earlier sessions. All the players should collaborate with the GM to plan how the campaign will work. Usually this is a conversation among all of you to decide what sort of heroes you want to play, what sort of world you live in, and what sorts of adversaries you'll have. Talk about how serious you want the game to be and how long you want it to last.

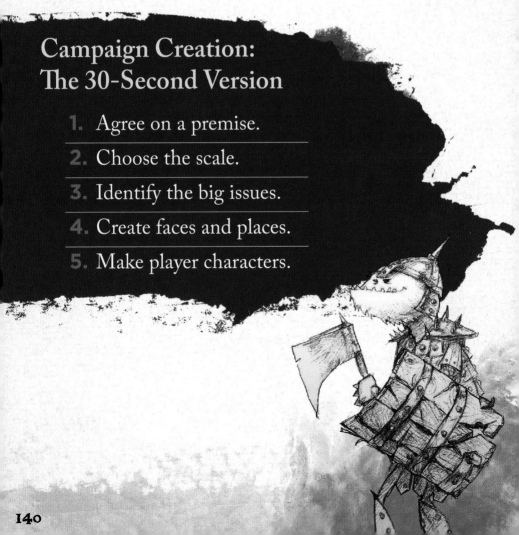

Campaign Creation: The 30-Second Version

1. Agree on a premise.
2. Choose the scale.
3. Identify the big issues.
4. Create faces and places.
5. Make player characters.

Once you decide who the GM will be, and what the framework of the story will be, it's time for the players to make their characters—that's detailed in the *"How Do I Make a Character?"* chapter on page 157.

Premise

The world of Agaptus and the War of Ashes are based on a *grimsical* aesthetic, which melds the grimness of brutal conflict with a whimsical, humorous attitude. When you plan a game you know you're going to be working with the following elements in your premise:

* Fantasy setting.

* Unpredictable magic and inept gods.

* Warfare and conflict as an important backdrop, even if your particular storyline concentrates on other facets.

* Technology and tactics levels comparable to early Middle Ages Europe. For example, no cannon powder or firearms.

* Lost knowledge of the Ancients and marvels that can no longer be replicated.

* Characters and societies that are blind to their own silliness.

* Despite the humor, there is real danger, drama, and death.

While there is nothing that prevents your group from removing or altering these elements, they are part of Agaptus. Make note of anything you want to change, and we'll talk more in a little bit about how you can customize the setting to your preferences.

Within this framework, your group should discuss some the **fundamental questions** about the stories you want to build, for example:

* **What tone you are hoping for?** Do you want to place the accent on humor, drama, danger, heroism, friendship, politics? Is Agaptus a doomed world, one on the cusp of change, or a place of hope?

* **What level of violence are you comfortable with?** Does your group want only humorous violence, "realistic" gore, or some point in between?

* **Are you okay with character death?** Is this a real and possible threat in your game, or are you going to have breathtakingly narrow escapes?

* **What kind of PCs and PC group do you want to play?** For example, will your player characters be champions writ large, unlikely allies, scoundrels, Chosen Ones, reluctant heroes? Will they all belong to one faction, or be mixed?

* **What kind of adventures you will have?** Does your group expect quests, political intrigue, dungeon-crawls, mysteries, con jobs?

Ask the group whether anyone has other such questions that should be discussed up-front.

Kim is going to be running a game for Ben, Sharlene, and Ian. They decide that they want a feeling of high adventure, and to visit a lot of the world rather than center their story in one place. Ben wants to play a Big Damn Hero but Ian feels like a bit more of a "grey area" character, and Sharlene just doesn't want to play a completely amoral character. They agree to use this to create some dramatic tension, but stay away from making characters too close to the extremes. They won't shy away from brutality if it shows up in the story, but they don't want to focus on it as a primary element.

Issues of Scale

Play in the War of Ashes is possible on a wide range of scale, from small local campaigns featuring young villagers to world-spanning campaigns where the (inept) gods of Agapta themselves intervene. In fact, if your players feel really ambitious, they can play the gods themselves!

Decide how epic or personal your story will be. In a small-scale game, characters deal with problems in a city or region, they don't travel a great deal, and the problems are local. A large-scale game involves dealing with problems that affect the entire kingdom, all of Agaptus, or even the rest of the world beyond.

Kim, Ben, Sharlene, and Ian decide that they would like to participate in world-changing events, but they would also like to start small so they can get a bit of a Hero's Journey feel.

A small-scale game will turn into a large-scale one over time, as you've probably seen in long-running novel series or television shows. We'll talk about re-scaling a mature campaign under *"Custom-Fitting and Expanding the World"* on page 316.

Big Issues

There are many global issues for the world of Agaptus, issues that most people there can't even see clearly because they are in the thick of the action. Is Agaptus a dying world, one on the verge of change, or a backdrop you're happy to keep more or less constant while you focus on local events? It depends on where you want the story to go.

But the issues for Agaptus may not be the ones your group will want to focus on in your campaign. Perhaps they are all about carving territory for a little lordling in the hills above Prolyus, exploring islands to the south where it's warmer, or salvaging Ancient knowledge from an unstable ruined city before it collapses. The default number of issues in a *Fate* game is two, and you can mix and match types.

Types of issues: The issues should reflect the scale of your game and what the characters will face. They're broad ideas; they don't just affect your characters, but many people in the world. Issues take two forms:

* **Current Issues:** The problems or threats that exist in the world already. Heroes tackling these issues are trying to change the world, to make it a better place. Examples: The ongoing War of Ashes, the Kuld invasion, the loss of Ancient knowledge, the ossification of Elvorix society, the cult of ignorance in Vidaar society, the Jaarl's loss of their Murmadon homeland.

* **Impending Issues:** These are things that have begun to rear their ugly heads, and threaten to make the world worse if they come to pass or achieve a goal. Heroes tackling these issues are trying to keep the world from slipping into chaos or destruction. Examples: The cooling of the climate, a pretender to the throne bent on seizing control, the imminent invasion of the heroes' town.

Now, **turn your issues into aspects**. You've already seen how we've done something like this for every story seed in this book. Distill your issues into aspects that you will use during play. Good aspects are ones for which you can readily think of both invoke and compel uses. For more on aspects, see *"Composing Good Aspects"* on page 198.

Expanding Story Seeds Into Issues: Speaking of the story seeds, maybe one grabbed your attention while thumbing through the book; why not expand it into more than a challenge or even an adventure, and make it part of your campaign? You may have to rephrase it to give it more scope.

*Kim likes the plot of **A Contract Is A Contract, And The Rules Are The Rules** from "Things That Can Happen" at the Elvora Bibulus Academy (see page 33). Not only is it an easy plot to twist as needed, but the aspect itself will make a good theme for an adventure in Elvorix society.*

Foreshadowing the Issues: As one issue is being resolved, a gamemaster can foreshadow a new issue that is gaining prominence. That way, the group of heroes always has its collective hands full (but not too full) and the story flows with crests and troughs, like in our favorite epic tales.

Sharlene is interested by the Great Catastrophe, its causes, and whether its effects can be stopped. Ben likes the heroic possibilities—saving the world!— and Isaac likes the scope. Isaac would really like to see some swashbuckling adventures at sea but doesn't have a specific issue. Since all three have shown some interest in Ancient technology, Kim suggests that maybe this idea of salvaging knowledge from an unstable Ancient site could take place on a small island off the coast of Sentia. Because she also wants more direct opposition, Kim also wants a shadowy group (often called a "seal" if acting in the name of their religion) also intent on collecting Ancient knowledge, but in order to get an edge in the War of Ashes.

*They boil this down to three issues and aspects: **Secrets of the Ice, Lost Island of Konaré, and The Seal of Prolyus.***

What's Really Going On?

What's the relationship between the various disasters that happened around the time of the Great Catastrophe? Can anything be done to improve the situation? What will the future bring if this is not investigated? Here are some options.

You want a fantasy explanation of what's happening with the world of Agaptus? The gods did it. They're powerful but inept and capricious, the Lord of the Sky got angry and screwed things up, and now neither he nor any of the other gods are too sure how to fix things without making them worse somehow.

You want a mechanist explanation of what happened? When the super-volcano of Murmadon Island erupted, it spewed enough ash and gases into the atmosphere to create a general cooling of the planet's surface, and now the world will have to go through an ice age until things return to equilibrium.

You want to mix that with cosmic, sword-and-sorcery, or science fiction explanations?

❋ Maybe the Jaarl caused the eruption by messing with the strange properties of the volcanic rock.

❋ Maybe the "gods" are just a powerful race squatting here from another planet and trying to improve the neighborhood.

❋ Maybe the gods are entities attracted from another plane by the devotion of mortals, but really bad at winning it; they must find a way to recruit followers or fade away.

❋ Maybe the volcano was a coincidence, they do happen after all; the problem is that the sun around which the planet orbits has just undergone a dramatic transition and is cooling off. Not only is the planet entering an ice age, but it will keep getting less suited to support life.

Faces and Places

Now that you have your issues figured out, decide who the important people and locations are. In discussing these issues, you probably thought of some organizations or groups that are implicitly part of your story, whether to provide support or opposition. You will also have important locations. All of these will be more vivid in your campaign if they are represented by *people*; assign a few characters to be their faces, give each a distinguishing aspect, and think of some relationships between these and the player characters you'll create in the next step.

The GM can guide this process by asking questions as the group formulates ideas, for example:

* ❋ "Who knows the most about X?"

* ❋ "Who is the biggest backer of X?"

* ❋ "Who is the biggest opponent to X?"

* ❋ "Who do people associate with X?"

* ❋ "Where do you go to find X?"

* ❋ "Where is X going?"

* ❋ "How do you get to X?"

Kim, Ben, Sharlene, and Ian agree that there will be some travel by sea to get to the island of Konaré, and perhaps a rival for the Ancient knowledge, a shadowy organization that doesn't plan on sharing. Ian would like this rival organization to include an enemy captain so there can be plenty of naval battles and boarding actions. Ben suggests that the heroes should also have some sponsor or sponsoring organization who put them onto the track of this island.

They create the following:

» The Seal of Prolyus, the rival organization for Ancient knowledge, dedicated to recovering science applicable to warfare to provide the Elvorix with an edge over their enemies.

» Rogue scholar Laetitia Bibulus ix Gailus, sponsored by the Seal of Prolyus; her aspect is *I'll Show Them All*.

» Captain Volo Troll-Axe, Laetitia's ally; his aspect is *Is This Thing Valuable?*

» The Stone-Seekers, a branch of the Virian Order that is trying to find out the truth about the eruption of Mount Murmadon and the Great Catastrophe.

» They've already identified the island of Konaré as a location, of course, and they know it will have Ancient ruins, but they want to leave it shrouded in mystery so they don't assign a face to it for now.

Creating the Heroes

Now that you've decided what kind of story you'll be telling in your game, decide who your character is—what they look like, what they're good at, and what they believe.

You'll probably find yourself discussing character concepts in parallel with the campaign creation steps discussed above. That's fine, just don't close your mind to changing details along the way. We'll talk about the nuts and bolts of character creation in *"How Do I Make A Character?"* on page 157, but let's consider character creation here as a group activity.

Think about the setting that you've decided to play in and make that your main guide. Are you playing the entourage of an Elvorix general? Play one of the general's underlings! Are you playing the adventures of the Jaarl Virian arcanists? Play a member of the elite Virian! Make sure your character has a reason to interact and cooperate with the characters the other players are making.

Mixed Nuts or All the Same?

Before you start creating player characters, you'll want to discuss party composition. Playing characters of all the same faction can be just as diverse as characters all different factions. We've provided some examples of each and a few tips on how to make it work.

How and why you would play characters from a single people: A group of heroes aligned with one of the factions—Elvorix, Vidaar, Jaarl, or Kuld—makes party cohesion easier, makes it easier to connect the characters, and provides impetus to readily accept certain types of missions as adventure seeds. Heroes from one faction will generally be welcomed or blend in among the lands of their own faction, and face grave danger and hostility in the other factions' lands.

A single faction does **not** mean sacrificing character individuality or niche protection.

For example:

» **A party of attendants to an Elvorix high mucky-muck, chosen for their ability to act as lightning rods away from their boss.** Roles could include resident scholar, foppish noble friend, jolly entertainer, spy posing as a servant, practical majordomo, poor relative, stalwart bodyguard, dour confessor, long-suffering tutor, etc., all probably chosen for their eccentricity or originality.

» **A splinter group of Vidaar Late-Comers left on some Island-That-Wasn't-Garigla or another and now finally catching up with everyone else.** Roles could include captain, shaman, navigator, freebooter, strange "pet" from a distant island, and the keeper of all oral history of the clan's voyages at sea. Because a ship is a world unto itself, everyone could have a variety of secondary abilities from cooking to carpentry.

» **Last Best Hope for the Jaarl to recover volcanium.** The Jaarl are looking for a way to forge swords and other volcanium objects; they would prefer a suitable volcano, but perhaps another sufficient source of heat can serve too. The heroes' mission is to find a solution. Roles could include elite military escort, arcane specialist studying the effect of Sacred Rock, metallurgist or smith from the Provider Guild, Preserver scholar who serves as the expert on pre-Catastrophe volcanium forging techniques, Elvorix or Vidaar captives serving as guides, porters, and interpreters in exchange for their freedom, etc.

» **An advance group seeking a new Kuld homeland.** The Kuld have been driven to more temperate locations by the cooling climate and the ash falling from the skies. Clearly the Source is pointing them somewhere new, but the noisy edible ones keep attacking the great horde. The heroes have been tasked with finding passage to a new Kuld home with plenty of food and warmth, and none of this tedious fighting all the time. Fighting just makes everyone hungrier. As a group of Kuld PCs, they are all considered "Wandering Kuld," but as a party of explorers they will need to represent important horde skills such as Shuda, Guldul Rider, and Augurst. See *"The Kuld Hordes"* on page 91 for a breakdown of battle roles.

Playing a party of all Kuld presents its own challenges (and fun!) as there would be no "in-character" dialogue; the Kuld communicate through scents and glyphs. Discuss as a group how you would represent this in-game while still being able to

How and why you would play characters from different factions or peoples: Maybe not everyone in your group shares the same interest in a particular faction. Mixed groups will likely face suspicion and a measure of struggle to get help almost everywhere, and some group members will face outright hostility in certain areas.

Kuld characters are hardest to mix with other factions because they employ a completely different mode of communication based on scents and because they tend to eat the rest of the party...

If your group wants to mix origins, you'll want to come up with a good solid reason the characters will hang out and have adventures together instead of killing one another or just splitting up.

For example:

» **Odd buck out:** If you have only one player character from a different faction, the onus is on the player of that character to come up with a good reason to be there, such as a war captive in a group of another faction if there are some bonds of obligation or friendship with other PCs.

» **A mixed Elvorix-Vidaar party from a region that has had a lot of inter-breeding:** Sure, the Pact of Prolyus collapsed three years ago, but that doesn't mean that family and friends were forgotten.

» **Descendants of Elvorix and Vidaar sent to check on Murmadon's mysterious cities and captured by the Jaarl:** Generations later, the descendants of the original prisoners had become part of Jaarl society, but after the Great Catastrophe and exodus their status was reduced again. The loyalties of current-day descendants, born in Agaptus but raised to think of Murmadon as the homeland and Jaarl as friends, are sorely tried.

» **A group of mismatched escapees from the advancing Kuld army:** The Kuld don't care about distinctions between Elvorix, Vidaar, and Jaarl; the heroes found themselves hiding and running away together, pooling their meager forces to defeat a small Kuld force, and bonded. You'd want to make this either part of the characters' backstory when making PCs, or tell the players upfront that this is what the first adventure will be about, and get their buy-in.

» **The Company of the Rock:** Not everyone in the lands of Agaptus is blind to the necessity of cooperation between peoples. The heroes are tasked with the epic mission of finding a way to slow, stop, or even reverse the effects of the Great Catastrophe. Theirs is a secret alliance that could save all of Agaptus!

» **A ragtag band of mercenaries:** A group of hard-bitten, elite mercenaries who will fight for whoever can hire them; think of Glen Cook's *Chronicles of the Black Company* for inspiration.

Iva: "It isn't easy these days putting together a group to go haring off on an adventure in the wilds. Times are tough and the world is dangerous."

Rustica: "Plus, everybody hates everybody else."

Ulf: "Aye. I took a big risk agreeing to work with an Elvorix and a Jaarl. If things had happened only a bit less profitably, I likely would have been banished from my clan."

Iva: "Wait—I thought you WERE banished from your clan."

Ulf: "Wealth is a powerful thing—it can change even history."

Iva: "In our case it was a bit easier than usual. Rustica and I were both interested in retrieving the lost Elvorix volumes so we had common cause to travel together."

Rustica: "I had the knowledge, she had the money. It was pretty simple."

Ulf: "Are you ever going to tell us where that money came from?"

Iva: "I would tell you—"

All: "—BUT THEN I'D HAVE TO KILL YOU!"

(General laughter)

Kuri: "HEE!"

Ulf: "Travelling with those not of my people proved to be a boon, not a hindrance. It was quite advantageous at times."

Rustica: "It's easy enough, no matter where you go, to find people who will hate you. At least in a mixed group you have a chance to find someone who won't try to rob, stab, or eat you."

Iva: "We talked our way past Elvorix guards by pretending to be the right sort of person and vouching for the others."

Rustica: "It would have worked on that Vidaar raiding party too if Ulf hadn't tripped over his own tongue."

Ulf: "I could not lie to my own people—it would not have been honorable!"

Rustica: "It wasn't honor, you're just the world's worst liar."

Ulf: (mumbles) "I take that as praise."

From interview notes for the volume "The Explorers," by Matia Bibulus. Transcribed by Bura Bibulus Ven Proudheart, 88 AGC.

Can You Play Something Unorthodox?

Some players look for their kicks on the margins of the game's society. Perhaps they will ask you if they can play a Nhilde troll or a member of a sentient species from one of the more distant islands. (For ideas on the latter, you may want to look at the skirmish miniatures game SHIELDBASH from ZombieSmith, which presents new factions for the setting.) The gamemaster may have some additional work to do, or the players may dislike the resulting "flavor"; but if the group agrees, this is doable. Look at the description and stats in *"Beasts of Agaptus"* on page 109 to get inspiration, then make your character as normal.

Just like the mixed party, you need to come up with a plausible rationale for this, such as:

* Visionary Kuld ostracized by its own people for wanting to make non-alimentary contact with other species.

* Nhilde troll with a party of Vidaar.

* Lizard-man or giant sentient bird with a party of seafaring explorers or pirates from any faction.

* Gods of the Elvorix Pantheon rivalling not only with each other, but to gain the proper adoration of the Sentians as well as "helping" the world of Agaptus.

Note that such creatures will provide special challenges in party balance if they have abilities or advantages other Agaptans do not. For example, a Nhilde troll would be expected to benefit from its size represented by the characteristic called *weight* (see page 222). In addition, the default factions get special aspects and stunts (see page 159 and 170). We'll talk more about compensating for such disparities in a bit (see page 318).

Factions, Species, Clans, and Guilds

Throughout this book we have talked about many possible groups your character might belong to, even discounting the unorthodox options: three species, Sentians, Kuld and Jaarl; four factions, Elvorix, Vidaar, Kuld, and Jaarl; a variety of affiliations for each faction based on family lines, region, politics, occupation, and more. When you want to represent this as something that sets your character apart from the other heroes, think about basing an aspect or stunt on these. See *"Aspects in a Nutshell"* on page 158 and *"Creating Stunts"* on page 170 for more information on personalizing your character.

In groups where everyone is from the same faction, characters' high concept aspects might include their guild—which, in turn, also suggests a campaign aspect (see page 144).

*An all-Elvorix group with an **Ambitious Vorix Scout**, an **Impoverished Highborn Third Son**, and a **Sarcastic Northerner Priest of Agaptus**, acting as the entourage of a foppish noble. Further, the gamemaster might decide to add the campaign aspect **The Hapless Retinue of Lord Limurax**, which the players could invoke to get some benefit, luxury, or contact from serving their vain patron, or compel in order to attract unwanted attention, receive tricky duties, or be forced to protect the foolish Limurax.*

In groups where characters are from different factions or species, characters' high concepts might include their origin and a stunt might further explore their background.

*A mixed group with an **Overachieving Elvorix Scholar**, a **Nostalgic Vidaar Privateer**, and a **Jaarl Wandering Virian Master**. The scholar is further defined by a stunt based on her Atronian origin, while the privateer has a stunt based on his clan. The Virian master's guild is implied from her high concept.*

Connecting

The better connected your characters are, the more fun the team will be. This doesn't mean you can't have rivalries, enmities, or other antagonistic relationships between PCs; in fact, the most dramatic relationships are those in which there is a certain tension, both something your character *wants* from another and something she *denies* them: approval, forgiveness, help, obedience, etc.

But you can start with straightforward connections of family, friendship, profession, politics, clan, and so forth. The important thing is for PCs to have a reason to work together. These connections are often expressed as aspects; see *"Aspects in a Nutshell"* on page 158 in the next chapter.

In addition to connections between the player characters, try grounding your character into the WAR OF ASHES setting in general, and the details of your campaign in particular; identify connections with the faces and places you just created.

The group opts for a mixed collection of heroes from diverse factions, adopting **The Company of the Rock** *as described above not only as their concept, but as the name of their group and an aspect for the campaign.*

Sharlene creates **Rustica Bibulus ix Atronia**, *an Elvorix scholar showing too much originality for her elders at the Academy. Rustica studies the mystery of the Great Catastrophe and the connections with the eruption of Mount Murmadon.*

Ian creates **Ulf Long-Teeth**, *a young Vidaar with a love for the old heroic sagas who longs to return to the life of swashbuckling seafaring adventures instead of this inhospitable land. He and Rustica are distantly related.*

Ben creates **Iva the Stubborn**, *a Jaarl Virian mother torn between fulfilling her duty to the Virian Order and the Stone-Seekers by assisting Rustica's quest, and the wish to go looking for her banished lover, who lost his sword. She carries her young fawn Kuri on her back throughout her travels.*

All three are young and gifted, well-versed in their own specialties, but not terribly experienced.

How Do I Make A Character?

Now it's time to start writing stuff down. Grab a pencil and a copy of the character sheet.

Creating Characters: The 30-Second Version

1. Write two aspects: a High Concept and a Trouble.

2. Select a faction aspect.

3. Give your character a name and describe their appearance.

4. Choose approaches.

5. Set your refresh to 3.

6. Set your weight to 1.

7. Choose your faction stunt and an equipment stunt.

8. Write up to two more aspects and a third stunt, or wait to complete during play.

Aspects in a Nutshell

An aspect is a word, phrase, or sentence that describes something centrally important to your character. It can be a motto your character lives by, a personality quirk, a description of a relationship you have with another character, an important possession or bit of equipment your character has, or any other part of your character that is vitally important.

Aspects allow you to change the story in ways that tie in with your character's tendencies, skills, or problems. You can also use them to establish facts about the setting, such as the presence of magic or the existence of a useful ally, dangerous enemy, or secret organization.

Your character will have a handful of aspects (between three and five), including a *high concept*, a *trouble*, and at least one aspect from a list specific to your character's faction (Elvorix, Vidaar, Jaarl, or Kuld).

We discuss aspects in detail in *"Aspects and Fate Points"* on page 190, but for now, this should help you get the idea.

High Concept

First, decide on your character's **high concept**. This is a single phrase or sentence that neatly sums up your character, saying who you are, what you do, what your "deal" is. When you think about your high concept, try to think of two things: how this aspect could help you, and how it might make things harder for you. Good high concept aspects do both.

Examples: **Overachieving Elvorix Scholar**, **Nostalgic Young Vidaar Privateer**, **Wandering Virian Master**.

Wandering Kuld PCs must include this idea as part of their high concept. At some point, you stopped gnawing on a fallen tree branch and realized that life would be better further south. You are filled with a new hunger—to meet creatures who are not Kuld, to communicate, and to learn.

Trouble

Next, decide on the thing that always gets you into **trouble**. It could be a personal weakness, or a recurring enemy, or an important obligation—anything that makes your life complicated.

Examples: **I'm Convinced That the Theory is Sound**, **Out to Make A Name for Himself!**, **Single Mother With A Fawn**.

Faction Aspect

Now pick an aspect reflecting your faction. Each faction offers five typical aspects you can choose from, and ways that they can be invoked and compelled. More on that in *"Aspects and Fate Points"* on page 190. Note that these faction aspects are not intended to represent an entire faction, but rather the type of members of that faction who end up becoming heroes—reluctant or willing, i.e., player characters.

With the GM's agreement, it's okay to rephrase your faction aspect a bit, for example, to replace **Conformity is Safety** with **Blend In With the Crowd** or **Bookworm** with **Tenured Academic**.

Elvorix:

Conformity is Safety: You know how dangerous it is to attract the attention of the gods by standing out in any way.

Invoke: You can easily hide in a crowd, be overlooked, or be forgotten by the authorities.

Compel: It's not always a good thing to be forgettable—waiting to be released from prison, for example, or when trying to impress an important personage; in addition, you are aghast when anyone else in your group plans anything spectacular, audacious, eccentric, etc.

159

Bookworm: You evoke the stereotype of the bookish Elvorix who Vidaar always mock.

Invoke: You have read widely on a range of topics and often have a ready answer when everyone else is stumped.

Compel: You often suffer from indecision and take too long, particularly when it comes to matters of action or questions that require quick resolution; you would prefer to research the question rather than act on incomplete information.

Beacon of Civilization: You embrace your heritage of civilization, honor, and chivalry to set an example for others. (Particularly appropriate for Highborn characters.)

Invoke: You tend to inspire respect and trust, at least as far as keeping your given oath or behaving honorably.

Compel: You carry this code of honor everywhere, even when it would be more advantageous to choose expediency over honor or dignity, such as when your group needs to wade through sewers, lie outrageously, or betray their given word. Worse, others expect you to live by this code of honor even when they have much more flexible morals, so you often get the worse end of a bargain.

Bucking the Trend: The rest of the herd might fall in step, but not you! You'll show them all. Or when you insist on doing something in a novel way, things go wrong: something breaks, people get angry, etc. (Particularly appropriate for Vorix characters.)

Invoke: When others least expect it, you pull something unexpected, even if that means attracting the attention of the gods.

Compel: People dare you to do things all the time, especially stupid things, and expect you to follow them. Or when you take an action and insist on doing it in a novel way, things sometimes go wrong: something breaks, people get angry, etc.

"Mix a little foolishness with your bloodlust: it's good to be silly at the right moment."
—Hlarn Pilum, *Spearbuck and poet*

Priest of ___: Pick a member of the Elvorix pantheon; while you are probably prudent enough to worship them all, you are dedicated to a particular deity.

Invoke: You serve the will of your divine patron by spreading their worship, protecting their domain, and opposing their enemies.

Compel: Your god has adversaries and foes among the pantheon; and those foes' servants take pride in opposing you. See *"The Nebulous Elvorix Pantheon"* on page 248 for more on the pantheon's interactions.

Vidaar:

A True Vidaar Acts First and Asks Questions Later!: Like Vidaarus the First, quick to decide and follow through.

Invoke: You have the edge in initiative or when it's time to act quickly and decisively.

Compel: It's not always a good idea to grab the prize, to confront a hostile NPC, or to step through the dark corridor…

We Don't Need No Education: Vidaar aren't known for their book learnin': a true warrior needs no Bookworm's advice!

Invoke: Raised in a tradition of learning by doing, you are good at figuring out how things work by simple observation or trial-and-error.

Compel: Did we mention error? Lots or error. You are also illiterate and thus baffled (intimidated, angered, etc.) by written knowledge.

Servant of the Only God: You are a militant devotee of Akka-Maas.

Invoke: Your devotion serves you well when you are acting directly in support of Akka-Maas' primacy (more on this in *"The Vidaar's Only God: Akka-Maas"* on page 254).

Compel: Other deities particularly have it in for you.

Roaring Barbarian: The quintessential uncouth barbarian of cheap Elvorix adventure tales, perhaps, but to other Vidaar, a pillar of strength and defiance.

Invoke: You are strong, rugged, and intimidating.

Compel: You are rude, vulgar, clumsy, and destructive when it's time to make a good impression with manners.

An Eye for Good Loot: You're the type of Vidaar who would still search for Garigla if you thought there was a chance to get its treasures.

Invoke: You have an eye for riches, you're good at estimating the market value of goods, and it's hard to hide valuables from you.

Compel: The promise of riches appears in the worst possible places. Or you realize taking the safe, practical, or smart option is going to mean missing out on treasure.

Jaarl:

Discipline Is the Core of a Jaarl's Soul: Ever since breaking from the shell, you have been relentlessly trained in the Jaarl's iron discipline.

Invoke: Whenever concentration, nerves of steel, following the chain of command, or long habit of practice would help, you have the edge.

Compel: Whenever gut instinct, spontaneity, willingness to question authority, or a mind unfettered by pre-conceptions is needed, you're at a disadvantage.

The Homeland Shall Be Rebuilt!: Murmadon is no more, but the Jaarl will have a new homeland!

Invoke: Your devotion inspires you whenever you act directly to support the new homeland, for example when protecting Jaarl citizens from danger or pursuing a mission given to you by your Jaarl superiors.

Compel: Your zeal is well-known and not only do you get assigned all the tricky missions, but you're constantly hearing the argument "But it's for the homeland!" from everyone trying to get something from you...

There Is No God: Jaarl are still mad at the god Murmadon for forsaking them and they have developed a militant kind of denial of all gods, with the vague notion that if it's devotion the gods crave, the worst punishment must be to ignore them.

Invoke: Whenever skepticism, cool-headed rationalism, and disdain of the supernatural are helpful, you carry the day.

Compel: When you attract the attention of the gods, you tend to annoy them and they really, really want to prove their existence to you—with all sorts of dangerous demonstrations. And even if it isn't your fault, non-Jaarl tend to blame you for the gods' fickleness anyway.

I Must Redeem My Family's Honor: Perhaps you broke or lost your sword in battle, perhaps you hopelessly bungled a mission, or maybe your parents were labeled as traitors. Whatever the reason, your status has been greatly affected in Jaarl society and you only live because the failure was not quite enough to require ritual suicide. Now you're on a quest to clear your family's name.

Invoke: Whenever you have an opportunity to do something dangerous, grandiose, honorable, or otherwise visible that would bring honor to your name, you're at your best.

Compel: Other Jaarl tend to view you poorly, discount your opinions, give you the crappiest jobs, and generally give you a hard time. In addition, you tend to be reckless in your pursuit of redemption.

Good, Bad—I'm the Jaarl with the Sword: You're very practical and not too encumbered with angst over what's right and what's wrong.

Invoke: You are not easily distracted from your path by clever arguments, moral quandaries, or tempting promises.

Compel: Because you tend to follow your own rules, even your allies don't always tell you the whole truth, to spare you from those pesky details.

"Every art and every investigation, and likewise every practical pursuit or undertaking, seems to aim at some good: hence it has been well said that the Good is that at which all things aim. Therefore, the good of the Jaarl must be the end of the science of war."

—Harri, Roccio and Barracks Philosopher

There is so much that is unknown about the Kuld. In order to play a Kuld PC in a mixed group, you need a clear explanation for why you will get along with the other heroes without eating them, and why they will hang out with you instead of trying to kill you. You are an unusual specimen, interested in reaching out to other species. Alas, this also makes you an outcast among your kind. In addition to your high concept explaining that you are a *Wandering Kuld*, these faction aspects provide the how and why.

Kuld:

Walkabout: You have left behind everything you knew and your personal journey of discovery has already taken you to many strange places.

Invoke: You have an eclectic acquaintance with little-traveled places such as secluded caves, deserted ruins, and isolated hamlets. You may even recognize the occasional Ancient artifact as something you've seen before.

Compel: You have trouble staying in one place too long when strange new scents are always calling to you. In addition, this strange need separates you from your origins even more than other "Wandering Kuld"; you know that you will never be home again, never walk to the Source with your brethren again, and this can leave you profoundly sad and melancholy at dangerously inopportune times.

Mysterious Agenda: You're pursuing your own goal, which is the entire reason you put up with non-Kulds. Some ideas are: You need to retrieve a particular lost stone inscribed with a sacred glyph; you have been directed by the Source (or so you think) to assemble a collection of particular smells; you are seeking a place to live where your clan can thrive without fighting the hairy ones.

Invoke: Unbeknownst to the non-Kuld PCs, you have done something inexplicable that will turn out useful, such as brought an odd item, prepared a hiding spot, eaten embarrassing evidence before it is discovered, etc.

Compel: At inconvenient times, your actions are completely misinterpreted and make others suspicious of you. Or you may receive strange instructions and even foreboding threats asking you to take action in incomprehensible ways.

Biding My Time: You will play nice and be docile, friendly, or otherwise seemingly harmless to non-Kulds until a certain task is accomplished or a result obtained, but once that result is reached all bets are off. The GM must approve the task or result, but it has to be something that could plausibly be achieved in the game. (This pairs well with *Mysterious Agenda*, if you choose a second faction aspect later.)

Invoke: You can resist what might seem an irresistible opportunity to devour a non-Kuld and may as a result appear trustworthy.

Compel: While you're fighting your hunger, you may wait a little too long and miss a golden opportunity.

Looks Like a Kuld, Smells Like a Kuld: When you eat anything up to and including corpses and garbage, and you use vomit as both weapon and means of communication, you're just not very appealing to other species.

Invoke: When it's time to create a negative impression—scare a prisoner, intimidate an adversary, repel passers-by with your stench before they walk down the alley where you're hidden—you have it nailed.

Compel: You generally evoke horror and disgust from non-Kulds, especially on first impression. Sorry, it's not you, it's—no wait, it is you. You're horrible.

Alien Communication: Kuld communicate through scent and through glyphs etched using their stomach acid; you're just particularly hard to understand for non-Kuld.

Invoke: Nigh-unbreakable cipher when trying to communicate with other Kuld and possibly, with difficulty, with dedicated scholars.

Compel: Nigh-incomprehensible jargon when trying to communicate complex ideas with anyone else, limiting what others can translate to isolated words.

Two Additional Aspects

Think of something really important or interesting about your character, and how that influences the way the world sees them (and how they see themselves.) This should be summed up in one sentence, but its meaning and application will unfold during the game.

* ❋ Are they the strongest person in their hometown? In a good way, or a bad way?

* ❋ Do they talk too much? Is it rambling, invasive, informative?

* ❋ Are they filthy rich? How did they get the money, how do they comport themselves?

* ❋ Do they have a catchphrase, or a firmly held superstition? How did they come by it?

Or these aspects might describe your character's relationship with other player characters or with an NPC: rivalry, friendship, family bond, apprentice and master, and so forth. See *"Composing Good Aspects"* on page 198 for more ideas. You can also opt to use another from the list of factions-specific aspects if you think it's particularly suited to your character.

If you prefer, you can leave one or both of these aspects blank right now and fill them in later, after the game has started. This is a good time to select aspects that will tie your characters together, or link them with the setting elements your group selected. See *"Creating the Heroes"* on page 148 for more details.

If you're stumped for ideas, you can browse the list of sample character aspects for inspiration.

Sample Character Aspects:

A Taste for the Finer Things

Always Have a Backup Plan

Beast-Tamer

Born Sailor

Dead-Ringer for Lord Maladros

Ever the Optimist

Explorer of the Great Ice Wastes

Faithful of Atronia

Family Comes First

Ferin Is My True Love

Flattery Will Get You Everywhere

Friends in Low Places

Glib Tongue

Half A Treasure Map

I Must Redeem My Name

I Swear It Was a Misunderstanding!

I Will Avenge My Defeat at Thul's Hands

I'm Not Stubborn, I'm Perseverant

In Case of Doubt, Deny Everything

Initiate of the Mysteries of Ilunus

It's My Own Invention

Last Heir to the Knowledge of Master Birina

Last Survivor of My Village

Measure Twice, Cut Once

My Faithful Kanid, Zupar

My Father's Broken Sword

My Word Is My Bond

Never Saw a Kogg Barrel I Didn't Like

Not the Marrying Type

Nothing Ventured, Nothing Gained

One Moss-berry in the Hand is Worth Two on the Bush

Searching for My Long-Lost Brother

Second-Best at Everything

Seventh and Smallest of My Family

Sworn to the Service of Lord Gerron

Wanderlust

Worry-Wart

167

Name and Appearance

Describe your character's appearance and give them a name. For convenience, we've listed a few examples. For the full information on the structure and creating of names, see the *"Names"* section in each Faction's description (page 26 for Elvorix, page 49 for Vidaar, page 76 for Jaarl, and page 95 for Kuld). We also have a cheat sheet in the appendices, *"Sample Names"* on page 346.

Elvorix:
Baseros, Caperna, Ficca, Semela, Ven.

Vorix:
Aguros Deathsong, Elantrix Proudheart, Gicca Quickstrike, Killim Arrowflight, Seadros Two-blades.

Vidaar:
Forlad, Gubba the Hearty, Sverra, Vaad of the Black Raiders, Vaad son of Vaad.

Jaarl:
Agirix, Ezzo, Lele, Tenghi, Ugolina.

Kuld:
Blubbous, Clubfoot, Kagaar, Meal-Finder, Waaanoooo.

Approaches

Choose your *approaches*.

Approaches are descriptions of *how* you accomplish tasks. Everyone has the same six approaches:

* Careful
* Clever
* Flashy
* Forceful
* Quick
* Sneaky

Each approach is rated with a bonus. Choose one at Good (+3), two at Fair (+2), two at Average (+1), and one at Mediocre (+0). You can improve these later. We talk about what each approach means and how you use them in *"Outcomes, Actions, and Approaches"* on page 177.

The Ladder

In Fate, we use a ladder of adjectives and numbers to rate a character's approaches, the result of a roll, difficulty ratings for simple checks, etc.

Value	Adjective
+9	Miraculous
+8	Legendary
+7	Epic
+6	Fantastic
+5	Superb
+4	Great
+3	Good
+2	Fair
+1	Average
+0	Mediocre
-1	Poor
-2	Terrible
-3	Awful
-4	Abysmal

Your approaches can say a lot about who you are. Here are some examples:

❉ **The Swordmaster:** Quick +3, Forceful and Flashy +2, Clever and Careful +1, Sneaky +0

❉ **The Guardian:** Careful +3, Forceful and Clever +2, Sneaky and Quick +1, Flashy +0

❉ **The Thief:** Sneaky +3, Careful and Quick +2, Clever and Flashy +1, Forceful +0

❉ **The Swashbuckler:** Flashy +3, Quick and Clever +2, Forceful and Careful +1, Sneaky +0

❉ **The Workhorse:** Forceful +3, Careful and Quick +2, Sneaky and Clever +1, Flashy +0

❉ **The Scholar:** Clever +3, Careful and Forceful +2, Sneaky and Flashy +1, Quick +0

The easiest way to pick is to envision what your character's preferred style looks like, and give the corresponding approach a +3; then think about the approach your character is poorest at, and give it a 0; you can think of these as the character's poles. Then distribute the other scores among the four remaining approaches without agonizing too much over them; you'll get chances to adjust them later (see *"Character Advancement"* on page 240).

Creating Stunts

A *stunt* is a special trait or piece of equipment that changes the way an approach works for your character. Generally, stunts give you a bonus (almost always +2) to a certain approach when used with a particular action under specific circumstances, or give you a special ability useable once per session. We'll talk more about stunts and the other ways they can be used in *"Stunts"* on page 198, but there is one particular type of stunt you need to come up with during character creation.

Faction Stunts

Choose one faction-related stunt to start, the same way you chose a faction-related aspect.

Elvorix:

Fierce when Cornered: Because I have a Savagebuck's Fierceness when Cornered, I have +2 to Forcefully attack in melee when I'm outnumbered. (Particularly appropriate for Vorix characters.)

Arts of Defense: Because I am trained in the Arts of Defense, I get +2 to Sneakily defend by using an improvised shield.

Master of the [Specify] Craft: Because I am a Master of my Craft, I get +2 to Carefully overcome when trying to create or repair something that falls under my particular expertise. (Pick a specific craft, e.g., pottery, basketry, book-binding, weaponsmithing, etc.)

Well-Read: Because I am Well-Read, once per scene I get +2 to Cleverly create an advantage involving my book learning.

Close-Knit House: Because I come from a Close-Knit House, once per session I can get unexpected help from my Elvorix community, such as reinforcements in the nick of time, a small loan, a piece of important information, etc.

Look, Over There!: Because I am trained in the divine rites, I get +2 to Quickly create an advantage when I cast a ritual to direct my god's gaze at my target—and away from me. (Of course, this means risking attracting the attention of the gods…)

Vidaar:

Vicious Fighter: Because I am a Vicious Fighter, I get +2 to Sneakily attack an opponent who has not yet noticed me, for example in an ambush or by backstabbing.

Valorous Bondee: Because I am a Valorous Bondee, I get +2 to Quickly defend against melee attacks when outnumbered.

Born Sailor: Because I am a Born Sailor, I get +2 to Cleverly overcome when sailing, climbing, maintaining my balance, or swinging from a line.

Prestigious Clan: Because I come from a Prestigious Clan, I get +2 to Flashily create an advantage by impressing other Vidaar.

Friends in Every Port: Because I have Friends in Every Port, once per session I can find a boat or ship to take me and my companions where I need to go.

Tyromancy: Because I am a trained priest of Akka-Maas, I get +2 to Carefully create an advantage with divination rituals that use smelly ylark cheese.

Jaarl:

Tactical Mind: Because I have a Tactical Mind, I get +2 to Cleverly attack using terrain advantage for my first attack in a fight (that's in addition to the bonus from any terrain aspect used).

Trained Builder: Because I am a Trained Builder, I get +2 to Carefully create an advantage by building, devising, or planning something of lasting benefit..

Fierceness: Because of my Fierceness, I get +2 to Flashily attack and defend when either attempting to intimidate or resisting intimidation.

Preserver's Foresight: Because of my Preserver's Foresight, I get +2 to Quickly create an advantage when reacting to an unexpected situation by using resources at hand.

Attuned to the Sacred Rock: Because I am Attuned to the Sacred Rock, once per session I can find the direction of the closest Murmadon rock. If I know its exact location (for example, a piece of rock I'm carrying with me), I can find the direction of the closest piece of Murmadon rock that is *larger* than the one I already know about.

Fragment of Murmadon Rock: Because I have a fragment of Murmadon rock, I get +1 to Forcefully overcome when casting a ritual. (Note that it's only a +1 because of the wider applicability; it's also recommended to take a related aspect. See also *"Murmadon Rock"* on page 268.)

Kuld:

Projectile Vomiting: Because I have Projectile Vomiting, once per session my attack affects everyone in an entire adjacent zone. One attack is made but everyone defends individually.

Tough Hide: Because I have a Kuld's Tough Hide, I get +2 to Forcefully defend against physical damage from blades.

Boulder Stance: When I hunker down and stay as still as a boulder for an action, I get +2 to Sneakily overcome or defend when trying to avoid detection. (The base difficulty varies by terrain and distance, from Mediocre (+0) in rocky terrain and at a distance, to Great (+4) in a city alley at a few paces, to Fantastic or just plain impossible up close with no boulders around.)

Vestigial Cavity: Because I have a Vestigial Cavity, once per scene I get +2 to Carefully create an advantage by hiding small items, storing them safe from being digested. With a success, I can use this retroactively to claim I have any such small item if I would reasonably have had a chance to hide it.

Relentless Hunger: Because I have a Kuld's Relentless Hunger, once per session I can devour an amount of organic matter equal to my own mass in mere moments, as long it's immobile and inert.

God-Scent: Because I am trained in the Source's rites, I get +2 to Flashily create an advantage when I cast a ritual using the smells from at least two different regurgitated substances. (See *"Religion"* on page 90 and *"The Kuld's All-Powerful Source"* on page 255 for descriptions of Kuld worshipping the Source.)

Equipment Stunts

In Agaptus it can make a big difference whether you hold a sword, a two-handed battle axe, or a potato peeler, so we use some rules for equipment, particularly weapons and armor. Choose one Equipment stunt to start with. Here are some examples:

Two-Handed Battle Axe "Nhildeslayer": Because my trusty two-handed battle axe "Nhildeslayer" has a mighty arc, I get a +2 when I Quickly attack from above (such as leaping off a building).

Vincius' Helmet: Because I have my father Vincius' helmet, I get a +2 bonus when I Flashily create an advantage by yelling a short encouragement to my troops on the battlefield.

Heavy Shield: Because I have a heavy shield on my right arm, I get +2 to Forcefully push an opponent into an adjacent zone.

Jaarl Sword: Because my volcanium Jaarl blade holds a fine edge that can pierce armor, once per session I deal lethal damage when I make a Clever attack successfully.

Great Spear: Because I whirl my great spear with flare, I can Flashily attack, create advantages, or overcome in my zone and adjacent zones.

Bow and Arrow: Because I have a bow and arrow, I can Carefully attack, create advantages, or overcome in up to three zones away, but not in my zone.

Round Buckler: Because I have a round buckler, I get a +2 when I Carefully defend when facing only one opponent.

For more examples of equipment stunts and how to make them, refer to *"Equipment Stunts"* on page 201.

Other Stunts

Next, you can choose a second or third stunt. This could be another faction stunt or something else unique to your character. Refer to *"Stunts"* on page 198 for more details.

If you don't feel inspired right now, you can wait and pick your equipment and "open" stunts during the game. Later, when your character advances, you can choose more.

Refresh

Your *refresh* is the number of fate points you begin each game session with—unless you ended the previous session with more unspent fate points than your refresh, in which case you start with the number you had left last time. By default, your refresh starts at three and is reduced by one for each stunt *after* the first three you choose—essentially, your first three stunts are free! As your character advances, you'll get opportunities to add to your refresh. Your refresh may never go below one.

Character Weight

Your *weight* describes how much force you bring to bear in a conflict. See *"Weight"* on page 222 for more information on how weight works. If you're playing a Sentian (an Elvorix, Vidaar, Jaarl, or Kuld) your weight is 1. If your group decides to play *stranger* characters you may need to take a stunt to reflect your weight being higher. See *"Stunts and Weight"* on page 205 for some examples.

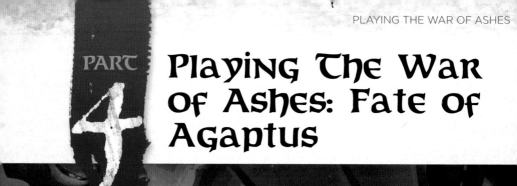

PART 4

Playing The War of Ashes: Fate of Agaptus

Ulf: "Now that is a tale well worth telling! There we were, trapped below decks, bound hand and foot with no one to save us! Things did indeed look grim, but I did not lose heart! I knew that all was not lost, for—"

Iva: "Kuri gnawed through his ropes."

Kuri: "HEE!"

Ulf: "Well, 'tis true that the buckie was first to gain freedom, but then I seized the opportunity—"

Iva: "And then he gnawed through my ropes and I untied everyone else."

Ulf: (sulky) "Your renditions of our sagas are distinctly lacking in heroic spirit."

Matia: "What happened next?"

Iva, Ulf, Rustica: (simultaneously) "There was a—" "I charged the nearest—" "We searched the hold—"

Kuri: "HEE!"

Ulf: "We fought them across the deck for control of the ship! Back and forth the battle swung with the advantage first being ours, then theirs. Until at last I came chest to chest with the Captain—a mighty Vidaar, tall as a tree, with muscles hard as stone. Our blades clashed, a sound like thunder!"

Rustica: "Wait. I thought the Captain knocked you flat."

Ulf: "'Twas just one pass of many—a momentary disadvantage!"

Iva: "The crew was desperate, but they weren't trained warriors—just fishermen given some rudimentary instruction and with a bit of experience. But there were a lot of them and a few of us, and things looked grim. Even a badly thrust spear is going to hit once in a while."

Ulf: "Meanwhile, the Captain and I exchanged blow for blow. How the fight would end would be decided by the god—"

(A momentary hush falls as everyone looks around for lightning bolts, inexplicable flames, or rains of carnivorous fish.)

Ulf: (clears throat) "... would be decided by luck more than skill."

Kuri: "HEE!" (Kuri belches.)

(Everyone visibly relaxes.)

Ulf: "And in the end it was I who struck the decisive blow, knocking the Captain from his feet and over the railing into the churning sea below!"

Iva: "He tripped over Kuri, actually."

(Kuri plays with pirate hat.)

From interview notes for the volume "The Explorers," by Matia Bibulus. Transcribed by Bura Bibulus Ven Proudheart, 88 AGC.

Outcomes, Actions, and Approaches

Now it's time to start doing something. You need to leap from the back of one galloping ylark to another. You need to search the entire Elvora Bibulus library for that one manuscript. You need to distract the guard so you can sneak into the fortress. How do you figure out what happens? First you narrate what your character is trying to do. Your character's own aspects provide a good guide for what you can do. If you have an aspect that suggests you can perform magic, then cast that ritual. If your aspects describe you as a swordsman, draw that blade and have at it. These story details don't have additional mechanical impact. You don't get a bonus from your magic or your sword unless you choose to spend a fate point to *invoke* an appropriate aspect. Often, the ability to use an aspect to make something true in the story is bonus enough!

How do you know if you're successful? Often, you just succeed, because the action isn't hard and nobody's trying to stop you. But if failure provides an interesting twist in the story, or if something unpredictable could happen, you need to break out the dice.

Taking Action: The 30-Second Version

1. Describe what you want your character to do. See if someone or something can stop you.

2. Decide what action you're taking: create an advantage, overcome, attack, or defend.

3. Decide on your approach.

4. Roll dice and add your approach's bonus.

5. Decide whether to modify your roll with aspects.

6. Figure out your outcome.

Dice or Cards

Part of determining your outcome is generating a random number, which is usually done in one of two ways: rolling four Fate dice, or drawing a card from a Deck of Fate.

Fate Dice: Fate dice are one way to determine outcomes. You always roll Fate dice in a set of four. Each die will come up as ⊞, ⊟, or ▇, and you add them together to get the total of the roll. For example:

⊟ ⊞ ▇ ⊞ = +1

⊞ ⊟ ▇ ▇ = 0

⊞ ⊞ ⊞ ⊟ = +2

⊟ ▇ ▇ ▇ = -1

Deck of Fate: The Deck of Fate is a deck of cards that copies the statistical spread of Fate dice. You can choose to use them instead of dice—either one works great.

These rules are written with the assumption that you're rolling Fate dice, but use whichever one your group prefers. Anytime you're told to roll dice, that also means you can draw from the Deck of Fate instead.

Outcomes

Once you roll your dice, add your approach bonus (we'll talk about that in a moment) and any bonuses from aspects or stunts. Compare the total to a target number, which is either a fixed difficulty or the result of the GM's roll for an NPC. Based on that comparison, your outcome is:

❊ You *fail* if your total is *less than* your target number.

❊ It's a *tie* if your total is *equal to* your target number.

❊ You *succeed* if your total is *greater than* your target number.

❊ You *succeed with style* if your total is at least *three greater than* your target number.

Now that we've covered outcomes, we can talk about actions and how the outcomes work with them.

Actions

So you've narrated what your PC is trying to do, and you've established that there's a chance you could fail. Next, figure out what *action* best describes what you're trying to do. There are four basic actions that cover anything you do in the game.

 ## Create an Advantage

Creating an advantage is anything you do to try to help yourself or one of your friends. Taking a moment to very carefully aim your arrow, spending several hours doing research in the Academy library, or tripping the bandit who's trying to rob you—these all count as creating an advantage. The target of your action may get a chance to use the defend action to stop you. The advantage you create lets you do one of the following three things:

* Create a new situation aspect.

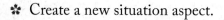

* Discover an existing situation aspect or another character's aspect that you didn't know about.

* Take advantage of an existing aspect.

See *"Magic"* on page 260 to read about creating aspects that would normally be beyond the reach of your character.

If you're creating a new aspect or discovering an existing one:

If you fail: Either you don't create or discover the aspect at all, or you create or discover it but an *opponent* gets to invoke the aspect for free. The second option works best if the aspect you create or discover is something that other people could take advantage of (like **Rough Terrain**). You may have to reword the aspect to show that it benefits the other character instead of you—work it out in whatever way makes the most sense with the player who gets the free invocation. You can still invoke the aspect if you'd like, but it'll cost you a fate point.

If you tie: If you're creating a new aspect, you get a *boost*. Name it and invoke it once for free—after that, the boost goes away. If you're trying to discover an existing aspect, treat this as a success (see below).

If you succeed: You create or discover the aspect and you or an ally may invoke it for free. Write the aspect on an index card or sticky note and place it on the table.

If you succeed with style: You create or discover the aspect and you or an ally may invoke it *twice* for free. Usually you can't invoke the same aspect twice on the same roll, but this is an exception; success with style gives you a BIG advantage!

A boost is a temporary aspect that you can only use once. See *"What Do You Do With Aspects?"* on page 192 for more info.

If you're trying to take advantage of an aspect you already know about:

If you fail: You don't get any additional benefit from the aspect. You can still invoke it in the future if you'd like, at the cost of a fate point.

If you tie or succeed: You get one free invocation on the aspect for you or an ally to use later. You might want to draw a circle or a box on the aspect's note card, and check it off when that invocation is used.

If you succeed with style: You get two free invocations on the aspect for you or an ally to use.

Actions & Outcomes:
The 30-Second Version

Create an advantage when creating or discovering aspects:

» **Fail:** Don't create or discover, or you do but your opponent (not you) gets a free invocation.

» **Tie:** Get a **boost** if creating new, or treat it as a success if looking for an existing aspect.

» **Succeed:** Create or discover the aspect, get a free invocation on it.

» **Succeed with Style:** Create or discover the aspect, get two free invocations on it.

Create an advantage on an aspect you already know about:

» **Fail:** No additional benefit.

» **Tie:** Generate one free invocation on the aspect.

» **Succeed:** Generate one free invocation on the aspect.

» **Succeed with Style:** Generate two free invocations on the aspect.

Overcome:

» **Fail:** Fail, or succeed at a serious cost.

» **Tie:** Succeed at minor cost.

» **Succeed:** You accomplish your goal.

» **Succeed with Style:** You accomplish your goal and generate a **boost**.

Attack:

» **Fail:** Attack doesn't harm the target and you take one point of stress.

» **Tie:** Attack doesn't harm the target, but you gain a **boost**.

» **Succeed:** Attack hits and causes damage.

» **Succeed with Style:** Attack hits and causes damage. You also gain a **boost**.

Defend:

» **Fail:** You suffer the consequences of your opponent's success.

» **Tie:** Look at your opponent's action to see what happens on a tie.

» **Succeed:** Your opponent doesn't get what they want.

» **Succeed with Style:** Your opponent doesn't get what they want, and you get a **boost**.

 **Overcome**

You use the **overcome** action when you have to get past something that's between you and a particular goal—picking a lock, escaping from handcuffs, leaping across a chasm, navigating a ship through dangerous shoals. Doing something to eliminate or change an inconvenient situation aspect is usually an overcome action; we'll talk more about that in *"Aspects and Fate Points."* Performing most maneuvers (see page 228) is done with an overcome action. The target of your action may get a chance to use the defend action to stop you.

If you fail: You have a tough choice to make. You can simply fail—the door is still locked, the brute still stands between you and the exit, the Vidaar ship is still *In Hot Pursuit*. Or you can succeed, but at a *serious cost*—maybe you drop something vital you were carrying, maybe you suffer harm. The GM helps you figure out an appropriate cost.

If you tie: You attain your goal, but at some *minor cost*. The GM could introduce a complication, or present you with a tough choice (you can rescue one of your friends, but not the other), or some other twist.

If you succeed: You accomplish what you were trying to do. The lock springs open, you duck around the bandit blocking the path, you manage to lose the Vidaar ship on your tail.

If you succeed with style: A success (above), but you also gain a boost.

Succeed at a Cost

GMs, you can offer to give the PCs what they want, but at a price—in this case, the failed roll means they weren't able to achieve their goals without consequence.

A *minor cost* should complicate the PC's life. This focuses on using failure as a means to change up the situation a bit, rather than just negating whatever the PC wanted.

> Foreshadow some imminent peril. *"The lock opens with a soft click, but the same can't be said for the heavy door. If they didn't know you were here before, they sure do now."*

> Introduce a new wrinkle. *"Yes, the acolyte is able to put you in touch with a scholar who can translate the withered scroll—a guy named Eludis Bibulus the Third. You know him, actually, but the last time you saw him was years ago, when he caught you with his daughter."*

> Present the player with a tough choice. *"You brace the collapsing tunnel ceiling long enough for two of the others to get through safely, but not the rest. Who's it going to be?"*

> Place an aspect on the PC or the scene. *"Somehow you manage to land on your feet, but with a* **Twisted Ankle** *as a souvenir."*

> Give an NPC a boost. *"Ragnhild surprises you a bit by agreeing to your offer, but she does so with a toothy smile that makes you uneasy. Clearly,* **Ragnhild Has A Plan.***"*

> Check one of the PC's stress boxes. Careful with this one— it's only a real cost if the PC's likely to take more hits in the same scene. If you don't think that's going to happen, go with another choice.

A **serious cost** does more than complicate the PC's life or promise something worse to come—it takes a serious and possibly irrevocable toll, right now.

One way you can do this is by taking a minor cost to the next level. Instead of suspecting that a guard heard them open the door, a few guards burst in the room, weapons drawn. Instead of being merely cut off from their allies by a collapsing tunnel, one or more of those allies ends up buried in the debris. Instead of merely having to face an awkward situation with Eludis Bibulus, he's still angry and out for blood.

Other options could include:

> Reinforce the opposition. You might clear one of an NPC's stress boxes, improve one of their approaches by one step for the scene, give the opposition a fate point, or give them a new aspect with a free invocation.

> Bring in new opposition or a new obstacle, such as additional enemies or a situation aspect that worsens the situation.

> Delay success. The task at hand will take much longer than expected.

> Give the PC a consequence that follows logically from the circumstances—mild if they have one available, moderate if they don't.

If you're stuck for just how serious a serious cost should be, you may want to use the margin of failure as a gauge. For instance, in the door-opening example, above—the one where the guards hear the PC and burst in the room—if the player failed their Sneaky roll by 1 or 2, the PCs outnumber the guards. Not a tough fight, but a fight nonetheless. If they failed it by 3 to 5, it's an even match, one that's likely to use up resources like fate points or consequences. But if they failed by 6 or more, they're outnumbered and in real danger.

Attack

Use an **attack** when you try to hurt someone, whether physically or mentally—swinging a sword, throwing a spear, or yelling a blistering insult with the intent to hurt your target. We'll talk about this in *"Ouch! Damage, Stress, and Consequences"* on page 231, but the important thing is: If someone gets hurt too badly, they're knocked out of the scene. The target of your attack gets a chance to use the defend action to stop you. (See also the *"Challenges, Contests, and Conflicts"* chapter on page 206.)

If you fail: Your attack doesn't connect. The target parries your sword, your spear misses, your target laughs off your insult. In addition, you take one point of stress from the exertion.

If you tie: Your attack doesn't connect strongly enough to cause any harm, but you gain a boost.

If you succeed: Your attack hits and you do damage. See *"Ouch! Damage, Stress, and Consequences"* on page 231.

If you succeed with style: You hit and do damage, plus you gain a boost.

Fate veterans will notice that an attack works a little differently in FATE OF AGAPTUS: a failed attack costs the attacker a point of stress, and a boost is gained automatically when the attacker succeeds with style. Grim!

Defend

Use **defend** when you're actively trying to stop someone from doing any of the other three actions—you're parrying a sword strike, trying to stay on your feet, blocking a doorway, and the like. Usually this action is performed on *someone else's turn*, reacting to their attempt to attack, overcome, or create an advantage. You may also roll to oppose some non-attack actions, or to defend against an attack on someone else, if you can explain why you're able to. Usually it's fine if most people at the table agree that it's reasonable, but you can also point to an relevant situation aspect to justify it. When you do, you become the target for any bad results.

If you fail: You're on the receiving end of whatever your opponent's success gives them.

If you tie: Things don't work out too badly for you; look at the description of your opponent's action to see what happens.

If you succeed: Your opponent doesn't get what they want; look at the description of your opponent's action to see what happens.

If you succeed with style: Your opponent doesn't get what they want, plus you gain a boost.

Captain Volo Troll-Axe charges forward and lunges at Ulf Long-Teeth, swinging his famous two-handed axe. Kim rolls for the NPC's attack and gets a total of +4. Ulf hurriedly raises his own axe to meet the blow as he sidesteps. Ian rolls for Ulf's defense and gets a +7—success with style! Captain Volo's blade misses Ulf and embeds itself in the wood of the bulkhead behind the younger Vidaar. Ian suggests, and Kim agrees, to a boost: **Stuck Axe.** *Ian will get to invoke the boost for a free +2 on his next action, then Volo frees his axe from the bulkhead and the boost vanishes (and because Volo failed his attack roll, he takes a point of stress). See "Conflicts" on page 208 for more on using attack and defense.*

Getting Help

An ally can help you perform your action. When an ally helps you, they give up their action for the exchange and describe how they're providing help; you get a +1 to your roll for each ally that assists this way. Usually only one or two people can help before they start getting in each other's way; the GM decides how many people can help at once.

In **conflicts**, however, an ally can provide help in a different way: by moving into your zone and facing the same opponent(s), they can increase your weight in the conflict. (See page 222 for more on how weight works.)

Choose Your Approach

There are six approaches that describe how you perform actions.

Careful: A Careful action is when you pay close attention to detail and take your time to do the job right. Lining up a long-range arrow shot. Attentively standing watch. Restoring a crumbling scroll.

Clever: A Clever action requires that you think fast, solve problems, or account for complex variables. Finding an opening in an enemy swordsman's style. Finding the weak point in a fortress wall. Figuring out how an Ancient device works.

Flashy: A Flashy action draws attention to you; it's full of style and panache. Delivering an inspiring speech to your army. Embarrassing your opponent in a duel. Producing a magical fireworks display.

Forceful: A Forceful action isn't subtle—it's brute strength. Wrestling a ylark. Staring down a Vidaar captain. Casting a big, powerful, magic ritual.

Quick: A Quick action requires that you move quickly and with dexterity. Dodging a Shuda's projectile vomiting. Getting in the first punch. Running away from an ilk swarm.

Sneaky: A Sneaky action is done with an emphasis on misdirection, stealth, or deceit. Talking your way out of getting arrested by the Town Watch. Picking a pocket. Feinting in a sword fight.

Each character has each approach rated with a bonus from +0 to +3. Add the bonus to your dice roll to determine how well your PC performs the action you described.

Approaches can be used **descriptively**, that is, by describing the character's action and behavior then selecting which approach to use based on this description:

Player: "I put my back into it and shove the door with everything I've got."
GM: "Cool, roll to open that door forcefully."

or **prescriptively**, by selecting an approach and then coming up with a description of what this would look like:

Player: "I want to do this forcefully."
GM: "Cool, describe how you use brute strength to do it."

Your first instinct is probably to pick the action that gives you the greatest bonus, right? It doesn't work like that. Would you Forcefully creep through a dark room, hiding from the guards? No, that's being Sneaky. Would you Quickly push that big rock out of the way of the cart? No, that's being Forceful. Circumstances constrain what approach you can use, so sometimes you have to go with an approach that might not play directly to your strengths.

The possible outcomes should also logically derive from the fiction: Forcefully opening a lock means smashing it, which means noise; Quickly doing it means using a shim that might get stuck in the door frame; Carefully means taking your time when guards might appear, and so forth.

Roll the Dice, Add Your Bonus

Time to take up dice and roll. Take the bonus associated with the approach you've chosen and add it to the result on the dice. If you have a stunt that applies, add that too. That's your total. Compare it to the target number, which could be a fixed number set by the GM or what your opponent's total.

Decide Whether to Modify the Roll

Finally, decide whether you want to alter your roll by invoking aspects—we'll talk about this a lot in *"Aspects and Fate Points"* on page 190.

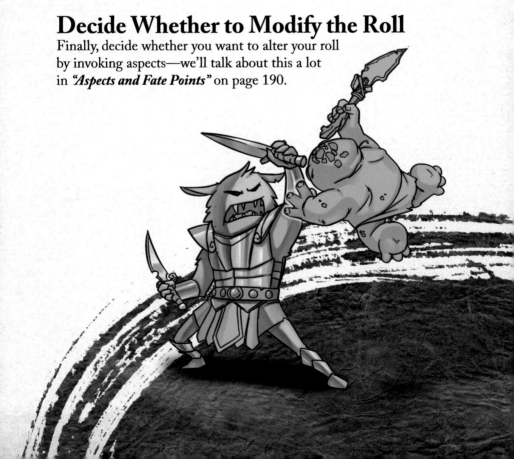

Engine of Narration: Aspects and Stunts

Aspects and Fate Points

An aspect is a word or phrase that describes something special about a person, place, thing, situation, or group. Almost anything you can think of can have aspects. A person might be the *Greatest Swordswoman on the Ashen Sea*. A room might be *On Fire* after you knock over an oil lamp. After an encounter with a Nhilde troll, you might be *Terrified*. Aspects let you change the story in ways that go along with your character's tendencies, skills, or problems.

You *spend fate points* to unlock the power of aspects and make them help you. You can keep track of fate points with tokens. We recommend Campaign Coins' Fate Tokens (see *"Inspirations and Resources"* on page 333), but pennies, glass beads, poker chips, or some other tokens will also do. The GM has her own fate points, which she can spend in similar ways on behalf of the NPCs.

You *earn fate points* by letting an aspect be compelled against you to complicate the situation or make your life harder. Be sure to keep track of the fate points you have left at the end of the session—if you have more than your refresh, you start the next session with the fate points you ended this session with.

You earned a lot of fate points during your game session, ending the day with five fate points. Your refresh is 2, so you'll start with five fate points the next time you play. But another player ends the same session with just one fate point. His refresh is 3, so he'll begin the next session with 3 fate points, not just the one he had left over.

What Kinds of Aspects Are There?

There's an endless variety of aspects, but no matter what they're called they all work pretty much the same way. The main difference is how long they stick around before going away.

Character Aspects: These aspects are on your character sheet, such as your high concept and trouble. They describe personality traits, important details about your past, relationships you have with others, important items or titles you possess, problems you're dealing with or goals you're working toward, or reputations and obligations you carry. These aspects only change under very unusual circumstances; most never will.

Examples: **Captain of the Ship Skyhammer**; *Hiding From the Agapta Town Watch*; *Attention to Detail*; *I Must Protect My Brother*.

Situation Aspects: These aspects describe the surroundings that the action is taking place in. This includes aspects you create or discover using the create an advantage action. A situation aspect usually vanishes at the end of the scene it was part of, or when someone takes an action that would change or get rid of it. Essentially, they last only as long as the situational element they represent lasts.

Examples: **On Fire**; *Bright Sunlight*; *Crowd of Angry People*; *Knocked to the Ground*.

To get rid of a situation aspect, you can attempt an overcome action to eliminate it, provided you can think of a way your character could accomplish it—dump a bucket of water on the *Raging Fire*, use evasive maneuvers to escape the enemy scout rider that's *On Your Tail*. An opponent may use a defend action to try to preserve the aspect, if they can describe how they do it.

Consequences: These aspects represent injuries or other lasting trauma that happen when you get hit by attacks. They go away slowly, as described in *"Ouch! Damage, Stress, and Consequences"* on page 231.

Examples: **Sprained Ankle**; **Fear of Falling**; **Concussion**; **Agaptus is Watching**.

Boosts: A boost is a temporary aspect that you get to use once, then it vanishes. Unused boosts vanish when the scene they were created in is over or when the advantage they represent no longer exists. These represent very brief and fleeting advantages you get in conflicts with others.

Examples: **Surprised**; **Distracted**; **Unstable Footing**; **Rock in His Boot**.

What Do You Do With Aspects?

There are three big things you can do with aspects: **invoke** aspects, **compel** aspects, and use aspects to **establish facts**.

Invoking Aspects

You **invoke** an aspect to give yourself a bonus or make things a bit harder for your opponent. You can invoke any aspect that you a) know about, and b) can explain how you use it to your advantage—including aspects on other characters or on the situation. Normally, invoking an aspect costs you a fate point—hand one of your fate points to the GM. To invoke an aspect, you need to describe how that aspect helps you in your current situation.

Player vs. Player

The only time that fate point might not go to the GM is when you're in conflict with another player. If you are, and you invoke one of that player's character's aspects to help you out against them, they will get the fate point instead of the GM once the scene is over. (Look at it from the other side: from the other player's perspective, you're compelling their aspect to your advantage, so they should get a fate point for it.)

If you invoke one of your own aspects to help yourself against another PC, then the fate point goes to the GM as usual.

> » *I attack the guldul with my sword. I know guldul are* **Slow Creeping Death**, *so I should be faster and have no trouble hitting.*

> » *I really want to scare this guy. I've heard he's* **Scared of Ilk**, *so I'll release an ilk in his bedroom.*

> » *Now that the guard's* **Distracted**, *I should be able to sneak right by him.*

> » *This ritual needs to be really powerful—I'm a* **Veteran Popio**, *and powerful rituals are my bread and butter.*

What does invoking the aspect get you? Choose one of the following effects:

* Add a +2 bonus to your total.

* Re-roll the dice. This option is best if you rolled really lousy (usually a –3 or –4 showing on the dice).

* Confront an opponent with the aspect. You use this option when your opponent is trying something and you think an existing aspect would make it harder for them. For instance, a Vidaar brigand wants to draw his bow, but he's **Buried in Debris**; you spend a fate point to invoke that aspect, and now your opponent's level of difficulty is increased by +2.

* Help an ally with the aspect. Use this option when a friend could use some help and you think an existing aspect would make it easier for them. You spend a fate point to invoke the aspect, and now your friend gets a +2 on their roll.

* For a specific mechanical effect tied to the aspect. See *"Invoking for Effect"* on the next page.

Important: You can only invoke any aspect once on a given dice roll; you can't spend a stack of fate points on one aspect and get a huge bonus from it. However, you can invoke several different aspects on the same roll. The only exception to this is that multiple *free* invocations of the same aspect (for example, earned on a success with style when creating an advantage) can be used to modify the same roll.

If you're invoking an aspect to add a bonus or re-roll your dice, wait until *after* you've rolled to do it. No sense spending a fate point if you don't need to!

Free invocations: Sometimes you can invoke an aspect for free, without paying a fate point. If you create or discover an aspect through the create an advantage action, the first invocation on it (by you or an ally) is free (if you succeeded with style, you get two freebies). If you cause a consequence through an attack, you or an ally can invoke it once for free. A boost is a special kind of aspect that grants one free invocation, then it vanishes.

Invoking for Effect

Sometimes an aspect should make something true in the world that needs a bit of mechanical justification. Let's say your Vorix soldier just found a **Stash of Bows** but doesn't have the stunt needed to hit a target more than one zone away, invoking for effect is a way to make sure the mechanics match up with the story.

When you invoke for effect, you're spending a fate point—or a free invocation—to create a specifically defined mechanical effect, something other than what a typical aspect is capable of. When you create an aspect, look at it and decide whether or not it needs a special effect attached to it. Maybe your Vidar Pirate can invoke *Captain of the Ship* Skyhammer to summon forth a crewmember to add to her weight (see *"Weight"* on page 222) in a conflict, or maybe your Kuld Guldul Rider can invoke **Sudden Burst of Speed** to move an extra zone before making an attack.

Mechanically, invoking an aspect for effect should be worth the fate point you're spending—the equivalent to two shifts' worth of potency, just like any other effect of invoking an aspect. Aspect effects should do something, like in the examples above, rather than provide a static bonus. A regular aspect invocation already provides a bonus, so you don't need a special effect that does that, too. An aspect effect is a bit like having an extra rules-exception stunt that you always have to pay for, both in terms of what the effect can accomplish and the amount of complexity it adds to your character.

Throughout **FATE OF AGAPTUS** there are a few examples of invoking an aspect for effect, such as using a battle ritual *Divine Wrath* to make an attack do lethal damage (see page 235) or *Pushed by a Divine Wind* to move an extra zone (see page 226), but the GM can allow this effect where they feel it appropriate. In general since the effect should be no more powerful than invoking an aspect, it should be something that you could accomplish using an overcome action with Fair (+2) difficulty.

Compelling Aspects

If you're in a situation where having or being around a certain aspect means your character's life is more dramatic or complicated, anyone can compel the aspect. You can even compel it on yourself—that's called a self-compel. Compels are the most common way for players to earn more fate points.

There are two types of compels.

Decision compels: This sort of compel suggests the answer to a decision your character has to make. You can model it off of this template:
You have **[aspect]**, so it makes sense that you'd decide to **[describe a situation]**.

*Iva is a **Wandering Virian Master**, so it makes sense that she would need to stay to lead the defense of the Virian Academy rather than fleeing to safety.*

*Ulf Long-Teeth is **Out to Make a Name for Himself!**, so it makes sense that he would accept a foolishly dangerous job.*

Event compels: Other times a compel reflects something happening that makes life more complicated for you. It looks something like this:
You have **[aspect]**, so it makes sense that, unfortunately, **[describe a situation]**. Damn your luck.

*Iva the Stubborn is a **Single Mother With A Fawn**, so it makes sense that, unfortunately, her fawn Kuri would go wandering off and get lost instead of staying near the hut. Damn her luck.*

*Rustica Bibulus **Owes Valius Nummus a Favor**, so it makes sense that, unfortunately, Valius Nummus would show up and demand that Rustica perform a service for him just when it's least convenient. Damn her luck.*

In any case, when an aspect is compelled against you, the person compelling it offers you a fate point and suggests that the aspect has a certain effect—that you'll make a certain decision or that a particular event will occur. You can discuss it back and forth, proposing tweaks or changes to the suggested compel. After a moment or two, you need to decide whether to accept the compel. If you agree, you take the fate point and your character makes the suggested decision or the event happens. If you refuse, you must pay a fate point from your own supply. Yes, this means that if you don't have any fate points, you can't refuse a compel!

If a player wants to compel an NPC, they can spend a fate point to compel one of their aspects. If the NPC is named, the fate point goes to them individually, otherwise it goes to the GM, who can spend it that scene.

Group Compels

Can the GM compel multiple PCs at the same time? Yes! If an aspect would apply to more than one character—for example, a story aspect or a scene aspect—and complicates the lives of each of these characters, then each character is compelled and receives a fate point if they accept.

If some accept the compel and some refuse, then perhaps a few heroes have escaped the trap, or not all of them have been noticed by the angry crowd, etc.; the GM can declare that it's all or nothing when she offers the compel.

Similarly, if a player comes up with a compel on the opposition and wants to affect multiple targets, it will cost one fate point per target. Note that groups of minions statted as a single entity (see "Groups of Minions" on page 304) count as one target.

How Many Fate Points Does the GM Get?

As GM, you don't need to track fate points for each NPC, but that doesn't mean you get an unlimited number. Start each scene with a pool of one fate point per PC that's in the scene. Spend fate points from this pool to invoke aspects (and consequences) against the PCs. When it's empty, you can't invoke aspects against them.

How can you increase the size of your pool? When a player compels one of an NPC's aspects, add the fate point to your pool. If that compel ends the scene, or when an NPC gives in, instead add those fate points to your pool at the start of the next scene. But then if you still don't use them in the next scene, they're gone.

Fate points you award for compels do NOT come from this pool. You never have to worry about running out of fate points to award for compels.

Establishing Facts

The final thing that aspects can do is establish facts in the game. You don't have to spend any fate points, roll dice, or anything to make this happen—just by virtue of having the aspect *Captain of the Ship* Skyhammer, you've established that your character is a captain and that you command a ship named the *Skyhammer*. Having the aspect *Mortal Enemy: Hand of Kuldarus* establishes that the setting has an organization called the Hand of Kuldarus and that they're after you for some reason.

When you establish facts of the setting this way, make sure you do it in cooperation with other players. Make sure that the facts you establish through your aspects make the game fun for everyone.

So if a player asks, "Cool! So I can create a character with the aspect *Emperor of Sentia*? Because I'm totally doing that!" the answer is "Yup, you totally can." But talk to the other players first, because you're making a BIG decision for the table, one that might take the game in an unwelcome direction for everyone. But if people are cool about it, then sure, go nuts. Aspects give players the potential to author or change large swaths of setting. If they want to do that, and if everyone at the table is happy with the resulting idea, then go for it.

Composing Good Aspects

When you need to think of a good aspect (we're mainly talking about character and situation aspects here), think about two things:

❋ How the aspect might help you—when you'd invoke it.

❋ How it might hurt you—when it would be compelled against you, and whether that would be fun for you.

I'll Get You, Krugar! *Invoke this when acting against Krugar to improve your chances. Get a fate point when your dislike for Krugar makes you do something foolish to try to get him.*

Hair-Trigger Nerves: *Invoke this when being extra vigilant and careful would help you. Get a fate point when this causes you to be jumpy and distracted by threats that aren't really there.*

Obviously, your Trouble aspect is supposed to cause problems—and thereby make your character's life more interesting and get you fate points—so it's okay if that one's a little more one-dimensional, but other character and situation aspects should be double-edged. If that idea makes you nervous, that's understandable. If you haven't played a Fate game before, the idea of building in "weaknesses" may seem counterintuitive. We can reassure you that they actually make things more fun, but don't take our word for it. Feel free to pick some more strongly positive aspects and just watch how play unfolds for the more interesting ones.

Stunts

Stunts are tricks, maneuvers, gear, or techniques your character has that change how an approach works for your character. Generally this means you get a bonus in certain situations, but sometimes it gives you some other ability or characteristic.

There's no definitive list of stunts that you pick from; much like aspects, everyone composes their own stunts. There are two basic templates to guide you in composing your stunts, so you do have something to work from.

The first type of stunt gives you a +2 bonus when you use a certain approach in a certain situation. Use this template:

Because I **[describe some way that you are exceptional, have a cool bit of gear, or are otherwise awesome]**, I get a +2 when I **[pick one: Carefully, Cleverly, Flashily, Forcefully, Quickly, Sneakily]** **[pick one: attack, defend, create advantages, overcome]** when **[describe a circumstance]**.

Smooth-Talker: *Because I am a Smooth Talker, I get a +2 when I Sneakily create advantages when I'm in conversation with someone.*

Lover of Puzzles: *Because I am a Lover of Puzzles, I get a +2 when I Cleverly overcome obstacles when I am presented with a puzzle, riddle, or similar conundrum.*

World Class-Duelist: *Because I am a World-Class Duelist, I get a +2 when I Flashily attack when engaged in a one-on-one swordfight.*

Pet Kanid: *Because I have a Pet Kanid helping me, I get a +2 when I Quickly defend when fighting against multiple opponents.*

Sometimes, if the circumstance is especially restrictive, you can apply the stunt to both the create an advantage action *and* the overcome action.

Paveo of the Stonemasons Guild: *Because I am a skilled Paveo, I get +2 when I Carefully create advantages or overcome when crafting stone works.*

Ylark Herder: *Because I am a patient Ylark herder I get +2 when I Cleverly create advantages or overcome when working with Ylark.*

The second type of stunt lets you make something true, do something cool, or otherwise ignore the usual rules in some way. Use this template:

Because I **[describe some way that you are exceptional, have a cool bit of gear, or are otherwise awesome]**, once per game session I can **[describe something cool you can do]**.

Well-Connected: *Because I am Well-Connected, once per game session I can find a helpful ally in just the right place.*

Quick on the Draw: *Because I am Quick on the Draw, once per game session I can choose to go first in a physical conflict.*

Can Run Circles Around a Runnigum: *Because I Can Run Circles Around a Runnigum, once per game session I can show up anywhere I want to, provided I can run there, no matter where I start.*

These templates exist to give you an idea of how stunts should be constructed, but don't feel constrained to follow them exactly if you have a good idea.

Going Beyond the Basic Stunt Format

While the "mad lib" format makes life easier for newcomers, astute readers will have noticed that ultimately, the first stunt structure above can be further simplified to:

Because I **[describe some way that you are exceptional, have a cool bit of gear, or are otherwise awesome]**, I get a +2 when I **[pick one: attack, defend, create advantages, overcome]** when **[describe a narrow set of circumstances]**.

Smooth-Talker: *Because I am a Smooth Talker, I get a +2 when I create advantages when I'm in conversation with someone.*

The purpose of pairing an approach with the stunt format is two-fold—showcase a character's signature style, and make sure the application of the stunt is narrow enough to remain balanced. Gamemasters can color outside the lines as needed, but we recommend paying careful attention to play balance by making sure the stunt's application is narrow enough.

Equipment Stunts

A stunt can also reflect specialized, high-quality, or exotic equipment that your character has access to that gives them a frequent edge over other characters.

Your character starts with one equipment stunt, which works like a normal stunt but has a few additional options. If a piece of equipment is such an important part of your character, you may even want to name it!

Basic Effects: *Equipment stunts can take a form similar to regular or innate stunts.*

Because I have **[describe item]**, I get +2 when I **[pick one: Carefully, Cleverly, Flashily, Forcefully, Quickly, Sneakily]** **[pick one: attack, defend, create advantages, overcome]** when **[describe a narrow circumstance]**.

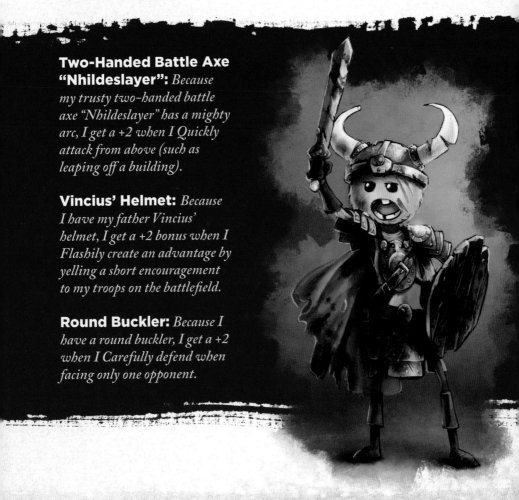

Two-Handed Battle Axe "Nhildeslayer": *Because my trusty two-handed battle axe "Nhildeslayer" has a mighty arc, I get a +2 when I Quickly attack from above (such as leaping off a building).*

Vincius' Helmet: *Because I have my father Vincius' helmet, I get a +2 bonus when I Flashily create an advantage by yelling a short encouragement to my troops on the battlefield.*

Round Buckler: *Because I have a round buckler, I get a +2 when I Carefully defend when facing only one opponent.*

Weapon Combinations: What if you are specifically trained with sword and shield, or are a master of the two-sword technique? Do you need to spend two stunts on the combination, one for each hand? Not necessarily. You could attach a stunt to the combination itself, using the same formula as above.

Two Swords: *Because I have Vaad's Swords of Triumph, I get +2 when I Quickly attack an opponent in single combat.*

Sword and Shield: *Because I have the Sword and Shield of Rumia, I get +2 when I Carefully defend against damage coming from my off-side.*

Lethal Damage: *Lethal* damage does not deal stress points—it goes directly to consequences. If you want to have a weapon stunt that lets you do lethal damage instead of one of the basic effects, it **must** have the form of:

Because I have **[weapon]**, once per session I deal lethal damage when I make a **[pick one: Careful, Clever, Flashy, Forceful, Quick, Sneaky]** attack successfully.

See *"Lethal Attacks"* on page 235 for more.

Jaarl Sword: *Because my volcanium Jaarl blade holds a fine edge that can pierce armor, once per session I deal lethal damage when I make a Clever attack successfully.*

Spiked Morningstar "Skullbreaker": *Because my heavy morningstar crushes my foes' bones, once per session I deal lethal damage when I make a Forceful attack successfully.*

Poisoned Dagger: *Because I have a hollow dagger with a poison reservoir, once per session I deal lethal damage when I make a Sneaky attack successfully.*

Zones and Ranged Weapons: An equipment stunt could also be used to affect opponents in other zones, or affect an entire zone with an attack.

Because I have **[weapon with long reach or range]** I can **[pick one: Carefully, Cleverly, Flashily, Forcefully, Quickly, Sneakily]** attack, create advantage, or overcome in **[pick one: my zone and adjacent zones, up to three zones away but not in my zone]**.

or

Because I have **[a weapon that affects multiple targets]**, once per session I can attack every opponent in **[pick one: my zone, an adjacent zone]**.

See also *"Zones and the Battlefield"* on page 209 for more info about zones.

Great Spear: *Because I whirl my great spear with flair, I can Flashily attack, create advantages, or overcome in my zone and adjacent zones.*

Bow and Arrow: *Because I have a bow and arrow, I can Carefully attack, create advantages, or overcome up to three zones away, but not in my zone.*

Throwing Knives: *Because I wield throwing knives, I can Quickly attack, create advantages, and overcome in my zone and adjacent zones.*

Alchemical Bombs: *Because I create volatile alchemical concoctions, once per session I can attack every opponent in my zone.*

Heavy Shield: *Because I have a heavy shield on my right arm, I get +2 to Forcefully push an opponent into an adjacent zone.*

Equipment Stunts and Weight: Equipment stunts can also add weight in conflicts. See *"Stunts and Weight"* on the next page for more detail and examples.

Repair and Replacement: Damaged or lost stunt equipment can be repaired in play, or replaced as a stunt transfer as part of normal milestone advancement.

Grolf had bad luck this session and his battle axe "Nhildeslayer" broke. Grolf gets his weapon repaired by a skilled weaponsmith and regains the stunt. When the session ends the GM announces that the group has reached a minor milestone; that's also a chance for Grolf's player to decide whether to get a different weapon instead, with a different stunt.

"See to your weapons—while you may tire and long for your hammock, rust sleeps not."

—*Vidaar proverb*

Stunts and Weight

Some stunts can also affect weight, a concept that is explained on page 222. They typically take the form of:

When I use my **[talent, advantage, equipment, or riding beast]** in **[pick as appropriate: social, mental, physical, etc.]** conflict, my weight counts as 2 in **[narrow circumstance]**.

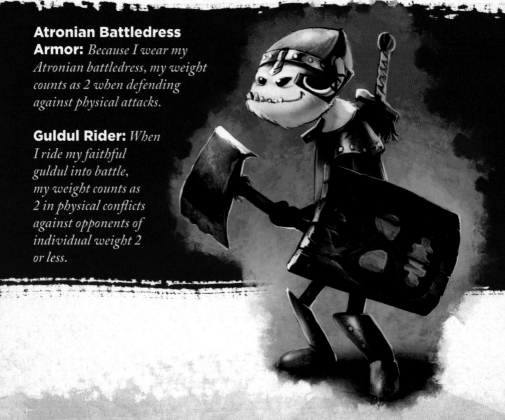

Atronian Battledress Armor: *Because I wear my Atronian battledress, my weight counts as 2 when defending against physical attacks.*

Guldul Rider: *When I ride my faithful guldul into battle, my weight counts as 2 in physical conflicts against opponents of individual weight 2 or less.*

Princeling: *Because I am a princeling by-blow of King Vidaarus, my weight counts as 2 in social conflicts involving Vidaar.*

Barbaric Yawp: *When I sound my barbaric yawp, my weight counts as 2 in the first round of physical conflicts.*

Big-Ass Axe: *Because I am a* **Giant Creature of Destruction** *that wields a* **Big-Ass Axe**, *in physical conflicts my weight counts as 4 when I Forcefully attack. (***Takes two stunts***. An appropriate stunt if playing a Nhilde troll for instance).*

The GM and player can decide at the table if this type of stunt would go into their equipment slot or not, if applicable. Is your guldul considered your only weapon, or do you have that *and* a great spear?

Challenges, Contests, and Conflicts

We've talked about the four actions (create an advantage, overcome, attack, and defend) and the four outcomes (fail, tie, succeed, and succeed with style). But in what framework do those happen?

Usually, when you want to do something straightforward—swim across a raging river, read a manuscript—all you need to do is make one overcome action against a difficulty level that the GM sets. You look at your outcome and go from there.

But sometimes things are a little more complex.

Challenges

A *challenge* is a series of overcome and create an advantage actions that you use to resolve an especially complicated situation. Each overcome action deals with one task or part of the situation, and you take the individual results together to figure out how the situation resolves.

To set up a challenge, decide what individual tasks or goals make up the situation, and treat each one as a separate overcome roll.

Depending on the situation, one character may be required to make several rolls, or multiple characters may be able to participate. GMs, you aren't obligated to announce all the stages in the challenge ahead of time—adjust the steps as the challenge unfolds to keep things exciting.

The PCs are the crew of a ship caught in a storm. They decide to press on to their destination despite the weather, and the GM suggests that this sounds like a challenge. Steps in resolving this challenge could be calming panicky passengers, repairing damaged rigging, and keeping the ship on the right heading.

Important: The challenge should never be, effectively, rolling the same thing multiple times. The ship only needs to be navigated once—if the GM really wants to push this in such a way as to make failure likely, that's a reason to use a compel, not to abuse the challenge system.

Contests

When two or more characters are competing against one another for the same goal, but not directly trying to hurt each other, you have a *contest*. Examples include a foot chase, a public debate, or an archery tournament.

A contest proceeds in a series of exchanges. In an exchange, every participant takes one overcome action to determine how well they do in that leg of the contest. Compare your result to everyone else's.

If you fail: You lose this exchange in the contest.

If you tie: No one gets a victory, and an unexpected twist occurs. This could mean several things, depending on the situation—the terrain or environment shifts somehow, the parameters of the contest change, or an unanticipated variable shows up and affects all the participants. The GM creates a new situation aspect reflecting this change and puts it into play. This may prematurely end or pause the contest before a winner is determined based on the twist.

If you succeed: You win the exchange—you score a victory (which you can represent with a tally or check mark on scratch paper) and describe how you take the lead.

If you succeed with style: you mark two victories.

The first participant to achieve three victories wins the contest.

Conflicts

Conflicts are used to resolve situations where characters are trying to harm one another, whether morally (hurting feelings), socially (demolishing reputations), physically (coming to blows), or through some other means. It could mean physical harm (a sword fight, a magic duel, a good old fashioned bar brawl), but it could also be mental harm (a shouting match, a tough interrogation, a debate between scholars).

Let's start with a quick overview of how conflict unfolds in FATE OF AGAPTUS, then we'll go into more detail showing you step-by-step how this plays out.

Conflicts: The 30-Second Version

1. Set the scene.

2. Determine turn order.

3. Roar phase.

4. Start the first exchange:

» On your turn, take an action.

» On other people's turns, defend against or respond to their actions as necessary.

» At the end of everyone's turn, start a new exchange or end the conflict.

Setting the Scene

Establish what's going on, where everyone is, and what the environment is like. Who is the opposition? The GM should write a couple of situation aspects on sticky notes or index cards and place them on the table. Players can suggest situation aspects, too.

The GM also establishes *zones*, loosely defined areas that tell you where characters are. Rather than limiting—as many other games would—how far in measurement units you can get in one unit of time, or how far you can shoot, then applying penalties for local conditions like terrain or visibility, it skips the math and looks at local conditions to *then* establish how far you can move or shoot.

This method is also part and parcel of *Fate*'s Fractal Adventure method (described in *"Gamemaster Advice"* on page 288), since it allows re-scaling; if you change the time unit, or the size of the map, or both, then naturally your zones are going to change too, while necessitating no change to the rules describing how things work.

Zones and the Battlefield

Even in physical conflict, zones aren't measured in yards in the fiction or inches on a map—they're much more abstract than that. Roughly speaking, if another combatant is close enough that you could take a few steps and attack them with a hand-to-hand weapon, like a spear, axe, or dagger, you're both in the same zone. In non-physical conflicts a zone might represent areas of political influence, a clan supporting one of their own, the various gods' attention, or groups of Sentians you can talk to.

You can visually represent zones using a number of different means, such as a series of connected squares drawn on a piece of paper, index cards arranged together on the table, elaborate 3-D terrain tiles, or anything in between. The only thing that really matters is that everyone has a clear idea of where the zones begin and end and how their spaces relate to one another.

Physical conflict: *Vidaar raiders are attacking the characters in an Elvorix farm house. The kitchen is one zone, the bedroom another, the front porch another, and the yard a fourth. Anyone in the same zone can easily throw punches at each other. You can also carry the fight from one room into another.*

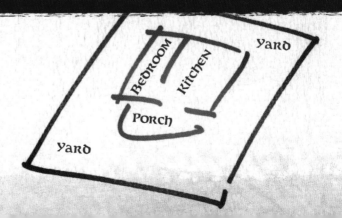

Zones for Non-Physical Conflicts

That's all nice and well for a battlefield, but what about conflicts that don't involve coming to blows? How do you establish zones for a social conflict (for example, about who will become the new leader of an Arcane faction) or a mental one (for example, a debate between scholars of the Elvora Bibulus Academy)?

The process is essentially the same, but the zones represent more abstract divisions of the metaphorical ground the opponents are fighting over.

Social conflict: *Jusipio and Meloria, respectively members of the Jaarl Builders and Providers, disagree about what to do with the limited supply of stones excavated from a quarry. Jusipio argues for a bridge across the river to ensure the new city's communications, while Meloria wants to build a new granary to protect the food reserves from Kuld incursions. The Builder and Provider Guilds form two zones, the city council a third in between them.*

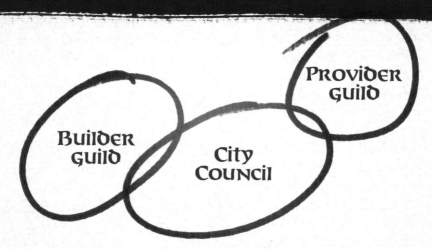

Zone Aspects

Of course, zones aren't merely abstract space—they're the very terrain of the battlefield. To that end, every zone can have a *zone aspect* that tells you what's in it. Unlike character aspects, zone aspects shouldn't be particularly nuanced. The simpler and more straightforward, the better. No matter what the terrain in the zone is like, it's going to be useful in some situations and a hindrance in others. An aspect that clearly communicates that in one or two words is ideal.

Keep it intuitive and broad—and short enough that it can easily fit on an index card. There are two good reasons for this rule of thumb. One, the battlefield is likely going to contain several zones and therefore several aspects, and you don't want things to look cluttered and confusing for the players or yourself. Two, time spent crafting the perfect zone aspect is time *not* spent actually playing the game. Better a good zone aspect now than a great one in 90 seconds.

*A zone might have **Trees** or a **Steep Slope**, or it might be a **Kitchen** or a* *Crumbling Stairway**, or even a **Waterfall** or **Bottomless Chasm**. Every* *zone needs a zone aspect. That flat, featureless meadow over there? Why, that's* *an **Open Field**.*

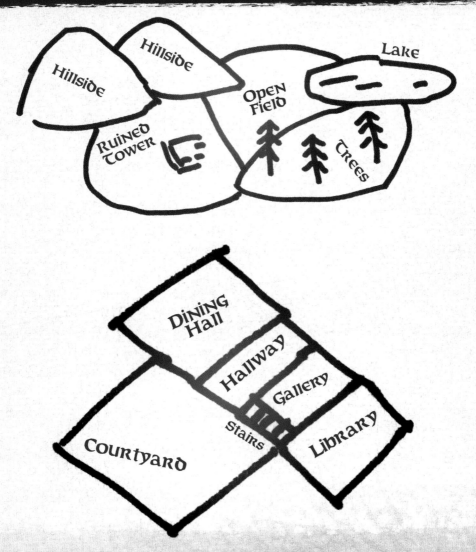

If a zone has more than one potentially interesting feature, either combine the two into one succinct aspect (like a **Farmhouse On Fire**) or pick the one that you think will be most entertaining or relevant to the scene and go with that (what feels more fun for this combat, a **Narrow Passage** or all those **Rocks and Boulders** in it?).

Normally it's the GM's job to assign zone aspects, but that doesn't mean they all have to be done in advance. If the PCs are in a starting position that prohibits them from seeing the entire battlefield—due to a closed door, outcropping of rock, heavy fog, or the like, feel free to leave them blank and fill them in as the PCs gain visibility to them.

Alternately, let the *players* define some of these aspects by exploring these zones. Handling zone aspects in this way gives the players more control over their situation and lends a little more unpredictability to the combat. This is a create an advantage action, typically using Clever or Careful, and can be done from another zone, provided the character in question can see into the unexplored zone. Generally speaking, you can't replace an existing zone aspect, unless the aspect itself is responsible for obscuring the zone in the first place. The difficulty for this task should be fairly low, such as Average (+1) or Fair (+2). If it makes sense that a zone aspect would make the task more difficult, increase it by +2 for every such aspect. Likewise, if the unexplored aspect is more than one zone away from the character, increase the difficulty by +2 for every zone that separates them.

Rustica wants to know what's hiding in the **Fog** *a couple zones over, so she takes time to Carefully peer into it and see what she can make out. Kim sets the difficulty at Average (+1), then bumps it up by +2 because of that* **Fog** *and another +2 for being two zones away. That doesn't sound so good to Rustica's player, Sharlene. Fortunately, she's able to move a zone closer, lowering the difficulty to Good (+3), and gets a result of Great (+4). Success! Since the scene takes place in a mountain pass, Sharlene suggests that the zone actually contains a* **Fog-Shrouded Chasm***, and Kim agrees. Someone's in for a surprise.*

Each pre-defined zone aspect starts the scene with one free invocation. Aspects "discovered" by the players (that is, by creating an advantage) start with one or two free invocations, as usual.

GMs are encouraged to use common sense when determining whether an aspect would affect a particular creature or character. For example, flying creatures such as uhyre would be affected by **Buffeting Wind** but not by **Icy Ground**, and a swamp dweller like a jormund would not mind **Marshy Terrain** but would be at a disadvantage on **High Rocky Ground**.

Number of Zones

Deciding the size of a battlefield—how many zones it contains—can be a tricky business. Too many and you have wasted space, or combatants spread so far apart that their spatial relationships to one another have little meaning. Too few, and everyone's crammed together into a too-small space, without a variety of terrain types to make things fun and interesting.

Start by visualizing the scene in your mind's eye. What does the surrounding area look like? Is it all on a flat plain, or is there varying elevation? What's of interest nearby? If the answer comes back "Uh... I dunno." then *put* something interesting in and expand outward from there.

In the course of their quest, Rustica, Ulf, Iva, and some hired mercenaries need to deal with a hostile Jaarl encampment. Kim wants the scene to take place in a tactically interesting location, but other than knowing that she wants the PCs to have to take care of some guards, she isn't sure where to start. Fighting guards in a flat plain would be pretty dull, and she can't imagine the Jaarl would camp in such a vulnerable location anyway. Maybe they're in some badlands where they can post lookouts on natural pillars of rock—it's a cool visual. Even better would be access via a narrow ravine cutting through a low cliffside. So far the battlefield looks like this:

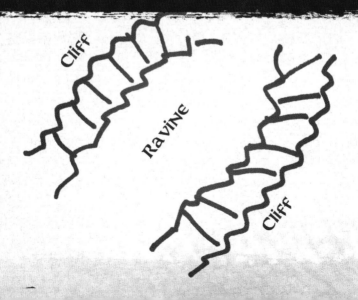

At the bottom of the cliff, Kim pictures a sparsely forested area with a clearing—so the lookouts can see intruders coming—but also a water feature of some kind, just to mix things up. A lake would be good. It's fun to throw people into, and it makes some sense with the ravine. And a waterfall flowing into it. Sure. Look, Kim isn't a professional geologist. She just wants a battlefield with interesting features.

That seems like enough for some variety, with enough space that missile weapons will make a difference. Kim imagines hidden Jaarl archers on the clifftops letting fly at the approaching PCs, a PC or two sniping back from cover of the trees, someone being pushed into the lake, or maybe even off the waterfall or a big jagged pillar....

Note that Kim hasn't assigned aspects to two zones. She figures the PCs can't see them from where they're starting (the **Sparse Trees** in the upper left), plus it'll be fun to define them during play.

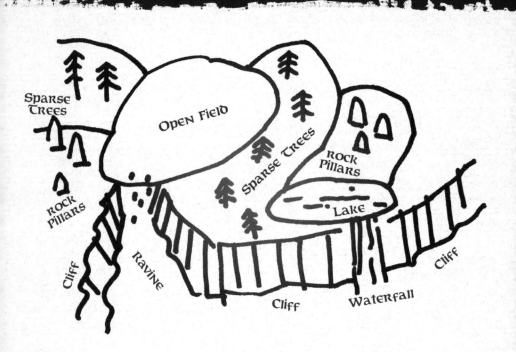

Determine Turn Order

Your turn order in a conflict is based on your approaches. In a physical conflict, compare your Quick approach to the other participants'—the one with the fastest reflexes goes first. In a mental conflict, compare your Careful approach—attention to detail will warn you of danger. Whoever has the highest approach goes first, and then everyone else goes in descending order.

Break ties in whatever manner makes sense, with the GM having the last word. For example, in an open fight, Forceful might break ties. In an ambush, it might be Sneaky. Of course, if the situation makes it clear who attacks first (such as an ambush, a ritual, or some sort of asymmetrical situation) then the situation should trump the approaches.

GMs, it's simplest if you pick your most advantageous NPC to determine your place in the turn order, and let all your NPCs go at that time. But if you have a good reason to determine turn order individually for all your NPCs, go right ahead.

Roar Phase

Whatever other cultural divides may separate them, the inhabitants of Agaptus are, like it or not, united in their ability to transcend their usual physical or mental limitations, to transform into enhanced versions of themselves. At the start of conflicts, Agaptans psych themselves up, call out challenges to each other, cast rituals, jockey for position, etc.; this is called the *Roar phase*, when opponents can enter a transcendent state.

This state may occur through intense concentration and focus, through wildly uncontrolled (and usually violent) emotions, through fearless derring-do, or the like. These higher states of consciousness go by many names, but are collectively referred to as *froth*.

One is said to "be frothing," or "in froth," or "taken by froth," or any number of other expressions. But they all mean the same thing: to be a paragon of one chosen facet of oneself. To outside eyes, the studiously intense Elvorix scholar would seem to have nothing in common with the literally-foaming-at-the-mouth Vidaar warrior, but both are, in fact, deep in froth.

How Froth Aspects Work

In *Fate* terms, Roar is an initial step of conflict during which anyone can create an advantage. With great reward, however, comes great risk, and frothing means not having access to the full range of your usual capabilities.

Creating a Froth Aspect

In one respect, creating a froth aspect is like creating any other situational aspect—they're both just using an approach to create an advantage. But there are three major differences when it comes to actually bringing one of these aspect extras into being.

For one, when you enter froth and as long as you are in this state, **you are limited to using the approach you used to create the froth advantage, and the two connected approaches** (see the diagram).

*Rustica is entering a conflict with Lord Tran Nummus and Sharlene wants her to froth with Careful, so she attempts to create the advantage **Intensely Focused**. Once she's frothing, she can use the free invoke from that aspect normally, but she's limited to the Careful, Sneaky, and Clever approaches.*

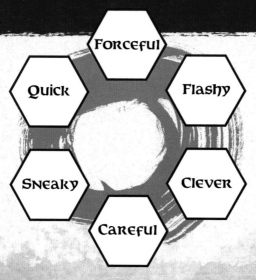

Second, **the base difficulty to create one of these froth aspects is +2**. The players and the GM take turns rolling for froth aspects—that's right, the GM can create as many aspects as the players do. How many free invocations are generated for each aspect, however, depends on the roll results.

Finally, **trying and failing to create a froth aspect means success at a cost**. The froth aspect will be created, but along with it will come a related consequence for the GM to use against the PC. On a tie, the GM only gets a boost against the PC rather than a consequence. It's a tricky business, transcending the bounds of mortal consciousness and capability. With great ambition comes great risk, and the gods don't take kindly to hubris. Note that minor NPCs who can't take consequences thus can't create a froth aspect at a cost; they simply fail altogether.

*Rustica fails the roll to create the froth aspect **Intensely Focused** for her debate against Lord Tran Nummus. Kim decides she will gain the mild consequence **Oblivious to her Surroundings**. Kim gains one free invocation of that consequence.*

Minor GM characters can froth with something they are skilled at, but lose the froth aspect automatically if they have to use an ability they are bad at.

Kim's NPC Lord Tran Nummus is skilled (+2) at appraising goods, negotiating contracts, and avoiding a straight answer, so he might froth by beating around the bush with a flowery opening speech to avoid getting to the point. He is bad (–2) at physical activity and admitting he's wrong, so he would automatically lose his froth aspect if he had to face evidence that he gave incorrect figures, or if Rustica managed to move around so that he is huffing and puffing to keep up with her pace.

Compelling a Froth Aspect

Naturally, a froth aspect can be compelled, either by the player who created it or the GM. If the player compels it, it's worth a fate point, as usual. If the GM compels a character's froth aspect, however, refusing a compel not only costs the player a fate point as usual, but also removes the froth aspect from play. See *"Losing a Froth Aspect"* on the next page.

Matia: "One topic we have not yet discussed is frothing."

(General laughter.)

Ulf: "Talk about frothing? We may as well be talking about breathing!"

Kuri: "Grr! Argh!" (Kuri stomps about.)

Iva: "It seems such a commonplace thing to talk about!"

Rustica: "The term comes from the Elvorix description of Vidaar Ulfryee, but different races and species are particularly known for expressing this in a specific way. Elvorix bravery and Jaarl discipline are both manifestations of it, even the Kuld's voracity."

Kuri: "Raarg!"

Iva: "Kuri, stop that! Like anything else, frothing has advantages and dangers."

Ulf: "But it can also be glorious! When frothing there is no doubt, only focus. To go into battle filled with froth is like floating on a calm sea. It is like—"

(Transcriber's Note: The remainder of Captain Longteeth's statement was lost, due to Kuri biting this humble scribe on the leg.—BBVP)

From interview notes for the volume "The Explorers," by Matia Bibulus. Transcribed by Bura Bibulus Ven Proudheart, 88 AGC.

Losing Your Froth Aspect

A froth aspect lasts until you choose to use a non-adjacent approach or until the end of the scene, whichever comes first. Barring any interference, of course. If the GM offers you a fate point to keep on **Raging** just as you're about to calm things down, for example, accepting means you're stuck with it for a while. You can pretty much count on the GM using this to your disfavor one way or another. What happens when the **Raging** Kuld can't stop raging, even though the only combatants still standing are his allies? Excellent question. Hopefully someone will survive to answer it.

As noted earlier, refusing a compel on a froth aspect not only costs a fate point, but immediately *removes* the froth aspect from play. There are no half-measures with froth—either you're in it or you're not. And as soon as you're not, it's over.

*Back to our earlier example, where Rustica was **Intensely Focused**. During their heated conversation, Rustica had started walking briskly to wear Nummus down. Their walk has led them to a glade outside of town. Unfortunately for the both of them, one lone Kuld has strayed from their pack to the same glade. If it notices them, more will soon follow. If Rustica wants to flee (Quick) or defend (Forceful), she will have to lose the froth aspect. Kim offers a shiny fate point if Rustica will keep frothing, and Rustica's player Sharlene accepts. She thinks she can Cleverly hide from the Kuld... Let's hope she has not underestimated their keen sense of smell.*

Froth isn't something to be entered into lightly. Froth can mean risk and loss just as easily as power and glory.

So Why Have the Roar Phase?

Fate veterans may wonder why we have a Roar phase and froth effects, if both sides can create an equal number of advantageous aspects. Here's why:

» **First**, it's part of the War of Ashes setting. Like ritual calling-out and boasting in many human societies from Western Europe to Western Africa to the Pacific Islands, it is a part of Agaptan conflict.

» **Second**, even when froth aspects aren't used directly against each other, it adds to the fiction by shining a spotlight on each character in conflict and what they're about. These aspects are used in a variety of ways; the Roar phase doesn't guarantee a zero sum between GM and players because some of them are won by way of taking a consequence before the battle even starts.

» **Third**, it lets you create lots of temporary aspects with free invocations you can stack later (see *"Invoking for Effect"* on page 194) at the moment in combat when the enemy is not trying to hurt you yet, so you don't have to worry about defending.

» **Finally**, it's the only way to create certain types of advantages, particularly battle rituals (see *"Magic"* on page 260).

Magic Rituals in the Roar Phase

Priests and others who bravely court the favor of the gods can create very special aspects through magic rituals during the Roar phase. See under *"Battle Rituals"* on page 275.

Exchanges

Next, each character takes a turn in order. On their turn, a character can take one of the four actions. Resolve the action to determine the outcome. The conflict is over when only one side has characters still in the fight.

Ulf has been challenged for leadership of his crew by First Mate Krog, in front of the assembled scurvy sailors of the good ship Blagaard. *This is a fairly dramatic point in the story and Kim decides to run it as a conflict. The two opponents will deal other stress through use of bombastic boasting, savage threats, well-crafted arguments, and base personal attacks. It's possible that they may come to blows, but what matters is convincing the crew to fall in behind one of them.*

Exchanges in Combat

While various types of conflict in *Fate*—social, mental, physical, etc.—use the same basic rules, *combat* and warfare can play out as a special type of conflict, relying much more than others on visual elements. When a conflict escalates into the physical, fur starts flying! FATE OF AGAPTUS details not only individual scraps, but skirmishes on a grand scale. It's time to go to the maps and the minis.

In FATE OF AGAPTUS, anyone in a fight is called a *fighter*. They don't literally have to be a career soldier or anything—it's just shorthand.

To keep track of things in a combat, every fighter is represented on the battlefield by a miniature or token of some kind. Miniatures are ideal, because they give the battlefield more color and visual interest. If they don't come pre-painted, they can be fun to paint, whether you're good at it or not. If you don't have any *War of Ashes* miniatures handy, distinctive markers such as cardstock standees or cardboard tokens will do the trick equally well. For nameless NPCs, you can even use coins of varying denominations. (Hey, they're nameless for a reason. Representing them with pennies is... apt.) As long as you can tell who's who, you're golden.

Why are miniatures so popular in roleplaying games and what do we use them for in physical conflict scenes?

Visualizing the action: Playing out scenes is visually exciting and focuses the attention of the players. Having a scaled-down model of the scene also helps the gamemaster define zones (see below) and the entire group stay on the same page as the events unfold.

Adjudicating movement and maneuvers: It helps to see what is going on in order to decide whether Ragnar can actually move past Salvia, or whether the sparse trees provides any cover against Goomba's ranged attack.

Suggesting actions and supporting tactical decisions: Just as the GM gets a better idea of what is possible, being able to see the action suggests to the players some of the cool actions their characters might take.

"Ooh, yeah, there's a kogg brewery in town! That begs for someone to roll some full barrels towards their foes, doesn't it?"

"Hey, Frigga is boxed in by those Kuld on one side and the river on the other—but Marko is obscured by the marshy reeds!"

"Whoa, that Marhn is huge! And it's right next to those tall trees with handy swinging vines!"

Weight

Weight represents how importance, influence, size, or numbers favor one side over the other. In **FATE OF AGAPTUS**, size *matters*!

Weight in Combat

Things like a fighter's facing and positioning within a zone don't really come into play—these rules don't care about that level of detail. Instead, it's the relative *weight* of combatants within a zone.

Add up the weights of all fighters on each side of a combat in a zone. If one side's total is greater than the other, that side *outweighs* the other side, or is "heavier." Unless a character has a specific stunt that would affect their weight (see page 204), the general size of the character determines weight. Sentians (Elvorix and Vidaar), Jaarl, and adult Kuld, including the typical "Wandering Kuld," have an individual weight of 1. (The run-of-the mill savage Kulds found in hungry hordes are usually smaller, immature specimens and have a weight of 0 individually; it takes several of them to form a swarm.) Other creatures can have different weights, as indicated in their profile under *"Beasts of Agaptus"* on page 109.

If the heavier side outweighs their opponents in the zone by at least two to one, they can replace any one of the dice they rolled with a ⊞.

If the heavier side attacker outweighs their target by at least four to one, they can replace *two* of the Fate dice results with ⊞.

It's a good idea to indicate weight advantage on the battle map using Fate dice, Campaign Coins' Fate Tokens, or Deck of Fate cards so you'll remember when it's time to roll dice.

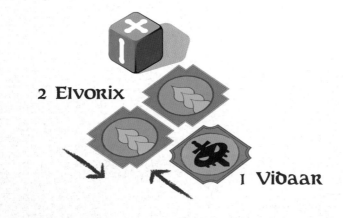

2 Elvorix

1 Vidaar

1 Elvorix

1 Marhn troll

Iva is facing off against a couple of Elvorix guards; they outweigh her two to one, so Kim sets down a Fate Token to mark a ⊞ *and rolls the dice for the guards' attack. She rolls* ▣ ▣ ⊟ ⊞ *, but replaces the* ⊟ *with a* ⊞ *, for a final result of* ▣ ▣ ⊞ ⊞ *. On her turn, Iva concentrates her attack on taking one guard out as fast as possible to gain a respite; by himself, the surviving guard no longer outweighs her and does not get the chance to change one die result to* ⊞ *.*

Alas for Iva, the guard hangs on long enough for reinforcements to show up, and she now faces four more Elvorix guards. They outweigh her at least four to one (five to one, really, but there's no additional bonus) so they now get to change results on **two** *dice, thus changing a* ▢ ⊟ ⊞ ⊟ *roll to* ▢ ⊞ ⊞ ⊞ *. Iva is in trouble.*

Weight comes into play whenever common sense dictates it would be relevant. Always include it when attacking or defending, but not necessarily when creating an advantage or overcoming. It depends entirely on context. Generally speaking, if the mere presence of allies in a zone would help accomplish something, it's reasonable to include the weight advantage.

Ulf wants to create an advantage against the horde of Kuld he's fighting by toppling a ruined wall onto them. He and his allies outweigh the Kuld in their zone, but in this case that's not really helping him since he's acting alone, so he'll roll as usual.

Later, channeling his ancestors of old, he attempts to create another advantage by intimidating their ravenous opponents with a savage battle cry. In this case, Kim rules that the presence of his allies around him makes his threats more credible, so he rolls the dice and can change one result to ➕ *.*

If the relative weights of two sides change during a round, adjust the dice accordingly on the *next* roll after they've changed. In other words, who outweighs whom can change on a turn-by-turn basis, no matter how things started out.

Our three heroes, along with a mercenary pal of theirs, face off against four Jaarl legionnaires in their zone. So far, their relative weights are equal, so everyone will roll normally on their attacks and defenses. Ulf acts first, and manages to take out two Jaarl fighters. Now the PCs outweigh the Jaarl two to one, so when the next player's turn comes around, they'll get the benefit of the ➕ *die on their roll.*

Weight in Social Conflicts

In social conflicts—for example, a debate between two leaders for control of a Guild—weight represents the importance, influence, and authority of the opponents. Rank, reputation, credibility, and circumstances will factor into this, and unlike physical conflicts, sheer numbers may not carry the day.

"If you do not know your enemy's strengths, and your own weaknesses, you are in certain peril."

—*General Khugg*

Example Weights

When addressing Elvorix:

- » Lord Maladros Bibulus ix Agapta co Agapta, Scholar King of the Elvorix, has a weight of 8;
- » A High Elvorix Houselord has a weight of 4;
- » The Houselord of a small Mercantile House has a weight of 2;
- » A commoner has a weight of 1, no matter how many are there.

In a scholarly debate:

- » A renowned academician might have a weight of 4.
- » A run-of-the mill professor might have a weight of 2;
- » A mere graduate student would have a weight of 1;
- » Commoners would have a weight of 0; it takes a swarm to add up to a weight of 1 and heckle enough to derail an argument.

Swarms

Some creatures, like ilk, are so small they have a weight of 0. They are too small to affect a creature of weight 1 or more unless there are a large number of them. Defeating an individual creature with weight 0 is handled using the overcome action instead of a conflict. So when creatures such as these attack *en masse*, they do so in a *swarm*.

Swarms come in three basic sizes. A *small swarm*, the size of an average Sentian, is weight 1. A *big swarm*, one about the size of an Ur-Kuld, is weight 2. A *huge swarm*, one as big as a Marhn, is weight 4.

If you want *really* huge swarms, the kind that can cover an entire farmstead, use several huge swarms. Five huge swarms are a lot more interesting and versatile in a fight than one gargantuan weight 20 swarm. Not only can five huge swarms spread out to five different zones, they can also work together to get a teamwork bonus. See *"Characters and Creatures"* on page 302 for more about groups of adversaries.

"What if I want to use swarms of something larger, like morgala or runnigum?"

Sure, you can do that too. See *"Groups of Minions"* on page 304 for more details.

While they outweigh their opponents, swarms can't be damaged by normal attacks that don't affect an entire zone, nor are they affected by opposed movement—there's just too many of them to try to make them go anywhere they don't want to go. Without a weapon like an alchemical explosion or a Shuda's vomit, you have to invoke an aspect for effect to make your attack affect a wide area, like **Boiling Oil** or **Flooded Room**.

Rustica and Ulf have run into three big (weight 2) swarms of ilk spread out around the Ancient ruins they were exploring. Right now the heroes are outweighed so their particular weapons are useless against the swarm. With all his might, Ulf knocks one of the giant pillars loose and uses the create an advantage action to add the aspect **Wobbly Pillar***. On her action Rustica invokes the aspect for effect and is able to attack one of the swarms by pushing the pillar and letting it crash down on the ilk.*

Movement on the Battlefield

A fighter can move to an adjacent, uncontested zone during their turn as a free action. This is made more difficult if:

❋ The zone the fighter is in or going into has an aspect that suggests an obstacle.

❋ The fighter is attempting to move more than one zone.

❋ Someone is blocking the fighter, by grabbing or otherwise trying to stop zone change.

If the first or second condition is met, the fighter will face **passive opposition** to moving into another zone. If the third condition is met, they'll face **active opposition**. Either way, it's an overcome action.

Note that **because this is an overcome action, the fighter will at the very least always have the option of succeeding with a serious cost**. This means that if they *really* want to get out of their current zone, they will always be able to do so—but the cost may be more than they're willing to bear.

*Ulf is on a **Narrow Mountain Path**, facing ranged attacks from bandits throwing javelins from the **Sparsely Wooded Slope** above. Ulf really wants to move into this adjacent zone to engage the bandits in melee, and the bandits oppose him. Unfortunately, Kim rolls well for the bandits and they tie with Ulf. Ulf's player Isaac still has the option to have Ulf succeed at a minor cost rather than remain an easy target; he offers to give the bandits a boost on Ulf, **Winded For A Moment**, and Kim agrees.*

Regardless of the opposition and the outcome, opposed movement costs the fighter their action for the turn.

Passive opposition means the fighter's struggling against the environment. If either the starting zone or destination zone has an aspect that suggests an obstacle to be overcome, the difficulty is Fair (+2). If *both* zones have such an aspect, the difficulty is Great (+4).

*Rustica is pinned in an **Icy** open zone by Vidaar archery volleys from a nearby cliff. She wants to get out and under cover of the nearby **Boulders**, so it's a passive roll and her difficulty is Great (+4) for the two adverse aspects.*

If the fighter is trying to move more than one zone, add +2 per additional zone to the difficulty. If these have adverse aspects, add +2 per adverse aspect as well.

*Ulf wants to move out of the **Avalanche!** zone, through the **Rockfall** zone, and into the **Tundra Plain** zone. The difficulty will be +2 for the extra zone and +4 for the two adverse aspects, for a total of +6. Difficult, but then again, so is recovering from being buried under falling rock...*

Active opposition means the fighter and their opponent(s) will make an opposed roll, with the opponent's total providing a difficulty for the fighter to overcome. Moreover, the opposition can invoke adverse terrain aspects, as appropriate, to increase the difficulty by +2 per invocation.

*Iva is struggling in melee with a Vidaar Bondee who tried to prevent her from moving out of the **Gaping Cliff Edge** zone and into the **Mountain Path** zone. It would be an opposed roll instead, and Kim can invoke the adverse aspect to add to the difficulty.*

Maneuvers

It's often important in combat to force your opponents to be where you want *them* to be—and to resist being moved where they want *you* to be.

We've included some examples below of how you can take advantage of the four basic actions to create specific *maneuvers*.

Most maneuvers allow your character to move to a more favorable location (e.g., adjacent zone with a useful aspect such as *Higher Ground* or *Good Footing*), or move an opponent to a less favorable location (adjacent zone with a troublesome aspect such as *Avalanche!* or where the opponent will be outweighed).

Maneuvers as Actions

Maneuvers as actions should be declared *before* rolling. The player should think about the specific flair they want to add, and choose the appropriate maneuver. If it's not on this list, the GM can assist in making up the maneuver on the fly. Here are some examples of maneuvers that can be performed with basic actions:

Push: When you and your opponent are in the same zone and you succeed in an opposed overcome action, you can push the opponent back one zone as your action. At your discretion, you can end in the same zone or choose to push only your opponent.

Pull: When you and your opponent are in the same zone and you succeed in an opposed overcome action, you can move and pull the opponent with you one zone as your action.

Charge: When you run into melee in an adjacent zone, you double your weight for one attack action. Additionally, if you succeed with style, you can force the opponent back one zone in a straight line at the end of your action (in addition to the attack). You both end in the same zone. However, if you fail in your attack, you give your opponent a free boost— that's in addition to taking one stress for failing the attack as normal; *and* also in addition to the boost they would normally gain if they defended with style.

*Ulf shouts a mighty battle cry and runs into the fray in the adjacent **Foredeck** zone, attacking two Jaarl sailors. He doubles his weight thanks to the charge, so no one is outweighed. Alas for Ulf, the Jaarl defend with style, gaining not only a boost as normal but an **additional** boost for the failed charge.*

Full Defense: When you create an advantage to improve your defenses against attacks this turn, you create a *Full Defense* aspect that you can invoke freely once for every attack made against you, but the advantage goes away once you take any other action.

Full Attack: When you fully commit to an attack while disregarding your own safety, you can make an attack lethal (see *"Lethal Attacks"* on page 235). To do this, you must describe what you are doing and overcome a Good (+2) difficulty using an appropriate approach; on a success, your next attack will be lethal. However, your give your opponent a boost that works in their favor when they attack you, such as *Exposed*. A risky trade-off for adding extra oomph to your attack.

Gicca decides to use a Full Attack against the skjeggy she unwittingly angered. She swings her skirra, a double-bladed polearm, in a dizzying spiral to briefly force the skjeggy backward, then with a great cry suddenly lunges with one blade aimed at the beast's neck. She rolls an overcome action using her Flashy approach; on a success, her next attack will cause lethal damage. However, the skjeggy gains an **In Range!** *boost for its next attack.*

Maneuvers as Boosts

Maneuvers as boosts are determined after the roll. Sometimes you land a lucky blow or make a skillful shot. Instead of taking a boost for succeeding with style on an attack, you can instead perform one of these maneuvers. Again, think about what you want to achieve, and interpret accordingly.

Knockback: When you succeed with style at a melee attack with a heavy weapon (e.g., two-handed mace), you can knock the opponent back one zone at the end of your action. You and the opponent end the action in two different zones.

Disarm: When you succeed with style at a melee attack, you can force your opponent to drop their weapon or shield. This prevents the use of any equipment stunt associated with it until they succeed at an overcome roll (difficulty +2) to pick it up or pick up another handy piece of equipment.

Footwork: When you succeed with style in a melee attack, you can move automatically one zone, even if someone is opposing your movement.

Iva is fighting a jormund at the water's edge, where it has an advantage. Next to her is a rocky upland terrain zone. Iva succeeds with style with her attack, so instead of a boost she can move one zone even though the rocky terrain would normally provide her opposition.

The astute reader will notice that maneuvers as boosts are examples of invoking aspects for effect. In this case the aspect is a boost so it goes away once it's used, and since it's used as soon as it's gained, we don't bother writing the boost down. See *"Invoking for Effect"* on page 194 for more about invoking aspects.

Ouch! Damage, Stress, and Consequences

When you're hit by an attack, the severity of the hit is the difference between the attack roll and your defense roll; we measure that in *shifts*. For instance, if your opponent gets Superb (+5) on their attack and you get Good (+3) on your defense, the attack deals a two shift hit (5 - 3 = 2).

Then, one of two things happens:

❈ You suffer *stress* and/or *consequences*, but you stay in the fight.

❈ You get *taken out*, which means you're out of the action for a while—or worse.

Stress & Consequences:
The 30-Second Version

Each character starts with three stress boxes.

Severity of hit (in shifts) = Attack Roll – Defense Roll

When you take a hit, you need to account for how that hit damages you. One way to absorb the damage is to take stress; you can check one stress box to handle some or all of a single hit. You can absorb a number of shifts equal to the number of the box you check: one for Box 1, two for Box 2, three for Box 3.

You may also take one or more consequences to deal with the hit, by marking off one or more consequence slots and writing a new aspect for each one. Mild consequence = 2 shifts, moderate = 4 shifts, severe = 6 shifts.

If you can't (or decide not to) handle the entire hit, you're taken out. Your opponent decides what happens to you. See **"What Happens When I Get Taken Out?"** on page 235 for more details.

Giving in before your opponent's roll allows you to control how you exit the scene. You also get one or more fate points for doing this!

Stress vanishes at the end of the scene, provided you get a chance to rest. Consequences take longer.

Lethal damage, however, can't be absorbed with stress; it goes straight to consequences. See *"Lethal Attacks"* on page 235, for more on dealing and taking lethal damage.

What Is Stress?

If you get hit and don't want to be taken out, you can choose to take stress. Stress represents you getting tired or annoyed, taking a superficial wound, or some other condition that goes away quickly.

Your character sheet has a *stress track*, a row of three boxes. When you take a hit and check a stress box, the box absorbs a number of shifts equal to its number: one shift for Box 1, two for Box 2, or three for Box 3. If that box is already checked, check off a higher value box. If there is no higher available box, and you can't take any consequences, you're taken out of the conflict.

You can only check one stress box for any single hit, but you can check a stress box and take one or more consequences at the same time. You can't check a stress box that already has a check mark in it!

What Are Consequences?

Consequences are new aspects that you take to reflect being seriously hurt in some way—mentally or physically. Your character sheet has three slots where you can write consequences. Each one is labeled with a number: 2 (mild consequence), 4 (moderate consequence), or 6 (severe consequence). This represents the number of shifts of the hit the consequence absorbs. You can mark off as many of these as you like to handle a single hit, but only if that slot was blank to start with. If you already have a moderate consequence written down, you can't take another one until you do something to make the first one go away!

A major downside of consequences is that each consequence is a new aspect that your opponents can invoke against you. The more you take, the more vulnerable you are. And just like situation aspects, the character that creates it (in this case, the character that hit you) gets one free invocation on that consequence. They can choose to let one of their allies use the free invocation.

Let's say that you get hit really hard and take a 4-shift hit. You check Box 2 on your stress track, which leaves you with two shifts to deal with. If you can't, you're taken out, so it's time for a consequence. You can choose to write a new aspect in the consequence slot labeled 2—say, **Sprained Ankle**. *Those final two shifts are taken care of and you can keep fighting! But your opponent gets one free invocation against you.*

If you're unable to absorb all of a hit's shifts—by checking a stress box, taking consequences, or both—you're taken out.

Naming a Consequence

Here are some guidelines for choosing what to name a consequence:

Mild consequences don't require immediate medical attention. They hurt, and they may present an inconvenience, but they aren't going to force you into a lot of bed rest. On the mental side, mild consequences express things like small social gaffes or changes in your surface emotions. Examples: *Black Eye, Bruised Hand, Winded, Flustered, Cranky, Seeing Double*.

Moderate consequences represent fairly serious impairments that require dedicated effort toward recovery (including medical attention). On the mental side, they express things like damage to your reputation or emotional problems that you can't just shrug off with an apology and a good night's sleep. Examples: *Deep Cut, First Degree Burn, Down With The Flu, Drunk, Terrified*.

Severe consequences go straight to the temple for healing and prayers—they're extremely nasty and prevent you from doing a lot of things, and will lay you out for a while. On the mental side, they express things like serious trauma or relationship-changing harm. Examples: *Horrible Burns, Compound Fracture, Guts Hanging Out, Crippling Shame, Trauma-Induced Phobia*.

What Happens When I Get Taken Out?

If you don't have any stress or consequences left to buy off all the shifts of a hit, that means you're taken out.

Taken out is bad—it means not only that you can't fight anymore, but that whoever took you out gets to decide what your loss looks like and what happens to you after the conflict. They can't narrate anything that wouldn't make sense in the conflict (like having you die from shame), but they have a lot of latitude. Whether **character death** is an option normally depends on what the group agreed to when deciding on a premise (see *"Premise"* on page 141).

Sometimes the premise decision may have been made by the GM alone, particularly for a one-off game. In that case, the GM has a duty to make it clear to the players what this premise is, including whether character death is on the table.

The world of Agaptus is a harsh place and it's not unreasonable to decide that death is an option; but we recommend that you save that possibility for conflicts that are pivotal, dramatic, and meaningful for that character—in other words, conflicts in which that character would knowingly and willingly risk dying in order to win.

Lethal Attacks

For a variety of reasons, some attacks are more deadly than others. They're less a matter of wearing your opponent down than of landing exceptional blows which can have an immediate and devastating effect on the defender. In game terms, we call these attacks *lethal*.

While an average attack can usually be mitigated by checking a stress box, lethal attacks go straight to the defender's consequences, bypassing their stress track entirely. This means that a successful lethal attack will always mean some sort of longer-lasting trauma for the defender—or, in the case of mere minions, who don't *have* consequences to begin with, instant defeat. (Probably by death. We don't call them "lethal attacks" for nothing.)

Making an Attack Lethal

Broadly speaking, there are five main ways to make an attack into a lethal attack.

* Using certain maneuvers.

* Having a relevant stunt.

* Using an appropriate magic ritual.

* Some deadly creatures have lethal attacks.

* Creating such excellent attack conditions that the GM judges the attack to be lethal.

Using Maneuvers

The Full Attack maneuver sets you up to deliver a lethal attack but makes you exposed as well. See the *"Maneuvers"* section on page 228 for more detail.

Having A Stunt

Certain stunts with a special weapon or using a particular technique can give particular attacks the ability to cause lethal damage. **Lethal damage is always a "once per session" stunt effect.** See the *"Equipment Stunts"* section on page 201 for more detail.

Using a Battle Ritual

Rituals essentially grant temporary stunts and some rituals, such as "Combat Fury," can grant the ability to cause lethal damage. **Lethal damage is always a "once per conflict" effect.** See the *"Battle Rituals"* section on page 275 for more detail.

Deadly Creatures

Some creatures like the Marhn are just naturally deadly! See the *"Beasts of Agaptus"* section on page 109 for examples.

GM's Discretion

Sometimes the players come up with a brilliant plan that leaves the enemy at a serious disadvantage. If they put serious (and successful) effort into creating conditions that would make their attack much more dangerous, the GM can decide to declare that an attack will do lethal damage.

The heroes know they are badly outnumbered by the Kuld pack roaming the area, so they decide to create an ambush to even things out. Kim offers to treat this as a challenge. They will have to create an advantage by locating a suitable ambush spot, create a second advantage by preparing the location, and overcome the Kuld's wariness to bring them into the prepared trap. Iva scouts out the perfect bottleneck in a narrow rocky pass; Ulf piles boulders above, ready to trigger an avalanche; and Rustica brews a fantastic-smelling stew that should attract the Kuld for leagues around. They prepared well and described their actions interestingly, so Kim declares that the ambush will indeed be lethal, both the direct damage caused by the avalanche and the heroes' first attack in battle.

Often such situations will be represented by lots of preparatory aspects and boosts, which will in turn convert into substantial bonuses. The GM should not give a deadly outcome in that situation—the bonuses will be damaging enough. But it may be useful in a situation where the GM knows the players will be able to do all that preparation, and just skip over it in favor of making the initial attacks lethal rather than stretching out an otherwise unimportant conflict.

Giving In

If things look grim for you, you can *give in* (or *concede* the fight)—but you have to say that's what you're going to do *before* your opponent rolls their dice.

This is different from being taken out, because you get a say in what happens to you. Your opponent gets some major concession from you—talk together about what makes sense in your situation—but it beats getting taken out and having no say at all. A reasonable concession gives your opponent what they wanted but leaves you in a position to live to fight another day (because you escape, get separated from the fight, get captured by a third party or the like).

Additionally, you get one fate point for conceding, and one fate point for each consequence you took in this conflict. This is your chance to say, "You have won the battle, but not the war!" and get a tall stack of fate points to back it up.

Ian can tell that his character Ulf Long-Teeth, who has already taken mild and moderate consequences, is going to be in bad shape if he receives another hit from Captain Volo Troll-Axe's signature weapon, a two-handed axe. It could result in a severe consequence, and Ian doesn't really want to drag it through the entire adventure. Instead, he offers to give in—that way he'll get a fate point and a chance to preserve a bit of advantage. Before the dice hit the table he makes his offer:

"Can Ulf concede the fight, but manage to keep a weapon hidden?"

Kim agrees and tosses the fate point. Ian narrates Ulf dropping his weapon, clattering on the deck, holding his arm and feigning to be hurt worse than he really is—while slipping a dagger in his sleeve.

Getting Better—Recovering from Stress and Consequences

At the end of each scene, clear all of your stress boxes. Recovery from a consequence is a bit more complicated; you need to **explain how you recover from it**—whether that's a visit to the local shaman, tending to your wounds, taking a walk to calm down, or whatever makes sense with the consequence. You also need to wait an appropriate length of time.

Mild consequence: Clear it at the end of the next scene, provided you get a chance to rest or get appropriate help. If you keep right on moving, for example from a battle scene to an escape scene, then the consequence sticks with you until you have had some rest.

Moderate consequence: Downgrade it to mild at the end of the next session, provided it makes sense within the story.

Severe consequence: Downgrade it to moderate at the end of the scenario or the next major milestone (see *"Milestones"* on page 240), whichever comes first, provided it makes sense within the story.

*Ulf suffered a **Sword Gash to the Side**, a moderate consequence. He keeps it for the rest of the session and until the end of the **next** session, at which point it becomes a mild consequence and he renames it **Still A Little Sore**. At the beginning of the next session, Kim can take advantage of this lingering wound in the first scene if she wants to make life more interesting for the characters; otherwise, it will go away after the opening scene and some rest.*

Renaming Moderate and Severe Consequences

Moderate and severe consequences stick around for a while. Therefore, at some point during the session you may want to change the name of the aspect to better fit what's going on in the story. For instance, after you get some medical help, *Painful Broken Leg* might make more sense if you change it to *Hobbling on Crutches*. This is a good way to handle a session where a lot of time has passed in play (such as a long sea voyage) where it might make sense that the character will have had time to heal. Converting the injury into some sort of lingering remnant is a nice way to reflect that time without giving an easy out. It will still downgrade at the

Character Advancement

You change over time. Your skills sharpen as you practice them. Your life experiences accumulate and shape your personality. FATE OF AGAPTUS reflects this with *character advancement*, which allows you to change your aspects, add or change stunts, and raise your approach bonuses. You do this when your character reaches a milestone.

Milestones

Stories in TV shows, comic books, movies, and even video games usually continue from episode to episode, season to season. It took Frodo three big books to take the Ring to the fiery mountain. It took Aang three seasons to defeat the Fire Lord. You get the idea. FATE OF AGAPTUS can tell those kinds of stories; you play many game sessions in a row using the same characters—this is often called a **campaign**—and the story builds on itself. But within these long stories, there are shorter story arcs, like single episodes of a TV show or single issues of a comic, where shorter stories are told and wrapped up. FATE OF AGAPTUS can do that too, even within a longer campaign.

In FATE OF AGAPTUS we call those wrap-ups *milestones*—whether they're small ones for short stories, or really big ones at the end of many sessions of play. FATE OF AGAPTUS recognizes four types of milestones, and each one allows you to change your character in certain ways.

Minor Milestones

A *minor milestone* usually occurs at the end of a session of play, or when one piece of a story has been resolved. Rather than making your character more powerful, this kind of milestone is more about changing your character, adjusting in response to whatever's going on in the story if you need to. Sometimes it won't really make sense to take advantage of a minor milestone, but you always have the opportunity in case you need to.

After a minor milestone, you can choose to do one (and only one) of the following:

* Switch the ratings of any two approaches.

* Rename one aspect that isn't your high concept.

* Attach an existing equipment stunt to a new, similar piece of equipment to replace one that was lost or damaged.

* Exchange one stunt for a different stunt.

* Choose a new stunt (and adjust your refresh, if you already have three stunts).

* Clear one mild Divine Interest consequence. (See *"Divine Interest"* on page 256.)

Also, if you have a moderate consequence, check to see if it's been around for at least one full session (i.e., you had it at the end of the previous session). If you've taken action to recover from it, you can rename it and change it to a mild consequence.

Significant Milestones

A *significant milestone* usually occurs at the end of a scenario or the conclusion of a big plot event (or, when in doubt, at the end of every two or three sessions). Unlike minor milestones, which are primarily about change, significant milestones are about learning new things—dealing with problems and challenges has made your character generally more capable at what they do.

In addition to the benefit of a minor milestone, you also gain *all* of the following:

* ❃ If you have a severe consequence that's been around for at least two sessions, and you've taken action to recover from it, you can rename it and downgrade it to a moderate consequence.

* ❃ Raise the bonus of one approach by one.

* ❃ The group as a whole may clear one mild Divine Interest consequence OR reduce a moderate Divine Interest consequence that has been around for at least two sessions to mild. (See *"Divine Interest"* on page 256.)

* ❃ "Flag" an aspect that you intend to change, including your high concept. This is letting the GM know you intend to make the change, so talk to the GM about what direction you're thinking of taking it.

* ❃ Change a previously flagged aspect (with GM approval).

Raising Approach Bonuses

When you raise the bonus of an approach, there's only one rule you need to remember: you can't raise an approach bonus above Superb (+5).

Major Milestones

Major milestones should only occur when something happens in the campaign that shakes it up a lot—the end of a big story arc, the final defeat of a main NPC villain, or any other large-scale change that reverberates around your game world.

These milestones are about gaining more power. The challenges of yesterday simply aren't sufficient to threaten these characters anymore, and the threats of tomorrow will need to be more adept, organized, and determined to stand against them.

Achieving a major milestone confers the benefits of a significant milestone *and* a minor milestone. In addition, you may do *all* of the following:

❊ Take an additional point of refresh, which you may immediately use to purchase a stunt if you wish.

❊ Rename your character's high concept (optional).

❊ If a Divine Interest consequence has been around since at least the previous significant milestone, you can reduce it from severe to moderate.

Divine Milestone

At the end of any session that you are taken out by Divine consequences, clear all the Divine Interest consequences and decide on a new permanent group aspect. (See *"Divine Interest"* on page 256.)

243

In Short

Rolling the Dice *(page 189)*
Result = Dice Roll

+ Approach bonus
+ Bonuses from stunts
+ Bonuses from invoked aspects

Four Actions *(page 180)*
» **Overcome** an obstacle.
» **Create an Advantage** (aspect).
» **Attack** another character.
» **Defend** against attacks or advantages.

Four Outcomes *(page 179)*
Versus opponent's result or target number.

» **Fail** if your result is lower. Take appropriate fallout or succeed at serious cost.
» **Tie** if your result is equal. Gain appropriate benefit or succeed at minor cost.
» **Success** if your result is higher by 1 or 2.
» **Success with Style** if your result is higher by 3 or more. Gain appropriate benefit.

Turn Order *(page 215)*
» **Physical Conflict:** Highest Quick goes first.
» **Mental Conflict:** Highest Careful goes first.
» **Everyone else** goes in descending order.
» **NPCs** go on the turn of the most advantageous NPC.

Roar Phase *(page 215)*
Create an advantage against a difficulty of Fair (+2).

» **Fail:** Create a froth aspect and gain a consequence.
» **Tie:** Creates a froth **boost**.
» **Success:** Create a froth aspect with one free invoke.
» **Success with Style:** Create a froth aspect with two free invokes.

While frothing, you are limited to the approach you used and the two adjacent approaches.

The froth aspect lasts until you use a non-adjacent approach or the scene ends.

Weight *(page 222)*
» If you outweigh your opponents in the zone by at least 2 to 1, replace any one of the dice rolled with a ⊞.
» If you outweigh the zone opposition by at least 4 to 1, replace two results with ⊞.

Stress & Consequences *(page 231)*
» Check one **stress box** to handle some or all of the shifts of a hit.
» Take one or more **consequences** to deal with the hit.
  » Mild = 2 shifts
  » Moderate = 4 shifts
  » Severe = 6 shifts
» If you don't handle the entire hit, you're **taken out** and your opponent decides what happens.
» **Give in** before your opponent's roll to control how you exit the scene and earn one or more fate points.

PART 5

Gods and Magic

Rustica: "One of the problems with being in a position to make big changes in the world is that it attracts unwanted attention, usually at the worst time and in the worst place. Aside from attracting the attention of footpads, robbers, con artists, beggars, and general hangers-on, if you are particularly successful even the gods will take an interest in you."

Ulf: "God. There is no god other than Akka-Maas."

Iva: (snorts) "It's all just superstition. Something happens and you can't explain it so it becomes the work of some supernatural entity. Coincidences are just coincidences—they aren't the workings of a bunch of bickering deities."

Ulf: "Deity!"

Rustica: "So when we brought the statue out of that old temple, all that happened was just coincidence?"

Iva: "Yes!"

Rustica: "Lightning from a clear sky?"

Iva: "Natural phenomenon!"

Rustica: "Tornadoes?"

Iva: "They happen!"

Rustica: "Rain of ylark?

Iva: "Unusual, but not unprecedented."

Rustica: "Glowing, hundred-foot-tall Elvorix dressed in a golden toga announcing in a booming voice 'I AM AGAPTUS, YOU WILL BOW DOWN BEFORE ME'?"

Iva: "Optical illusion. Happens all the time."

Ulf: "Agreed."

From interview notes for the volume "The Explorers," by Matia Bibulus. Transcribed by Bura Bibulus Ven Proudheart, 88 AGC.

The Gods

The Elvorix believe in many gods, the Vidaar in only one, the Jaarl have turned their backs on the gods, and the Kuld worship a diffuse, impersonal universal force. Which one is right? All of them, or none of them as fits your game. Gamemasters are free to decide whether all these deities co-exist, are just facets of a same entity, or are just very powerful beings hitching a free ride from naïve Sentian worshipers.

Boons: Whatever the gods are, each is reputed to offers certain boons... and certain risks to devotees. Whenever you get favorable attention from a god by pleasing, entertaining, or at least vaguely distracting one from utter boredom, you can use a free invocation of any of the god's aspects for one scene while the deity's attention is on you. However, for every free invocation you claim, the gamemaster can use a free invocation of the god's trouble aspect against you. This scene, and access to the boon, ends when the god's attention wanders or you offend the deity.

The Elvorix priest Caperna Aedituus has managed to get Agaptus' attention. Although since the Great Catastrophe the god is still too angry at his people to show himself, he was mildly roused from his blue funk by Caperna's adventures and took an interest. For the scene, Caperna's player can call on free invocations of the god's aspects—as long as Caperna is willing to risk the god's trouble.

*Caperna invokes **Ruler Of The Sky And Stars** to cast a Combat Fury battle ritual (see page 275) during the Roar phase that will create a **Divine Wrath** advantage against an approaching party of hungry Kuld, making one hero's attack lethal for each invocation. However, Caperna will later have to roll to Quickly defend to avoid being accidentally singed by the near-sighted god when the GM gets one free use of **Poor Eyesight and Worse Aim**.*

The Nebulous Elvorix Pantheon

Only the five greatest of the sixteen Elvorix gods are still remembered with any certainty: Agaptus, Atronia, Gailus, Ilunus, and Prolyus. We'll also discuss Kuldarus, lesser-known but no less important.

Agaptus: God of the Sky and Stars

According to Elvorix scholar-priests, Agaptus is the god of the sky and the first-born of his family. He seems to take a special interest in the activities of Sentians, ever since he first met with their ancestor Sentius over 2,400 years ago. When he manifests himself to his faithful, he usually descends in a cloud of light and fire; this generally causes them to be blinded, suffer burns of varying severity, and flee in terror. Agaptus' keen interest has thus on more than one occasion caused the decimation of his flock.

The god's interest waxes and wanes with distractions available, and over the centuries his clergy has made great efforts not to be too interesting, providing enough deference and worship to avoid angering Agaptus but making themselves and their temples as unattractive as possible to discourage him from visiting too much. The temples are always painted in garish, clashing colors, and the clergy burns potent, foul-smelling incense day and night.

Thanks to these practices, they managed to reduce the frequency of divine visitations to the Great Temple of Agaptus from once a year or so in the early years of the kingdom to about once every twenty years by the time of the Great Catastrophe. Of course, it has been 87 years now since any confirmed visit of the god to his faithful. Some argue that this means the god must be getting very bored by now, and thus we are overdue for "the Big One," by which they mean that they expect the return of the Agaptus to be both imminent and particularly destructive.

Agaptus' chief celebration is the annual sacrifice of a ylark by fire. Proper care must be taken that the ylark is well-secured, so as to avoid any risk of a stampeding, flaming beast. Failure to do so is exactly what caused the Great Catastrophe that so offended the god.

Agaptus usually ignores those who worship his siblings—unless he's in a particularly cantankerous mood, in which case he is wont to roast them for fun. And then roast his own followers for allowing the heresy in the first place. He sometimes argues with his siblings, but is overall pretty satisfied with the way he's running things and is certain everyone else is too.

AGAPTUS
High Concept: *Ruler of the Sky and Stars*.
Trouble: *Poor Eyesight and Worse Aim*.
Other Aspects: *I Had Good Intentions*, *Flattery Will Get You Everywhere*.

Atronia: God of the Soil

Atronia is Agaptus' sister, next oldest of the siblings. She often feels she would do a much better job of being in charge, and is constantly starting new "projects"— then all too often abandoning them partway when another idea sounds more interesting. Nevertheless, she is generous and warm-hearted, if a bit arrogant.

Atronia is usually described as a very tall, glowing, supremely beautiful Sentian doe with flowers in her long hair. When she is angry, she may appear wearing golden armor and bearing wicked-looking weapons.

Her followers dedicate wreaths of plants, baskets of fruit, and weavings of mosses to her, and perform ceremonies involving singing and dancing.

Atronia is generally on good terms with her siblings Gailus and Ilunus, frequently bickers with Agaptus, has furious, bitter fights with Prolyus, and takes pains to oppose anything Kuldarus supports.

ATRONIA
High Concept: *Tender to the Soil and its Bounties of Grain and Moss.*
Trouble: *Distracted.*
Other Aspects: *Take Charge, Always One More Project.*

Gailus: God of the Wilderness

Gruff and awkward, Gailus appears as a towering, burly Elvorix buck with leaves and twigs snarled in his shaggy golden fur, his head sporting a pair of curved ylark horns. He often carries a barrel of kogg under his arm.

Gailus likes the wilderness and its creatures much more than the Sentians in which his siblings are so interested. He has some benevolence for hunters and herders in rural areas, but little interest in urban Elvorix. Moreover, he's disgruntled that the clergy of Agaptus sacrifices ylark, his favorite beasts, to his elder brother; he takes very poorly to such sacrifices in his territory and may cause herds of ylark to stampede when a priest of Agaptus is nearby.

Nevertheless, his followers appreciate his generosity and pray to him for a good season by raising wilderness shrines made of wood and stones in the approximate shape of a ylark, and making offerings of kogg and other strong drink, often partaking in the process. However, while Gailus himself enjoys wanton revelry, his followers are in grave trouble indeed if they inadvertently damage the wilderness he so loves during their celebrations.

GAILUS
High Concept: *Ruler of the Great Herds of Ylark that Wander Free Across the Plains.*
Trouble: *Not a People Person.*
Other Aspects: *One Idea at a Time, Wild Partier.*

Ilunus: God of the Sea

There is some debate among scholars regarding
Ilunus' appearance, motives, and powers. However,
this debate is fairly specialized, of interest
primarily to the inhabitants of coastal towns. No
two reported appearances of the god have produced
exactly the same description, but a tall willowy form
(usually female but not always, suggesting the god
is genderfluid) seemingly made of water and
fog has been reported several times, as have
talking fishes and disappearing islands.

Meanwhile, Ilunus doesn't understand why
she is not more revered, especially by the
Vidaar who are sailors but have chosen instead
to worship Akka-Maas, and by the Jaarl who
build splendid ships but spurn all her efforts
at showing them her might. After all, she rules
much more territory than any other god! From time
to time Ilunus generously attempts to share her great wisdom by showing
sailors the secrets of the deep, but they rarely seem grateful.

Elvorix fisher communities and sailors prudently worship the god by
offering sacrifices of precious or significant objects and dropping them
into the sea at particular locations Ilunus is known to visit. It's a dangerous
task and only the bravest crews volunteer for the annual ceremony. If there
are not enough volunteers, crews may be enlisted by hook or by crook and
forced to make the run. Delaying too much may cause Ilunus to come
personally to check on progress, and no one will like the result.

Ilunus doesn't particularly care about whom mainlanders worship, but
would really like to get more respect at sea. She gets along well enough
with her siblings, except for Agaptus, whom she resents. On occasion, she
has been known to support Kuldarus, but she may then turn and oppose
her sister on her next project.

Iʟᴜɴᴜs
High Concept: *God of the Sea And Waves*.
Trouble: *Failure to Communicate*.
Other Aspects: *Unsolicited Cryptic Wisdom*, *Ambiguous Nature*.

Prolyus: God of War

Prolyus appears as a proud buck with pure Atronian blue fur wearing ornate, glossy black armor, and bristling with weapons. His eyes reportedly glow brightly, but the color varies. He usually speaks in a sinister, thunderous voice that he is quite pleased with.

Prolyus claims that the Great Catastrophe and the War of Ashes mark the time of his ascendancy; indeed, he argues, Agaptus was merely stepping aside when he recognized that the time had come for a new god to lead. Since Agaptus hasn't been around lately, there isn't as much argument about the issue as one might think. In fact, some fringe Elvorix scholars have suggested that perhaps Prolyus found a way to hold Agaptus at bay, explaining the Lord of the Sky's conspicuous absence.

Those who worship Prolyus tend, unsurprisingly, to be career military. They carry small portable shrines to which they give offerings of their own blood before battle—and large offerings of troops **in** battle; nothing dispirits Elvorix soldiers like learning that their commander is a worshiper of Prolyus. Larger temples are few; the best known and most splendid is in the city of Prolyus, of course—at the very center of the conflict between Elvorix, Vidaar, and Jaarl forces, and the occasional Kuld incursion.

> ### PROLYUS
> High Concept: *The God of War and Conquest.*
> Trouble: *Worship Me or Die!*
> Other Aspects: *My Time Has Come!*, *Needy*.

Kuldarus: Ruler of the Underworld

The legends describe Kuldarus as a grimacing, malodorous, unkempt, snarling creature with patchy lichen-eaten fur. Least and last of her family, she was relegated to the cold depths of the Underworld and promptly forgotten.

The same legends ascribe the creation of the Kuld to her, in revenge against her siblings and especially against Agaptus, charging her creations with the mission to destroy her brother's children (hence the name "Kuld," given to them by Ancient Sentian scholars).

No one would ever openly claim to worship her, and if she has devotees, they remain hidden. In fact, the average Elvorix has never heard of her; she is but an essay topic for obscure scholars. However, shepherds and foresters have sometimes stumbled upon hidden caves and found rough drawings on the stone walls, which they whisper are the likeness of the god of the Underworld, drawn by her secret worshipers in dark ceremonies.

> **KULDARUS**
> High Concept: *Ruler of the Underworld.*
> Trouble: *All Too Often Forgotten and Kind of Bitter About It.*
> Other Aspects: *Seventeenth of Her Family, Frightening to Behold.*

Other Gods?

The rest of the pantheon causes many a scholarly argument, as nearly forty different names have been cited authoritatively for the remaining eleven divine siblings. More objective researchers admit that several of these names probably refer to the same few gods, although they cannot agree on which or what their particular areas of rulership are. More partisan theologians who favor a particular candidate to godhood refuse such accommodationism, however.

GMs should take this as free license to add whichever gods best fit their campaign. See *"New Gods"* on page 325, for an example of how to do it.

The Vidaar's Only God: Akka-Maas

According to Elvorix scholars, Akka-Maas is merely the Vidaar's name for Agaptus. According to Vidaar priests, Elvorix scholars are presumptuous pansies who will soon learn how the One God feels about their blathering.

Akka-Maas appears as a gigantic Vidaar warrior bathed in blinding light, throwing lightning bolts left and right with a booming laugh. Since he has exactly the same tendency to accidentally crisp his devotees as Agaptus—supporting the Elvorix position in the debate, as long as argued at a safe distance from their Vidaar detractors—he is not worshiped in temples but out in open areas from which flammable materials are removed.

Ceremonies involve booming music, wild gyrating dancing, and, optionally but popularly, libations of kogg. However, since no one wants too close a visit, the clergy of Akka-Maas is famous for its use of foul-smelling ylark cheese, which they use in lieu of incense. It also serves as the base for augury and as ammunition in war.

Vidaar theology is rather weak on the finer points of what, exactly, Akka-Maas wants except to be entertained.

> ### Akka-Maas
> High Concept: *Ruler Of Everything Important.*
> Trouble: *Oops! Was That One of Mine?*
> Other Aspects: *The Only God, Akka-Maas Loves a Good Tail-Shaking.*

The Jaarl's Scorned God: Murmadon

The former god of the Jaarl was the fiery Murmadon, both deity and mountain. He was glimpsed as a fierce silhouette in the glowing lava at the volcano's core, and gave the Jaarl the secrets of the mystical Murmadon rock and the mighty metal they call volcanium.

Something went wrong—the Jaarl are very silent about this—and Mount Murmadon exploded, destroying the Jaarl homeland and the majority of its population; the survivors have not forgiven their erstwhile god for this betrayal. If he was to be worshipped again, no doubt it would be in the caldera of volcanoes or in the fires of blacksmiths' forges.

> **MURMADON**
> High Concept: *Heart of the Volcano*.
> Trouble: *It Was An Accident!*
> Other Aspects: *Scorned God, The Very Essence of Magic*.

The Kuld's All-Powerful Source

Are the Source and Kuldarus the same, the way that scholars say Agaptus and Akka-Maas are aspects of the same god? It's difficult to say. According to the Kuld glyphs which have been deciphered to date, the Source is not a being and is never shown as personified; it is a natural force.

The Kuld worship this Source by raising scent-pillars etched with symbols, on top of which they place great stone bowls. The ceremonies consist of teachings, for which the Augurst regurgitates specific morsels into the bowl to instruct younger Kuld in their smell and savor. According to Kuld wisdom, the more substances one can digest, the closer one is to the Source.

Needless to say, worshipers have not sprung forth so far among non-Kuld.

THE SOURCE
High Concept: *All Things Flow from the Source, All Things Flow to the Source*.
Trouble: *Boundless Hunger*.
Other Aspects: *Perfect Scent Recall, This Too is Edible*.

DIVINE INTEREST

The gods are fickle and dangerous—whether Agaptus and his fifteen (or sixteen) siblings in the Elvorix pantheon, the Vidaar's single god Akka-Maas, the mysterious personified entity behind the Jaarl's Mount Murmadon, or the Kuld's diffuse Source, their benevolent attention is nearly as dangerous for devotees as their anger.

Think of Agaptans as pets, and the gods as their lackadaisical owners. There's not that much communication going on, and every once in a while the owners remember to put some food down, but all too frequently they completely misunderstand whether you wanted the litterbox cleaned, more water, or walkies. But pee on the carpet or ignore them for too long, and oh boy! It might be off to the pound with you. Or worse.

To represent this, the GM uses a method that looks similar to the character sheet's consequence boxes to track *Divine Interest*. It functions like a set of consequences for the entire group of heroes, recording how much attention they have attracted among the gods. Note that Divine Interest consequences cannot be used in conflicts between two player characters.

Attracting Divine Interest: Examples of things that would cause Divine Interest (i.e., add to the next lowest open Divine consequence) include:

* Rolling ⊞⊞⊞⊞ or ⊟⊟⊟⊟ on the dice. Even if a fate point is used to re-roll, the point will be incurred although the result of the action will be changed.

* Obtaining a Miraculous (+9) or better result— a.k.a. succeeding catastrophically.

* Obtaining an Abysmal (-4) or worse result— a.k.a. heroic calamity.

* Performing a magic ritual.

* Certain costs associated with magical stunts (see *"Magic"* on page 269).

* Doing something extravagant, extraordinary, eccentric, or otherwise distinguishing you from those around you, in place of taking a personal consequence.

When Rustica rolls a ⊟⊟⊟⊟ on her Clever roll to decipher an old grimoire containing useful nautical charts, her player Sharlene invokes an aspect and spends one fate point to re-roll. She rolls a +1 instead so the failure is averted, but the GM still marks a Divine consequence for the group.

Ulf has bitten off more than he can chew. When a group of rowdy pirates takes him up on his challenge to fight them all at once, one of them lands a terrible blow that would result in a severe consequence. Rather than take it himself, Ulf's player Ian opts to have the group gain a Divine consequence instead. Ulf prays to Akka-Maas for strength. And he answers... with lightning bolts!

The GM tracks four Divine Interest consequences—two mild consequences, one moderate, and one severe—for the group of adventurers, each of which represents on-going attention from the gods; you can attract the attention of different gods this way, or get the same one more and more excited about your adventure. They're not watching you constantly, but occasionally they remember your existence and intervene in your favor or against it, depending on the relationship.

Sample Divine Interest Consequences and their Deity:

Mild Consequences:
Clamor of Armies (Prolyus)
Fur Turning Bright Green (Atronia)
Persistent Localized Thunderstorm (Agaptus)
Rivers Running Backwards (Ilunus)
Rotting Ylark Cheese Smell Whenever Someone Is Lying (Akka-Maas)
Singing Rocks (Gailus)

Moderate Consequences:
Maelstrom (Ilunus)
Rain of Ylark (Gailus)
Swarms of Talking Dirkus (Atronia)
Turn Kogg Into Water (Akka-Maas)
Visions of Death (Prolyus)

Severe Consequences:
Attracts Kuld Hordes (Kuldarus)
Belch Lightning (Akka-Maas)
Fireblast (Agaptus)
Shipwreck (Ilunus)
Withering Crops (Atronia)

Recovery: Mild Divine Interest consequences are easily cleared; a minor milestone will allow one mild consequence to be cleared. But a moderate one will last at least two sessions and until a significant milestone, at which point it can be reduced to mild (see *"Milestones"* on page 240).

Severe Divine Interest consequences stick with the heroes and change them: the gods' attention is now firmly on you. They will keep continuously watching you and they will use you as their pawn, champion, martyr, or prize in their schemes and struggles. Sure, they will forget about you for long stretches of time, but the gods' divine gaze is now firmly fixed. A severe Divine Interest consequence will last at least through one significant milestone and until the next major milestone.

*A while ago, the heroes took the severe consequence **Displeased Atronia** by failing to serve her diligently enough. When Kim declares a major milestone, the group decides to change the consequence to **Atoning to Atronia** and decide to make some amends, perhaps go on a quest to appease her. The consequence is reduced to moderate.*

Being Taken out by Divine Interest: When you've already filled all four of the Divine Interest consequence slots for the group without a chance to clear them, and get one more such consequence, you are taken out just like with regular stress. At the end of the session, you will have a Divine milestone (see page 243). Clear all Divine Interest consequences and discuss a new group aspect, which can be invoked and compelled as usual. This should be an aspect the entire group, players and GM, agrees will make sense and be fun in the campaign.

Pawn of ___: When the god needs a cut-up for some reason, you end up being at hand. You find yourself in some cockamamie situation you are spectacularly not suited to because the god needs a marker of some sort.

Marked by ___: When there is nothing more interesting going on, the god checks on you, causing alarm and repercussions. You may develop a reputation for being bad luck.

Embroiled in Divine Plots: After one god showed interest, others also paid attention. You're like the ball in this game, and the winner will probably spike you before forgetting about you and going out to celebrate.

If you gain mostly favorable attention by doing something the gods think is neat, they will appear to you with a message—probably accidentally setting the place on fire or causing other collateral damage in the process. They may be trying to impress their benevolence upon you, and generally trying to help you, but are in fact being as useful as you are when you help ants build their little ant hill.

If you manage to anger, disappoint, or vex the gods, they will send you the occasional lightning bolt strike, put dangerous and ridiculous obstacles in your path, cause storms, floods, or earthquakes to follow you, or turn you into a talking ylark. The only thing that will provide any respite is the gods' gaze turning to someone else.

Being taken out by Divine Interest consequences can be the signal for a major milestone (see *"Milestones"* on page 240) and possibly even a re-scaling of the campaign (see *"Re-Scaling the Campaign"* on page 327). The heroes are now embroiled in world-spanning shenanigans. In that case, combine the effects of both the major and Divine milestones.

The Many Gods: It is perfectly possible to attract the Divine Interest of more than one deity, which may in turn result in many different group aspects.

*After many adventures, the heroes managed to attract the **Wrath of Prolyus**, the **Benevolence of Atronia**, and probably the attention of a few other deities as well...*

Magic

Magic in Agaptus is in many ways more trickery and taking credit for fortuitous success than actual arcane workings; after all, no one wants the gods to get too close. Priests mostly *pretend* to perform rituals without actually attracting attention from the gods, whose appearance is dangerous even to their devotees.

So why do magic-users risk it? One: it works. Sort of. Sometimes. In battle it can make all the difference. Two: the gods get very, very touchy when you neglect them, and they react badly. Then it's not ambiguous, two-edged, or risky at all: it's all bad.

Priests' objectives, then, are to minimize the amount of actual god involvement in mortals' affairs while maximizing the satisfaction of their flocks and patrons. They try to do just enough actual magic and no more, covering the rest with a mix of sooth-saying, show-boating, quackery, and blind luck.

Each variant works within a set of limits; effects (counterfeited or real) are accomplished through rituals. These are mostly used to encourage and motivate troops on the battlefield.

❋ The polytheistic Elvorix use sacrifices, especially animal sacrifices to Agaptus, to convince the populace that their deity has noticed them and blesses their endeavors. These sacrifices double as flaming shock troops when the ylark are set on fire and pointed at the enemy.

❋ The monotheistic Vidaar primarily use augury through the interpretation of cheese, loud music, dancing, and the occasional drunken party to "interpret" the will of Akka-Maas. The moldy cheese also doubles as ammunition for the stinkiest artillery ever.

❋ The Jaarl carry large chunks of Sacred Stone from Mount Murmadon, which they use to power their rituals, but invoke no god. They believe the god Murmadon forsook or double-crossed them, or perhaps just bungled his blessings, and they no longer invoke him by name.

❋ The Kuld cast rituals based on the subtle scents from items they regurgitate in order to interpret the will of the Source, a diffuse entity they believe powers everything in the world but lavishes special attention on the Kuld.

Magic: The 30-Second Version

1. Take an appropriate aspect at character creation.

2. Choose a ritual and perform the required chanting, dancing, and so forth.

3. Make an appropriate approach roll to overcome against the target of the ritual.

4. The GM marks a Divine Interest consequence.

5. Cast the ritual:

   General ritual: Use to create a temporary stunt on a target individual or item;

   Battle ritual: Use during Roar phase to create an aspect appropriate to a curse or blessing on the target group.

Use an Appropriate Aspect

Not everyone can perform magic rituals; you need an aspect that grants permission such as *Priest of Akka-Maas*, *Trained at the Virian Academy*, *Augurst of the Square-Stone Horde*, or even *Self-Trained Hedge Priest of Atronia*.

In addition, an aspect that includes *Jaarl* or any magical aspect grants the Sixth Sense, which is the ability to sense the presence of Sacred Stone from Mount Murmadon. An aspect that includes *Kuld* grants the ability to perceive the workings of a Kuld ritual, though not necessarily to understand its purpose.

Choose a Ritual

Some *rituals* have similar working in all versions of Agaptan magic, although their trappings will be vastly different from one faction to the next and even one school to the next. In addition, each has its own exclusive rituals.

Notes for rituals can be literal pieces of writing for Elvorix or Jaarl casters, but they can also be recorded as complex series of knots in a string for Vidaar, scent glyphs from previous regurgitations for Kuld, etc. It's difficult for a priest to decipher rituals from another school, and painstakingly difficult to even guess at another faction's rituals.

There is no tradition of creating new rituals—the list is the list. Really, who wants to be experimenting or improvising with something this dangerous? Every once in a great while, though, a scholar will claim to have rediscovered or reconstructed a ritual from some Ancient tome. Said scholar is usually invited to take a long sabbatical far, far away in order to study this in peace and quiet. If she comes back alive and not too singed, she may generate some interest in the "new" ritual.

Rituals' primary effect is to allow a blessing or curse to be placed on a *target*—the person, place, or thing it's being cast on. Sometimes a ritual will also have a *subject*—the person, place, group, or thing which will be the focus of the ritual's effect on the target.

A Rage ritual to make Flautul angry at Lilia would be cast on Flautul (the target) and focused on Lilia (the subject).

Casting A Ritual

In order to cast a ritual, the priest must use one or more actions to **overcome** the target difficulty. With a success, the ritual creates a temporary stunt (see the list on page 269). Rituals that produce good luck or beneficial effects for the target can either give a +2 bonus in narrow circumstances for one scene, *or* give a one-time special effect before dissipating. Rituals that produce bad luck or negative effects for the target produce a one-time special effect lasting up to one scene, then dissipate.

Assuming a single target—a person, or a thing perhaps as large as a hut—enough time to chant or mumble the sacred words, and the appropriate ritual trappings, the roll is made against a difficulty of Average (+1). So long as the character succeeds, then the target gains the blessing or curse—see below for details—for the scene or until it is no longer dramatically appropriate, whichever comes first. Further modifications follow:

TARGET	DIFFICULTY
Base difficulty *(self, object, or other person within contact range)*	Average (+1)
Object, area, or person is in sight but not touch range	Add +1
Target person not present, but a powerful symbolic tie to them is present *(their blood, a treasured possession)*	Add +2
Target person not present, but is known and named, or is a known location	Add +3
Target is as big as a ship or small building	Add +1
Target is as big as a large building or arena	Add +2
Target is as big as a small town	Add +3
Unforeseen difficulties *(performing the ritual in a rush, while underwater, at spear point)*	Add +1 to +3 *(GM's discretion)*
Praying to a god you have angered *(having unfavorable Divine Interest consequences or aspects)*	Add +2
Unwilling target	Add +1

❋ Larger targets require much more time, the efforts of several priests, and luck.

❋ Some rituals have a subject, such as a ritual that makes your Houselord mad at his son. The absence of that subject similarly impacts the difficulty: +0 if present, +3 if you only have a name, as above. The one qualifier is that if the subject can be made to accept some token of the ritual—a potion, a trinket—then they are effectively "present." Such tokens must be used within a short time, typically three days.

❋ Success with style on a ritual generates a boost as normal.

❋ No target can be the focus of more than one ritual at a time. The newest ritual replaces the existing one.

❋ Some blessings and curses have their own additional modifiers.

❋ High difficulties can be beaten by having multiple priests working together and by treating the ritual as a challenge (see *"Challenges"* on page 206). Create as many steps as you need, assigning static difficulties; the sum of these difficulties must be **equal to or greater than** the ritual difficulty you calculated.

*Chorten, high tyromancer of Akka-Maas, is performing a ritual to bless his brother Vaad with good luck; however Vaad is halfway across Sentia, doesn't **want** Chorten's help (or any attention from Akka-Maas for that matter), and Chorten has recently displeased Akka-Maas by fleeing from battle. He has the Divine consequence **Coward in Akka-Maas' Eyes**. The difficulty to cast the spell therefore is +1 (starting), +1 (unwilling target), +3 (Chorten has no link to Vaad), +2 (Akka-Maas is displeased), for a total of Epic (+7). Vaad won't go into combat for another day, and Chorten has two other Tyromancers nearby to help him out. They cast the ritual together and break the difficult ritual into three smaller challenges. First, one of them Flashily prays to Akka-Maas to forgive Chorten, a Fair (+2) difficulty, then another Carefully focuses the ritual on Vaad at a Fair (+2) difficulty, and finally Chorten Forcefully **forces** his no-good stubborn brother to accept the blessing at a Good (+3) difficulty.*

❋ Casting a ritual incurs a Divine Interest consequence. The priest can eliminate this cost—in other words, avoid Divine Interest—by performing the ritual as a challenge instead of a single overcome action: one roll to avoid the god's attention, one roll to cast the ritual, and one roll to make it look coincidental.

Chorten is at it again! He's trying to perform another difficult ritual but this time he's all alone, and terrified of incurring more of Akaa-Maas' wrath. The ritual's difficulty is Superb (+5) but Chorten is going to try it anyway. First he Sneakily avoids the god's attention. Since Akka-Maas is often forgetful and is distracted by a war, Kim sets the difficulty at only Average (+1). Then Chorten casts the ritual itself, Quickly this time so nobody notices, at the Superb (+5) difficulty. Finally, he Cleverly pretends like he had nothing to do with the storms overhead. Akka-Maas may have not been paying attention, but his fellow Vidaar sure are wary of him, so Kim sets that at a Good (+3) difficulty. If he succeeds at all three, the ritual is cast without anyone being the wiser and he doesn't gain a Divine consequence. Phew!

❋ Casting a ritual in the presence of Sacred Rock from Mount Murmadon incurs additional special rules (see page 268).

Why would your priest character bother to cast a ritual and thus get a Divine Interest consequence for the group to worry about?

» Because this allows you to create effects that would not be possible otherwise, like a **Sudden Gust of Wind** created by using (Bad) Luck on enemy archers, harmlessly dispersing a volley of arrows.

» Because if you are very Careful and don't mind anonymity, you can cast without attracting attention to yourself.

» Because attracting a god's attention can get you a boon!

» Because sometimes it's do or die.

» Because it's fun! Divine Interest is part of the flavor of the world of Agaptus, and if your characters are going to be heroes—even reluctant ones—then sooner or later they will attract Divine Interest. Embrace the risk!

You Can Always Cheat…

Agaptan priests do it all the time. Your character tells onlookers that you are casting a ritual, you chant some nonsense, and do *nothing*. But if you really want them to believe you, consider using Flashy to overcome an obstacle, and put on a good show. If you are getting paid to cast the ritual, you pocket the money and go to the nearest tavern to have a drink. Naturally, you can only use this trick so many times before your deception catches up with you. Perhaps your customers become angry, or perhaps the gods are starting to notice anyway…

Murmadon Rock

Rituals cast in the presence of Sacred Rock of Murmadon suffer strange warping effects. Jaarl priests have mastered the art of turning the stones' power into fuel for their rituals, but priests of other gods have not and take the full brunt of the effect.

First, the GM should determine how large the amount of Sacred Rock present is, using the Fate Ladder. The larger the accumulation, the more significant the effect.

RATING	DESCRIPTION	AMOUNT
+9	Miraculous	Mount Murmadon itself, now gone
+8	Legendary	As much as Mount Murmadon ejected when it erupted
+7	Epic	As much as the Jaarl currently hold
+6	Fantastic	As much as is found in Karthak
+5	Superb	As much as is stored in the Murmadolunagh
+4	Great	As much as a Jaarl army can assemble for a crucial battle
+3	Good	As much as a Segino can carry
+2	Fair	Head-sized chunk
+1	Average	Pebble
+0	Mediocre	A few grains of sand

The rating is added to the result of the roll when performing a ritual. For those foolish enough to try to use Sacred Rock to fuel rituals without the necessary training, i.e. without an aspect indicating that the character is a member of the Jaarl Arcane, the rating is *also* taken in stress points, minimum one point—meaning that even a few grains cause stress.

Starting Jaarl player characters **can have a pebble of Murmadon rock if they take it as a stunt** (see *"Faction Stunts"* on page 172). Non-Jaarl cannot start with Murmadon rock.

General Rituals

Magic rituals typically influence luck in small ways or push and pull on the target's emotions.

Annoyance: The target rubs people the wrong way. If the ritual has a subject, then this particular subject is more easily annoyed by the target of the ritual. Creates temporary stunts like:

Grating Voice: As a one-time effect lasting one scene, the target's voice is so irritating that those they speak to can hardly remember the actual words.

Looks Like This Jerk I Used to Know: As a one-time effect lasting one scene, the target creates a bad impression on someone they just met.

Sounds Fishy to Me: As a one-time effect lasting one scene, the target is refused the assistance they asked for.

Charisma: While related to love, this turns it on its head by improving the target's general presence and demeanor. It's sometimes a subject of ridicule—specifically, ridiculing those who would need such a ritual—but it sees a lot of quiet use. Creates temporary stunts like:

Great Fur: For one scene, the target gets +2 to Flashily create an advantage when good looks would matter.

Isn't That the Famous Guy?: As a one-time effect lasting one scene, the target is treated like a Very Important Person by those they meet.

Charming Wit: For one scene, that target gets +2 to Cleverly overcome social opposition when they have a chance to impart a witty comment to their audience.

Clarity: Popular among those who fancy themselves cutting-edge scholars, for some this ritual is their cup of coffee, sharpening their thoughts and senses and allowing them to study all night. It's also a popular "counter-ritual," used to remove curses. Creates temporary stunts like:

Ready for a Long Night of Study!: For one scene, the target gets +2 to Carefully create advantages based on detail and research.

Sharp As a Tack: For one scene, the target gets +2 to Forcefully overcome obstacles that would dull their wits, like fatigue or too much kogg.

Can't Fool Me: For one scene, the target gets +2 to Cleverly defend against social or verbal attacks based on deception.

Clumsiness: You know those days where you dropped a glass, spilled your kogg in your lap, and ripped your shirt on a latch? This makes for that kind of day. Creates temporary stunts like:

All Thumbs: As a one-time effect lasting one scene, anyone picking up the target object acts unusually clumsy and awkward.

I Never Even Saw It: As a one-time effect, the target collides while in motion (walking, running, riding, etc.) with someone or something they had not noticed.

It Could Happen to Anyone: As a one-time effect, the target missteps, or drops an object they were holding.

Confusion: People tend to misunderstand the target if it's a person, or get easily lost if it's a place. Creates temporary stunts like:

It's That Accent: As a one-time effect lasting one scene, the target has difficulty getting understood, and everyone misinterprets their speech.

Was It Left or Right?: As a one-time effect lasting one scene, people reaching the target location become disoriented and tend to retrace their steps or take the wrong path.

What Was the Middle Part Again?: As a one-time effect lasting one scene, the target forgets or jumbles the instructions they received and commits a rookie mistake.

Health: The magical equivalent of your mom's river-berry soup. Creates temporary stunts like:

Feeling Better Now: As a one-time effect, the target can immediately clear a mild health-related consequence (injury or illness). For a +2 difficulty, the target can immediately downgrade a moderate consequence to mild; for a +4 difficulty, the target can downgrade one severe consequence to moderate. Only one target can be affected per scene, and consequences can only be improved once per session this way.

Top Form: As a one-time effect lasting one scene, the target gets an extra mild consequence slot. If the extra mild consequence scene is not used in the scene, it vanishes at the end of the scene. If the target takes two mild consequences in the scene, they both last until the end of the next scene.

Strong as a Fedtik: For one scene, the target gets +2 to Forcefully overcome physical obstacles that require feats of strength.

Love: One of the better-known but also most contentious rituals, especially when used with a subject. Without a subject, it simply makes the target more friendly towards the world, but with a subject, it inclines the target toward the subject. A lot of people view this as skeezy at best. It's a touchy topic, and a number of priests get around this by deliberately casting dud rituals. Creates temporary stunts like:

Be Still, My Heart!: As a one-time effect lasting one scene, the target is distracted with interest for the subject, eager to make a good impression on them.

Hey, Check This Out!: For one scene, the subject gets +2 to Flashily create advantages by befriending, charming, or flattering the target.

What A Wonderful Day!: As a one-time effect lasting one scene, the target is as cheerful and well-disposed as circumstances allow. If in an adverse situation (pursued by hungry Kuld, chained at the oars of a Vidaar galley, etc.), the target keeps up their spirits and see the silver lining to every cloud.

Luck: This is the most common ritual in circulation, and it can take the form of good or bad luck. Creates temporary stunts like:

This Is My Day: For one scene, the target gets +2 to Quickly overcoming dangerous obstacles.

I Should Have Stayed in Bed: As a one-time effect lasting one scene, the target is the victim of a mishap such as mistaken identity, lost purse, stolen cart, mud splash, etc.

Wow, Really?: As a one-time effect lasting one scene, the target benefits from a happy coincidence such as finding a long-lost item, being favorably noticed by their superior, or getting the best seat in the theater.

Obscurity: The target is easily overlooked—by the subject, if appropriate. Whether this is a blessing or a curse depends a lot on your perspective. Creates temporary stunts like:

Not Worth Paying Attention To: For one scene, the target gets +2 to Sneakily create advantages based on remaining in the background.

This Has Been There Forever: As a one-time effect lasting one scene, the target item is overlooked by passers-by.

Ho-Hum: For one scene, the target gets +2 to Carefully defend against attempts to discover their true identity.

Prosperity: Another popular blessing, financial things fall the target's way. It's rare that this turns into a large windfall, but it can show up as a loan extension or free kogg. Creates temporary stunts like:

Next One's On Me: As a one-time effect, someone buys the target a meal or a drink.

It Must Have Been in the Lining of My Pocket: As a one-time effect, the target finds a small, useful object in a pocket, usually a coin.

Ride That Streak: For one scene, the target gets +2 to Cleverly overcome while gambling. Naturally, a priest caught casting this sort of ritual will be run out of town with extreme prejudice…

Rage: Small things annoy the target more than usual, as if they'd woken up on the wrong side of the bed. If the ritual has a subject, then the target of the ritual is more easily enraged by that subject. Creates temporary stunts like:

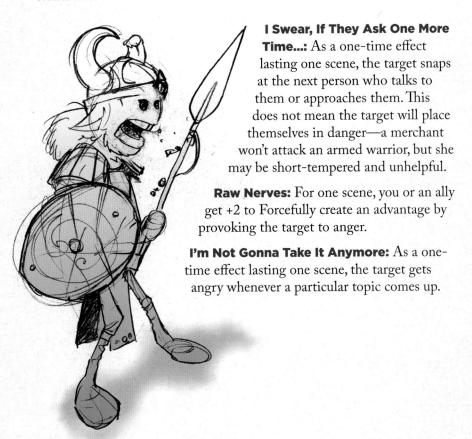

I Swear, If They Ask One More Time...: As a one-time effect lasting one scene, the target snaps at the next person who talks to them or approaches them. This does not mean the target will place themselves in danger—a merchant won't attack an armed warrior, but she may be short-tempered and unhelpful.

Raw Nerves: For one scene, you or an ally get +2 to Forcefully create an advantage by provoking the target to anger.

I'm Not Gonna Take It Anymore: As a one-time effect lasting one scene, the target gets angry whenever a particular topic comes up.

Safety: Keeps the target or area safer than it would be. Creates temporary stunts like:

Not Worth Attacking: For one scene, the target gets +2 to Carefully defend against search attempts.

Nothing Going On Here: As a one-time effect lasting one scene, the target location attracts no attention unless and until someone does something noteworthy, like screaming for help, having a fight, etc.

Snug As a Bug in a Rug: For one scene, the target gets +2 to Sneakily create an advantage by hiding.

Tyromancy: A form of augury using smelly ylark cheese, practiced only by Vidaar priests. Creates temporary stunts like:

I Saw This Coming: As a one-time effect, the target can choose to completely avoid the effects of one attack instead of rolling defense.

I Had a Hunch: As a one-time effect, the target can claim to have made any preparation for the scene such as bringing an object, speaking to a contact, prepared a meal, etc., if they could reasonably have done so by knowing in advance this situation was coming.

Two Steps Ahead of You: For one scene, the target gets +2 to Quickly overcome obstacles and challenges that are also based on speed.

A band of soldiers are pounding on the door of the abandoned farm house where our heroes are spending the night. Iva the Stubborn asks her fawn Kuri to hide in the root cellar while she goes out to check the source of ominous noises. Before she leaves, she casts a Safety ritual.

The target (Kuri) is present (+0), normal size (+0), there is no specific subject because Iva doesn't know who the threat is, so the difficulty would normally be Average (+1). However, time is of the essence so Iva wants to shorten the ritual; Kim says this will increase the difficulty to Fair (+2) and require the use of the Quick approach.

Iva's player Ben agrees and rolls for Iva's ritual, to Quickly create an advantage, and uses a fragment of Murmadon rock she acquired earlier (+1); the dice roll 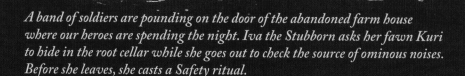 *and Iva's Quick approach is +2, for a total of +4 (Great), which beats the difficulty. Iva's ritual gives Kuri the stunt* **Nothing Going On Here**.

Kim notes a mild Divine Interest consequence for casting a ritual; the roll and result did not generate additional points.

Iva does not take regular stress for the use of Murmadon rock because of her training as a **Wandering Viridian Master**.

Battle Rituals

A particular type of ritual, called *battle rituals*, are used during the Roar phase and call on the power of the transcendent froth state to affect the priest's entire side of the conflict. They work differently: instead of creating temporary stunts, the priest enters froth and uses the ritual to create magical situation aspects with free invocations. Battle rituals' effects typically last until the end of the conflict scene. Just like frothing, battle rituals have a fixed difficulty of Fair (+2) to cast.

After the Roar phase, priests can still cast general rituals that provide temporary stunts for individual targets, but the time for froth is passed.

Combat Fury: The priest intercedes to the unit's god, asking to lend special strength and savagery in combat. Very similar to the Rage ritual below, but fine-tuned for the battlefield. Creates advantages like *Divine Savagery*, *Divine Wrath*, or *Divine Strength*. By spending a fate point or using a free invocation and invoking for effect (see page 194), the targets of the ritual can also make one attack lethal (see *"Lethal Attacks"* on page 235).

Troop Movement: A priest may ask the unit's god for assistance in moving them across the battlefield. Hopefully the god will move them in the intended direction. Creates advantages like *Pushed by a Divine Wind*, *A Burst of Speed*, or *Right Where They Should Be*. By spending a fate point or using a free invocation and invoking for effect, the targets can also move an extra zone for free.

Agaptus Avoid Us, Seek Out Those We Fight: This Elvorix battle ritual is similar to the (Bad) Luck ritual above, but placing a temporary mild Divine Interest consequence on the enemy for the scene. Weapons miss, the sun glints off the enemy's armor, etc. Creates advantages like *Agaptus Disapproves*, *How Could This Have Missed?*, or *Nope, Not Today*. By spending a fate point or using a free invocation and invoking for effect, force the next consequence that would result from an attack to be taken as a Divine Interest consequence.

Akka-Maas Will Smite Them All!: Udvlag (Vidaar priests) use this ritual to whip Vidaar troops into a frenzy for the scene. Creates advantages like *Smite, SMITE!*, *Our Blows Land True*, or *All At Once!*. By spending a fate point or using a free invocation and invoking for effect, the targets can also take one additional mild consequence before being taken out (useable only once per conflict per target). After the conflict, the extra mild consequence remains until cleared normally. See page 238 for more on recovering from consequences.

We Are Roccio!: Popio (Jaarl priests) use this ritual to bolster the focus and discipline of Jaarl units for the scene, helping them through the often complex battlefield maneuvers required by commanders. Creates advantages like *Roccio, Advance!*, *Form Up the Ranks!*, or *To Me, Roccio!*. By spending a fate point or using a free invocation and invoking for effect, the targets can also ignore adverse terrain aspects for all zones they move through this turn. In other words, these aspects cannot be invoked against them to oppose movement.

The Endless: Augurst use their strange, scent-based magic to summon Kuld horde reinforcements far and wide for the scene. Creates advantages like *Nom Nom Nom!*, *That Smells Yummy*, or *So Hungry....* By spending a fate point or using a free invocation and invoking for effect, the targets can also increase their weight by 2 for one conflict round.

During the Roar phase, Udvlag Chorten casts the ritual "Akka–Maas Will Smite Them All!" on the crew of the Skyhammer *to get them ready to fight in the upcoming boarding action against the* Blagaard. *The difficulty is Fair (+2).*

Chorten yells to the sky and sea for aid and the group agrees that sounds like the Flashy approach. Chorten's player rolls an amazing ⊞ ⊞ ⊞ ⊞ , *for a total of +5 (Superb) and succeeds with style.*

Chorten is now frothing with the aspect **Smite, SMITE!** *and is limited to using the Forceful, Flashy, and Clever approaches to maintain the ritual during the conflict.*

The crew of the Skyhammer *rejoice and can use the* **Smite, SMITE!** *aspect normally or invoke it for effect to gain an extra mild consequence for the fight.*

The gods take notice of course. It could be Akka–Maas excited by the battle, but Kim thinks it will be more fun for Ilunus to take notice, lamenting that even on the sea, Sentians don't pray to the sea god! The group gets one consequence for Chorten casting the ritual and a second for the natural ⊞ ⊞ ⊞ ⊞ *that was rolled.*

Wonɒrous Artifacts of the Ancients

The Ancient ruins are to current-day Elvorix and Vidaar what abandoned Roman roads, bridges, temples, and aqueducts would have been to inhabitants of the British Isles circa 900 A.D. They also borrow flavors from ancient marvels of architecture from around the world like the ones left by the Mayans, Inca, Zhou Chinese, Ancient Egyptians, Khmer, etc., and from fiction like legendary Atlantis, Mu, Shambhala, and so forth.

They are forgotten, made nearly invisible by their ubiquity; everywhere in Sentia one sees ruins, and entire villages and cities are built among these. In addition, the incipient ice age has driven the land's inhabitants to live underground more and more often; what better place than the catacombs, vaults, and half-buried palaces of the Ancients, with their unmatched masonry?

Is it Magic?

These marvels are not magic, except in the sense of Arthur C. Clarke's Third Law ("Any sufficiently advanced technology is indistinguishable from magic."); they come from advanced but forgotten knowledge. Based on real-world knowledge developed millennia ago but either forgotten or never applied to practical uses, we could picture advances in:

- » architecture
- » civil engineering
- » mining and metallurgy
- » cartography
- » navigation, including instruments like the compass, backstaff, astrolabe, quadrants, sextant, tide tables
- » astronomy, including instruments like ephemerids, simple telescopes, and armillary spheres
- » medicine and anatomy
- » mathematics
- » textiles and dyes
- » printing
- » paints and lacquers
- » physics and chemistry
- » masonry, stone-cutting, and mosaic
- » glass-blowing, ceramics, glazes
- » ship-building

And probably many more; mysterious, poorly understood knowledge. No magic need be involved.

Mechanics

In game, Ancient wonders work primarily as plot drivers, influencing the story: MacGuffins, *deus ex machina*, objects of quests, and the chance for sweeping changes in the balance of power if some of those secrets are unlocked.

Most of the time, this can be represented entirely by using aspects. A few practical devices may provide a stunt, and if durability or damage absorption is an issue, the device may get a stress track. In order to decide how an Ancient wonder works, we need to answer a few questions:

1. **How complex is the item's function?** The more complex, the more mechanical details may be needed; for example, an astrolabe is going to need more detailed definition than a sword.

2. **How general is the players' understanding of the item, and how much do they agree?** If it's likely that everyone at the table will clearly understand and agree, you need little in the way of mechanical details, but if it's unfamiliar to at least some of the players, you may need more mechanical detail. For example, ephemerids and maps are about equally complex items, but the map is much better understood by most people, so it may not need more than an aspect, while the ephemerids might deserve a stunt.

3. **How versatile will the item be in the story?** If the item is going to be used to do many different things, it potentially requires more definition. For example, a manuscript on medicinal properties of Agaptan plants may be used more often than one on creating rare colors of ceramic glaze.

4. **How prominently will the item feature in the story?** If an item is to be prominent and frequently used—not merely seen, like the ruins of a temple, but used for some story purpose with mechanical effects—then the GM may want to define it more precisely, for example by creating a stress track and perhaps giving the item a minor consequence to absorb damage.

Here are some guidelines for GMs:

Usability: Most of the Ancient technology will get very little actual use in play.

Scale: Most of it is represented by large-scale buildings and ruins: public buildings, bridges, aqueducts, sewers, public baths, roads, lighthouses, ports, monuments, and sometimes temples—temples tend to get damaged more and quicker in the War of Ashes.

Mystery: So much knowledge is missing that the primary purpose of any artifact discovered is probably unclear; the GM should probably give it a few mystery stats, such as unassigned aspects and/or stunts, even a stress track that gets marked off at unexpected times.

Function: Most of the time, the primary purpose should be something practical or logical which you can imagine in the real world, not "boots of flying" and "belts of ogre strength." But the features which are first discovered may in fact be secondary or by-products, just like you can have a whistle on a key chain or a clock readout and a camera on your telephone.

The best way to work through this is to work through a few examples. First, let's look at the most common Ancient wonder, the ruins of some large building or public works. They can generally be handled by aspects, some of which may be obvious and others that the players may have to work to discover.

Example 1: An Ancient lighthouse.

*If the site is still in fairly good shape, it may be easy to discover the high concept aspect **Ancient Lighthouse**, or the aspect can even be known already without the need to create an advantage to discover it.*

*However, the GM may add one to three less obvious aspects if the site is important to the adventure. For example, it might have **Hidden Crypt Deep Below** if you want a scene or even a whole adventure about poking in the depths beneath the lighthouse, or **Line Up the Two Fires to Navigate Through the Reefs** if the lighthouse is a navigation clue to help the heroes reach their destination, or **Secret of the Undying Flame** if this is really about the liquid fuel which the Ancients had devised to keep the beacon lit.*

Note that these additional aspects could also be flaws, but they should be intrinsic to the Ancient location or device. In Example 1, *Dangerous Vermin* or *Dripping Flammable Liquid* could exist, but they would be more scene aspects than item aspects. The next time your heroes visit the site, you might emphasize something different. See the *"Creating Adventures"* section on page 288 for more on scene aspects.

Don't stack too many aspects, though; use the minimum you need to get the story moving. First, too many aspects may leave the scene a confused mess, and dilute the importance of any single aspect. Second, you can always come back some other time, in some other story, and use different aspects for the same location to emphasize what is of interest in the current adventure. Finally, if you don't define more than you strictly need to, you are left free to pounce on any great ideas the players may come up with and use that instead in your next scenario!

Let's look at a second example, something that is still a building but where the original function is versatile and harder to guess at.

Example 2: The ruins of an Ancient apothecary shop.

*When you open the scene, you may have this listed as a **Small Half-Collapsed Building** and let the players do a bit of snooping—perhaps treated as a challenge—before they can discover the aspect **Half-Collapsed Apothecary Shop**. Note that we've now replaced or redefined what was a scene aspect. Now, every time they return, the PCs will find the **Half-Collapsed Apothecary Shop**, at least until they manage to demolish it further...*

The players may want to get some practical use out of a location like this, so if this is meant to be a chance for them to reduce some consequences they have taken previously, you could assign it the stunt:

Ancient Apothecary Shop: *Because this is an Ancient apothecary shop, heroes get +2 to Cleverly overcome the effects of an illness.*

You may want to limit such a location's use if you don't want to see it become the convenience store open all night which they keep visiting to fix problems. One way to do this is to assign narrower circumstances for use, such as a specific illness or type of illness. Another is to assign a number of uses after which, the supplies or equipment are exhausted. **Once** is a perfectly valid number!

Here is an example of public works where the original function might seem very difficult to understand at first. Its function is specialized but potentially very important to the setting.

Example 3: The ruins of a canal and lock system.

Depending on how damaged it is, it may not contain water when the heroes first see it; or it might be iced over if it's located in the north or the adventure takes place at some time other than the short summer months. At each end is a body of water, at different elevations.

The high concept to discover would be **Canal and Lock System**. *If the PCs succeed in restoring it to a working state and the climate conditions allow it, a stunt would become available:*

Ancient Canal and Lock System: *Because this is an Ancient lock system, once per session (or twice a day, or other reasonable time increment that the GM wants) it allows a ship to move between Water Body A and Water Body B.*

However, the importance of such a site is not just about moving a ship where you couldn't before; it's about acquiring that knowledge and using it in other locations.

What about something portable, specialized, and arcane?

Example 4: Ancient compass.

This device might be very damaged; if of the wet type, it would probably have dried up and requires refilling with water or clear alcohol and resealing; if of the dry type, the needle might need re-mounting and the moving parts cleaning and waxing.

*Understanding, refurbishing, and using the device can be handled as a challenge, perhaps over a long period. Even after the compass is in working order again, its usefulness for navigation might not be obvious. The high concept could be simply called **Compass**, or **A Device That Always Points in the Same Direction**. Understanding its usefulness would make a stunt available:*

Ancient Compass: *Because this device always points north, heroes get +2 to Carefully overcome obstacles when orienting their course.*

Now let's look at something portable, versatile, and fairly complex but relatively easy to figure out.

Example 5: Ancient multi-tool.

Did you know the Romans had invented multi-tools? It's true! If the tool is in good shape, it becomes fairly easy to guess at the purpose of a few of the attachments; if it's very damaged and partly disintegrated due to rust, it may be much more difficult.

*The primary aspect will be something like **Folding Multi-Tool**. Once a hero figures out how to make the various parts move, some potential stunts may come to mind; but now we're looking at many different stunts that apply in many different circumstances.*

*Instead of trying to list them, it may make more sense to just grant a number of free invocations of the high concept aspect, say one or two per session. It can of course be invoked as normal at the cost of a fate point. For flavor, it might be renamed to something like **I Have the Tool for That!**.*

Because it might be a coveted item that sees a lot of use, the GM might also want to give it a stress track, say one or two boxes, and even a minor consequence to represent some of the tools getting warped or broken.

If you need more in-depth discussion of creating wondrous artifacts, we recommend you check out the FATE CORE section *"Creating An Extra"* on page 271; and even the FATE SYSTEM TOOLKIT section *"Gadgets and Gear"* on page 154. Both are available as pay-what-you-want downloads at *evilhat.com*.

Creating Wonders: The 30-Second Version

1. Give the Wondrous Creation a high concept representing its purpose or nature, and a Flaw representing its dangers or weaknesses.

2. If it will be important enough to feature significantly in more than one scene, give it one or two other aspects such as a descriptive aspect, or a secret representing hidden characteristics. If the heroes discover the secret in play, rephrase it as a known aspect.

3. If it is still able to perform its function, or restored to a working state, give it a stunt— something that will give a bonus to those using it or allow a special effect once a day.

4. If you want to limit the use of such stunt, give it a number of uses and check one off after every use. When all the use boxes are checked off, the stunt stops working for good.

5. If the Wondrous Creation is a coveted item that sees a lot of use, the GM might also want to give it a stress track, say one or two boxes, and even a minor consequence to represent some of its parts getting warped or broken.

PART **6**

Running the War of Ashes: Fate of Agaptus

Gamemaster Advice

Now let's talk about the other main parts of being a gamemaster:

* *Fate*'s backbone: the Gold, Silver, and Bronze Rules

* Creating adventures for the player characters

* Creating the opposition

* Running games

* Adjudicating the rules

* Expanding or re-scaling the campaign as it matures

In this chapter, we'll also talk about tailoring the material from this book so it can fit in the campaign your group wants to play, and how to fit more closely with other games set in the world of Agaptus like **War of Ashes: Shieldwall** and **War of Ashes: Shieldbash**.

Learning How to Be a GM

Being a GM and running games can seem intimidating and difficult at first. It's a skill that takes some practice to master, so don't worry—you'll get better the more you do it. If you'd like to read more about the art of GMing *Fate*, there are several chapters in the **Fate Core** rules that you should check out: *Running the Game*; *Scenes, Sessions, and Scenarios*; and *The Long Game* are particularly helpful.

Fate's Backbone: The Gold, Silver, and Bronze Rules

The Golden Rule

Here's the first thing to think about, the general *Golden Rule* of *Fate*:

Decide what you're trying to accomplish first, then consult the rules to help you do it.

This might seem like common sense, but we call it out because the order is important. In other words, don't look at the rules as a predetermined limit on what you create. Instead, use them as a variety of potential tools to model whatever you're trying to do. Your intent, whatever it is, always takes precedence over the mechanics.

But you have to know what it is you're trying to do before you can pick the right tools to do it.

This applies whether you're a player creating a character—what is the character's core concept?—or whether you are writing an adventure—what is the adventure going to be about?—and even when you're creating a whole new magic system—what does this magic style look like?

The Silver Rule

Never let the rules get in the way of what makes narrative sense.
The *Silver Rule* is really a corollary to the Golden Rule: if you or the players narrate something in the game and it makes sense to apply a certain rule outside of the normal circumstances where you would do so, go ahead and do it.

Rules are written to cover general situations as reasonably and consistently as possible, but it's impossible to anticipate all the situations a group will come up with in play; sometimes, the story will develop in ways that aren't perfectly modeled by the rules. Go with the story, making adjustments as needed.

The Bronze Rule

In *Fate*, you can treat anything in the game world like it's a character. Anything can have aspects, approaches, stunts, stress tracks, and consequences if you need it to.

We call this the *Bronze Rule*, but you may also have heard of it as the *Fate Fractal*. The term "fractal" comes from a branch of mathematics that deals with structures in which similar patterns recur at progressively smaller scales, such as eroded coastlines or snowflakes.

In our case, it means that no matter what scale you're looking at—two characters in a duel, the back-and-forth of war between factions over the course of decades, the struggles of a pantheon—you can model it using the same tools. We've already seen some examples of this earlier in the book: you give your game its own aspects during creation, you place situation aspects on the environment and equipment as well as on characters, and the GM can let environmental hazards attack as if they had skills. Zones in combat are as big or small as you need them to be.

This rule will be handy as we create adventures and opposition for our PCs.

Creating Adventures

A *scenario* or *adventure* is one short story arc, the sort of thing you might see wrapped up in one or two sessions of an adventure television show, even if it's a smaller part of a bigger story. Usually you can wrap up a scenario in one to three game sessions, assuming you play for three or four hours at a time. But what is a scenario, and how do you build one?

Creating A Scenario: The 30-Second Version

1. Pick a Goal and High Concept Aspect

2. Find Problems

3. Pick a Trouble Aspect

4. Scene List: Ask Story Questions

5. Pick Adventure Aspects and Approaches

6. Establish the Opposition

7. Set the First Scene

Here is a method for writing scenarios called Fractal Adventures, which relies heavily on the Bronze Rule of *Fate*. It was created by author Ryan M. Danks, and a more detailed discussion of the method can be found in the *Fate* edition of Ryan's game JADEPUNK: TALES FROM KAUSAO CITY (Reroll Productions).

Once you get the hang of it, writing an adventure should take about twenty minutes, assuming you already know what the story will be about.

Goal and High Concept Aspect

First, you need a goal; this is the problem(s) the story will center around. What is it the PCs want? Create an aspect to represent the goal; you can call it the adventure's high concept.

Once you know the goal, decide whether or not the PCs will obtain their goal—"maybe" is a sufficient answer here, relying on the PCs to determine success or failure on their own. It isn't always necessary that they succeed; failure leads to more adventures.

Find Problems

Scenarios are centered around a problem which the heroes will try to solve, encountering twists and turns as they move towards resolution.

A scenario needs two things: An adversary with a goal and a reason the PCs can't ignore it.

> **Adversary with a goal:** You've probably figured this out already. The campaign's main opposition, or one of his allies, is probably your adversary.

> **Something the PCs can't ignore:** Now you have to give the PCs a reason to care. Make sure the adversary's goal is up in the PCs' faces, where they need to do something about it or bad things will happen to them, or to people or things they value.

And that's how your "problem" is born.

Here's the best tool to make sure the PCs can't ignore the hook: go fishing from their character sheets for problems they *want* to interact with, and from the campaign aspects for problems which they are *bribed* to tackle.

In case of doubt: think of a Muppet cast playing pirate tales or *Hamlet* for the Vidaar, Roman legions for the Jaarl, or King Harold and the Battle of Hastings for the Elvorix.

Problems and Character Aspects:
Look at the characters' aspects and see if anything can make a nice juicy core problem for an adventure. When you're trying to get a problem from a character aspect, try fitting it into this sentence:

> You have **[aspect]**, which implies that **[fact about that character or the world]**. Because of that, it would be probably be a big problem if **[describe a situation]**.

The second blank is what makes this a little harder than an event compel—you have to think about all the different potential implications of an aspect (and this may be a list of things, by the way). Here are some questions to help with that.

Who might have a problem with the character because of this aspect?

Does the aspect point to a potential threat to that character?

Does the aspect describe a connection or relationship that could cause trouble for the character?

Does the aspect speak to a backstory element that could come back to haunt the character?

Does the aspect describe something or someone important to the character that you can threaten?

As long as whatever you put in the third blank makes a nice story problem, you're good to go.

Ulf Long-Teeth has **The Good Ship Blaggard,** *which implies that he inherited his ship from somewhere. Because of that, it would be a problem for him if he was challenged for command.*

Iva the Stubborn is **Searching for Her Banished Lover,** *which implies that her lover has enemies at home. Because of this, it would be a problem for her if she needed help from one of his enemies to find her lover's whereabouts.*

Rustica Bibulus is a **Connoisseur of Atronian Folklore,** *which implies that such folklore may contain elements of truth that have been overlooked by scholars. Because of this, it would be a problem for her if the pursuit of an obscure legend brought her face to snout with a mythical monster.*

Problems and Game Aspects: Problems you get from a game's current and impending issues (See *"Big Issues"* on page 144) will be a little wider in scope than character-driven problems, affecting all your PCs and possibly a significant number of NPCs as well. The game aspects include the ones you chose in your campaign creation process, any scenario or adventure aspects, and perhaps some lingering aspects from a previous adventure.

Attach one or two aspects to the adventure you're designing; you can use the aspects suggested with every story seed in this book such as the ones attached to location descriptions, or come up with ones that are tailored for your group. As an incentive for players to get involved, you can allow one free invoke per adventure, or even one per game session for multi-session scenarios; alternately, you can use it as a compel on the PCs, offering them fate points for going along with the problem.

When you're trying to get a problem from a game aspect, try fitting it into this sentence:

> Because **[aspect]** is an issue, it implies **[fact about the character or the world]**. Therefore, **[describe a situation]** would probably create a big problem for the heroes.

Ask yourself:

> What threats does the issue present to the PCs?

> Who are the driving forces behind the issue, and what messed up thing might they be willing to do to advance their agenda?

> Who else cares about dealing with the issue, and how might their "solution" be bad for the PCs?

> What's a good next step for resolving the issue, and what makes accomplishing that step hard?

Because the **Lost Island of Konaré** is an issue, it implies that the location is both hard to find and dangerous. Therefore, having to retrieve a map from Kuld–infested territory would probably create a big problem for the heroes.

Because **Secrets of the Ice** is an issue, it implies that the information is valuable, coveted, and protected. Therefore, reaching an elderly scholar and protecting him before rivals capture him would probably create a big problem for the heroes.

Because **The Seal of Prolyus** is an issue, it implies that the organization has gathered temporal power. Therefore, an alliance of the organization with a powerful Merchant House would probably create a big problem for the heroes.

Problems and Aspect Pairs: You can also create problems from the relationship between two aspects instead of relying on just one. That lets you keep things personal, but broaden the scope of your problem to impact multiple characters, or thread a particular PC's story into the story of the game.

There are two main forms of aspect pairing: connecting two character aspects, and connecting a character aspect to an issue. They look like this:

Two Character Aspects:

> Because **[character]** has **[aspect]** and **[another character]** has **[aspect]**, it implies that **[fact about the characters or the world]**. Therefore, **[describe a situation]** would probably be a big problem for the heroes.

Ask yourself:

> Do the two aspects put those characters at odds or suggest a point of tension between them?
>
> Is there a particular kind of problem or trouble that both would be likely to get into because of the aspects?
>
> Does one character have a relationship or a connection that could become problematic for the other?
>
> Do the aspects point to backstory elements that can intersect in the present?
>
> Is there a way for one PC's fortune to become another's misfortune, because of the aspects?

> *Because Ulf has* **Family Trumps Everything. Almost.** *and Iva has* **Single Mother With A Fawn**, *it implies that Ulf is loyal to his family but also understands family loyalty in others. Therefore, siblings of Ulf hired to kidnap Iva's fawn to blackmail her would probably be a big problem for heroes.*

> *Because Rustica has* **Overachieving Elvorix Scholar** *and Ulf has* **Out to Make A Name for Himself!**, *it implies that they are both ambitious and competitive. Therefore, finding the clues to a treasure trove of Ancient artifacts, which Rustica wants to remain secret to all but the Academy, and which Ulf wants to describe in heroic tales of his mighty deeds, would probably be a big problem for the heroes.*

Because Iva has **Sponsored by the Stone-Seekers** *and Rustica has* **Owes Valius Nummus a Favor**, *it implies that their patrons have their own agendas. Therefore, Iva and Rustica both promising to bring back the same Ancient artifact, the Mask of Kuldarus, to their respective sponsors would probably be a big problem for the heroes.*

Character Aspect and Game Aspect:

Because you have **[aspect]** and **[aspect]** is an issue, it implies that **[fact about the character or the world]**. Therefore, **[describe a situation]** would probably be a big problem for you.

Ask yourself:

Does the issue suggest a threat to any of the PC's relationships?

Is the next step to dealing with the issue something that impacts a particular character personally because of their aspects?

Does someone connected to the issue have a particular reason to target the PC because of an aspect?

Because Rustica has **The Collected Notes of Peony the Elder** *and* **The Seal of Prolyus** *is an issue, it implies that the manuscript might be worth much to the secret organization. Therefore, the Seal of Prolyus trying to steal the notes from Rustica would probably be a big problem for her.*

Because Ulf has **The Good Ship** Blagaard *and* **Lost Island of Konaré** *is an issue, it implies that Ulf will face some challenges when he sails his ship in search of the lost island. Therefore, the* Blagaard *becoming trapped in a Bermuda Triangle–like area of sea would probably be a big problem for him.*

Because Iva has **I Can See Further Than You Ever Have** *and* **Secrets of the Ice** *is an issue, it implies that Iva will be interested in the long-term effects of the Great Catastrophe on the ice. Therefore, choosing between pursuing the mission the heroes undertook or dropping it to pursue new information about the cause of the new ice age would probably be a big problem for her.*

You can also browse the story seeds in this book and see if any of them generate ideas for connections with your character aspects, issues, and campaign aspects.

Trouble Aspect

How will you make it inevitable that the PCs will act toward that goal? To keep tension as you move from scene to scene, create a trouble aspect. This should represent the danger or death that's overhanging in the adventure; again, if there's no chance of physical, psychological, or professional death at all times, there is no tension, which means a boring game. The trouble is what happens if the PCs ignore the adventure, and also what will step in from time to time and remind them why what they are doing matters.

Kim picks a few ideas from her list and lays the bare bones out in detail as a Fractal Adventure:

The Mask of Betrayal: Aspects
Goal: *The Mask of Kuldarus*
The PCs must locate and retrieve this item to prevent it from falling in the wrong hands.
Trouble Overhanging: *The Seal of Prolyus Is On the Trail!*
The wrong hands, or at least some wrong hands…

Reinforcing the Themes
If you want the adventure's aspects to strongly color the action, make them known to the players and allow the players to invoke these adventure aspects like any other.

Scene List: Ask Story Questions

Once you have your goal, work backwards to create the scene list—scenes are where players get to play; without them, you have no game. This is where you need to create a list of story questions.

How do you flesh out the situation which you created with the problems? You start by asking lots of story questions as yes/no questions, in the general format of:

"Can/Will **[character]** accomplish **[goal]**?"

You don't have to follow that phrasing exactly, and you can embellish on the basic question format in a number of ways. The first question you will ask for a given adventure, but probably the last you will answer, is:

"Can the heroes resolve the adventure problem?"

All the other story questions will be the dotted line, the stepping stones leading to this one. Each can explore a specific facet of the problem, including who, what, where, when, why, and how.

The Mask of Betrayal: Problem and Story Questions

*Because Iva is **Sponsored by the Stone-Seekers** and Rustica **Owes Valius Nummus a Favor**, it implies that their patrons have their own agendas. Therefore, Iva and Rustica both agreeing to find the same Ancient artifact, the Mask of Kuldarus, and bring it back to their respective sponsors would probably be a big problem for them.*

*Some questions immediately pop to mind because they are implied in the choice of aspects used to create the problem: Will Iva get the mask for the Stone-Seekers? or Will Rustica repay Valius Nummus? These are the questions we will be answering by the **end** of the scenario.*

In order to get there, we have to answer some other questions. We're reasonably confident that both Iva and Rustica will be interested in finding the mask, but Will Rustica agree to bring the mask back to Valius Nummus? If the answer is "no" right at the start, then Valius Nummus might decide to force the issue through some other means—persuasion, blackmail, threats—or he might try to locate the artifact himself, or hire a rival team.

Will Iva and Rustica share with the group the requests their respective sponsors have made? Perhaps one or both will choose to keep it a secret. And if they share the information, Can the PCs come to an agreement on what to do with the mask? This might take the whole adventure to resolve, or they might immediately decide that one faction has better title to the prize.

Do the heroes know where to find the mask? If not, then that's probably a chunk of the adventure right there, finding out the artifact's whereabouts. This is a good place in the adventure to use Rustica's scholarly abilities, Iva's arcane connections, and Ulf's mundane ones.

Can they get there? Sometimes getting there is half the fun. Or all the fun. The players have shown interest for lost islands and sea adventures, and this will hook Ulf into the scenario, so Kim decides that there must be a sea voyage to a dangerous location protected by teeth-like reef formations and treacherous breakers.

Is there a reason why neither the Stone-Seekers nor Valius Nummus have already obtained the artifact? There must be great difficulties in recovering the mask, otherwise it wouldn't be an adventure. Difficulty of access, dangers, guardians, even magical protection shield the mysterious artifact.

Is there a reason to search for the mask now? If the group prefers to limit the amount of investigation in a given scenario, then perhaps a manuscript has just been discovered that talks about the location of the mask; that way, the problem is reduced to obtaining the manuscript and deciphering it. If on the other hand the players love investigation but tend to dissolve into analysis paralysis, perhaps the clock is driven by the fact that a rival team—say, Laetitia Bibulus and the Seal of Prolyus—is already on its way to retrieve the mask and put it to ill use.

Do the PCs know what the mask's properties are? There is ample room for secrets and surprises. What does the thing do? Under what circumstances?

Is Valius Nummus friend or traitor? To what ends does he wish to acquire the mask?

Pro Tip: Multiple Solutions

When you're asking your story questions that will lead to scene ideas, try to think of several different ways of completing a segment and several different paths to get the end questions, the ones that are wrapped up in the problem. One way to do this is to ask, *How would a player or a group complete this if:*

- » They want to investigate their way through?
- » They want to fight their way through?
- » They want to negotiate their way through?
- » They want to sneak their way through?

Jot down your answers for later use. As a rule of thumb, if you can't think of at least two or three ways to get the job done, then your scenes or adventure may be too narrow.

Assembling the List

What steps will the players need to take to achieve their goal? To bring a killer to justice, they might first have to discover his whereabouts, which requires discovering who he is, which may require questioning witnesses and following clues, which requires investigating the crime scene, which requires being alerted to the crime.

Read that backwards and you have your scene list: hear about the crime, investigate the scene, talk to witnesses and follow clues, discover the killer's identity, discover his whereabouts, take him down.

While reading this list, you might decide to increase the tension somewhere in the middle. Maybe a witness turns up dead, or a fight ensues between a masked killer and the PCs as they arrive just before a witness is murdered. This is logical, as the killer would want to throw off the investigation.

You can mark some scenes as core and others as optional; you can also jot down notes when some scenes need to be played in a specific order. Witness interviews and clue investigation can probably be played out in any order, for example, but the last few scenes may need to happen sequentially. If you know you will be limited by time when you run your game, you can concentrate on the core scenes and watch the clock to decide whether to lead into one of the optional scenes, such as the murder of a witness.

Kim uses her story questions to create a list of possible scenes:

The Mask of Betrayal: Scenes

» **The Theft:** *Valius Nummus' shop has been burglarized and the Teran manuscript stolen. Attributed to Tera Bibulus, the manuscript may contain clues to the location of the Mask of Kuldarus. Valius asks Rustica for help retrieving both manuscript and mask.*

» **Recovering the Manuscript:** *Discovering the identity of the thieves and getting the manuscript back. Since the thieves used violence, there is probably going to be a physical confrontation.*

» **The Stone-Seekers' Interest:** *The Stone-Seekers approach Iva and offer help in finding the Mask of Kuldarus, but ask her to bring it back to them, not Valius Nummus.*

» **Researching the Mask:** *The PCs—most likely Rustica—will probably want to do a little background research into the history, location, and nature of the mask.*

» **Race for the Prize:** *The PCs learn that another group is already on its way to recover the mask from its resting place. Set sail!*

» **Nautical Adventures:** *Good time to encounter the rough climate of the World of Agaptus, pirates, sea monsters, and a fight against the rival team. This can become several scenes, depending on how much fun the players are having.*

» **The Forbidden Temple:** *The PCs reach the location of the mask, brave its defenses, and face the competition for possession of the artifact.*

» **Who Gets the Mask?:** *Valius Nummus wants it, as do the Stone-Seekers and the Seal of Prolyus, and perhaps a secret cult dedicated to protecting or using the mask. Some of these factions may be covert allies.*

Important Note:
No plan survives contact with the PCs. If the scenes don't unfold in that particular order, that's perfectly normal. The PCs will manage to skip a scene through ingenuity, or make a scene irrelevant, or create a new scene by following some tangent they came up with. Go with it! You can always bring them back on track, or modify a previous scene on the fly to create the new scene.

In fact, it makes your life easier to plan on scenes that can be shuffled, combined, or removed so you can adjust them to fit the rhythm at which your game is unfolding.

Adventure Aspects

Now you can come up with your adventure aspects. Write two for each scene: one for the location/setting, and one for the obstacle the PCs will face. You can write more, but include at least these two. If the PCs will face no obstacle, then there is no tension. The scene will be boring and you need to delete it from your list. Even searching an abandoned war camp for information is an obstacle, *Hidden Clues*.

Kim thinks about who stole Valius Nummus' manuscript and how hard it should be to track them. She wants to bring in some physical confrontation early on and also point to the waterfront so Isaac, whose character Ulf is not directly tied to the Mask of Kuldarus, will not be left out.

Recovering the Manuscript: *Discovering the identity of the thieves and getting the manuscript back. Since the thieves used violence, there is probably going to be a physical confrontation.*
Obstacle Aspect: **Cheap Hired Brutes**
Environmental Aspect: **Dark Alleys Near the Waterfront**

The Opposition

Adventure Approaches

Adventures use the following "approaches":

❊ **Combat:** This governs NPCs attacking, defending, and creating advantages using combative maneuvers.

❊ **Exploration:** This sets the difficulty of (or opposes) PC attempts to interact with or move through the environment, whether that opposition comes from an NPC or another obstacle in the setting. This covers movement, investigating clues, discovering details, determining NPC initiative, allowing something to remain hidden from the PCs, etc.

❊ **Interaction:** This is rolled to have the NPCs interact with the PCs.

❊ **Lore:** Governs how difficult it is to know some relevant information that comes up in the adventure.

To set the adventure's approach ratings, set one of them at the same level as the PC's highest approach rating +1 (called Hard difficulty), then choose two to be at the same level as the PC's highest approach rating -1 (called Average difficulty) and one to be -3 lower (called Easy difficulty). For instance, if the PCs' highest approach score is Good (+3), then you'd have a set-up of +4, +2, +2, +0. If you have an experienced group of PCs that have raised their approaches to Great (+4), then you would have a spread of +5, +3, +3, +1.

Choose the scores so that they highlight the important aspects you have in mind for the adventure. Do you want this adventure to be a tough fight with low social interaction? Have Combat be your Hard approach and Interaction be Easy. Do you want a game of intrigue with next to no fighting? Use Lore or Interaction as your Hard approaches and Combat as your Easy approach.

This is what you'll be rolling for every NPC or setting element that comes into play against the PCs.

The campaign is just beginning and the PCs' top approach score is Good (+3), so Kim assigns +4, +2, +2, and +0 to the adventure "approaches." She doesn't want to make it too difficult to find the mask, so she sets Exploration at Mediocre (+0), and she wants a lot of the questions left at the end to revolve around motives and factions, so she sets Interaction at Great (+4). Combat and Lore will thus be at Fair (+2).

Divine Interest: Bear in mind that in order to beat a Hard adventure approach of +5, your group of heroes will have to roll high enough to routinely risk "catastrophic success," a roll of +9 or higher, which incurs Divine Interest (see page 256). When you, the GM, select the Hard approach, you're essentially deciding what, in this adventure, most risks attracting the attention of the gods.

Conversely, when selecting the Easy adventure approach, you're nudging the flow of the story by offering a place where the adventurers will have an easier time succeeding.

Characters and Creatures

The GM gets to play all the non-players characters or NPCs, be they support, allies, contacts, etc. But some of the most important will be those who present opposition for the PCs. You don't need to fill in a character sheet for every one of them; jot down only what matters. We have two main types of characters to track in the opposition: recurring adversaries and minions.

Adversaries: When you make an adversary, you can choose to stat them out exactly like the PCs, with approaches, aspects, stress, and consequences. You should do this for important or recurring adversaries who are intended to give the PCs some real difficulties, but you shouldn't need more than one or two of these in a given scenario.

Laetitia Bibulus ix Gailus and her ally Captain Volo Troll-Axe will definitely be recurring adversaries, so Kim thinks she will write fairly complete character sheets for them.

Minions: Other opponents are *minions*—unnamed soldiers, monsters, or brutes that are there to make the PCs' day a little more difficult, but they're designed to be more or less easily swept aside, especially by powerful PCs. Here's how you create their stats:

1. Make a list of what this minion is skilled at. They get a Fair (+2) to all rolls dealing with these things.

2. Make a list of what this minion is bad at. They get a Terrible (−2) to all rolls dealing with these things.

3. Everything else gets a Mediocre (+0).

4. Minions use the Fractal Adventure's approaches (Combat, Exploration, Interaction, and Lore) as modified by their abilities.

5. Give the minion an aspect or two to reinforce what they're good and bad at, or if they have a particular strength or vulnerability. It's okay if a minion's aspects are really simple.

6. Minions have zero, one, or two boxes in their stress track, depending on how tough you imagine them to be.

7. Minions can't take consequences. If they run out of stress boxes (or don't have any), the next hit takes them down.

8. Give the minion a weight 0 if they are smaller than a Sentian, 1 if they are Sentian-sized, 2 if they are bigger than a Sentian, 4 if they are the size of a small building, and more if they are even bigger! Note: This weight represents their physical size. If they have a particularly impressive intellect or social skills you can mark their weight in other arenas as well. See the *"Weight"* section on page 222 for more details.

Since Volo Troll-Axe is captain of the Skyhammer, *he must have a crew, but we don't need much detail on any of them; they are rank-and-file minions.*

VIDAAR SAILOR
Weight: 1 (Sentian-sized)
Vidaar Sailor; We Are Skyhammers!
Skilled (+2) at: Sailing, fighting with boarding axes, climbing in the rigging.
Bad (-2) at: Planning, social situations.

STRESS
○

Astute gamers will have noticed that using "skilled at" and "bad at" are roughly the equivalent of giving minions a few stunts and flaws.

Groups of Minions (a.k.a. Mobs): If you have a lot of low-level opponents facing the PCs, you can make your job easier by treating them as a group—or maybe a few groups. Instead of tracking a dozen individual opponents, you track three groups of four minions each. Each of these groups acts like a single character and has a set of stats just like a single minion would:

1. Choose a couple of things they're skilled at. You might designate "ganging up" as one of the things the group is good at.

2. Choose a couple of things they're not so good at.

3. Give them an aspect.

4. Give them the same stress an individual would have plus one stress box for every two individuals in the group.

5. Give the group a weight by adding up the weight of the individuals. This shouldn't go above 8. If it does, split them up into smaller groups.

When several crew members are acting together against the PCs, Kim will treat them as a group of rank-and-file minions. For example, a press gang might look like this:

PRESS GANG OF THE *SKYHAMMER*

Weight: 6 (6 crew members that are Sentian-sized)

Press Gang; *Vidaar Sailors*; *We Are Skyhammers!*

Skilled (+2) at: Finding derelict shore parties, fighting with belaying pins, pressing civilians into service, ganging up.

Bad (-2) at: Standing up to organized groups, fighting when outnumbered.

STRESS

〇〇〇〇 (6 crew members)

A mob of minions can use its weight to surround or split the the group of PCs. When it makes sense, the GM can treat a mob as a single unit—instead of rolling dice individually for each of three Vidaar brutes, just roll once for the whole mob.

Mobs typically have two to four stress boxes. When a mob takes enough stress to reduce it to a single minion, try to have that orphaned minion join up with another mob in the scene, if it makes sense. (If it doesn't, just have them flee. Minions are good at that.)

Swarms: Remember swarms? We talked about them on page 225. Swarms are groups of creatures which individually have a weight of 0, meaning they're too small to be a serious threat to the average character (annoying, yes; a threat, no). But when they swarm, they can increase their weight: a **small swarm**, the size of an average Sentian, is weight 1; a **big swarm**, one about the size of an Ur-Kuld, is weight 2; and a **huge swarm**, one as big as a Marhn, is weight 4.

Well, that's not the only thing they can increase: they can also increase their capacity to take harm. Small swarms typically have no stress boxes (meaning they are taken out by the first point of harm), big swarms have one stress box, and huge swarms have two or three.

Adding Opposition to the Adventure

Go through the list of obstacle aspects you assigned to each scene, and turn them into adversaries, minions, or at least adventure stunts (for example, for a violent storm).

In this adventure, Kim knows she wants Laetitia Bibulus and Captain Volo Troll-Axe as antagonists during the race to get the mask.

She has also listed as "live" opponents the cheap hired brutes who are **Skilled (+2) at ganging up, scaring innocent people,** *and* **Bad (-2) at thinking ahead, fighting when outnumbered**; *and a tentacled sea monster who is* **Skilled (+2) at grabbing people off ships, sinking small boats,** *and* **Bad (-2) at everything else.** *The tentacle monster has a weight of 4 and the special monster stunt* **It's Everywhere**: *No penalty for up to three attacks per turn.*

There is also a school of nasty carnivorous little fish that can attack anyone who falls overboard at sea; Kim treats them as a medium swarm, giving them a weight of 2 and one stress box. She decides they are **Skilled (+2) at swimming and biting** *and* **Bad (-2) at avoiding attacks from above**.

Finally, she wants the environment of the Forbidden Temple and its surroundings to be very hostile, so she stats it like an antagonist and she gives it the stunt **Skilled (+2) at creating physical danger advantages using Exploration and Hiding its Secrets** *and* **Bad (-2) at avoiding attention from explorers.**

Set the First Scene

You've got the problem, the scenes, and the opposition. All you need now is to open with a strong scene that will make the players want to jump in and act. You want to create a strong opening situation that ties to the problem, and some good antagonist characters with agendas. The players' interactions with these will create the fiction.

Pick a book from your shelf of favorites that has a really good opening, say within the first ten pages, and ask yourself why you think it was strong. Usually, a scene that gets your attention swiftly has some intriguing setting, some questions that pique the reader's curiosity and are left open, and some sort of action scene or exciting event.

Now adapt these concepts to your adventure as needed. Look at your story questions and pick one which you think will get the players' attention immediately. If you don't see one in the list, it's time to ask more questions! Whatever question you ask in the opening must make the players want to answer.

Note that **you don't actually have to start at the beginning**. Sometimes it's good to open with a short prologue, a flashback, even a flash forward that will be followed by "Ten days earlier..." in the next scene. All of these are good, but you have to articulate them clearly so the players can understand what you are doing.

Finally, remember that the game is about characters who are proactive, competent, and dramatic. Even if you start with a scene that puts the PCs on the defensive, don't describe them as being belittled or disempowered.

The Mask of Betrayal: Opening Scene

Kim really wants for Rustica to take this seriously, and she wants the favor owed to Valius Nummus to be more than a business obligation. She's also not sure how much investigation her players are up for tonight, so she decides she will set things up so she can feed them useful information as needed if they don't feel like researching the history of the Mask of Kuldarus, by creating a manuscript that sheds light on the artifact.

She opens with Rustica making a routine visit to the establishment of Valius Nummus, purveyor of books, scrolls, fine writing implements, rare texts, and occasional antiques—and finding the merchant amidst the wreckage of his shop, getting his bleeding head bandaged. As a conversation with him will rapidly reveal, Valius' shop was broken into and ransacked during the wee hours of the night.

After shooing away his assistants, Valius confidentially tells Rustica that a manuscript he had recently acquired has been stolen. He tells her he was studying the badly damaged manuscript in the hope of learning the location of the Mask of Kuldarus. Clearly, someone learned of his studies and wants to reach the mask first. Valius asks Rustica to help him retrieve the manuscript and find the mask. This is a compel of Rustica's **Owes Valius Nummus a Favor** *aspect.*

That's it! You have your completed adventure, ready to share with your players. Don't forget to roll with their punches, and keep things fluid. Like most good outlines, this one is subject to change at a moment's notice. Don't force the issue of your perfectly devised plans. If the PCs get off-track, find a way to get them back to their goal—the adventure's trouble aspect, the reason it was inevitable or imperative that they pursue the goal, is a good motivator to get them back on track. But if they are merely pursuing the goal in a way you had not expected, let them!

Getting Better At It

Once you grasp how it works, the Fractal Adventure method is quick and straightforward to use when creating scenarios. The unified view makes it easy for the GM to react quickly since there is no sheaf of notes to thumb through, and having the adventure statted like a character makes the GM more like another player at the game table, less like the CEO of the gaming group.

Ultimately, if you are comfortable improvising in response to your players' ideas, all you really need in an adventure is a strong opening situation that ties to one of your issues, and some good antagonist characters with agendas. The players' interactions with these will create the fiction; the entire group will create scenes on the fly.

One-Page Adventures

You can find the full version of *The Mask of Betrayal* in the appendices, and more one-page adventures will be posted on Evil Hat Productions' website. However, these may not be as much fun as the ones you'll create for your own group, simply because it's not possible to tie them to the characters' aspects. Look them over to get inspiration, or tailor them to fit your campaign.

More Story Seeds

Here are a few more story seeds that can be used for different factions or for a mixed group of Agaptan heroes.

Raise the Titanic! The ships that sank in King Vidaarus the Thirty-First's original attempts to leave for the fabled island of Garigla are still out there off the coast, not too far. Is there something precious, like a famous weapon, on board one of the wrecks? Are there ghosts at sea? Are the gods of Agaptus poking around the site of the disaster? Do some of the wrecks shake loose from the bottom and go adrift?

You Shall Be My Chosen. A nearly-forgotten god decides to try a new approach at recruiting followers before falling into complete oblivion. Hilarity and destruction ensue. We have the perfect setup here to have the *Iliad* and the *Odyssey*, as reenacted by Muppets…

Enemy Brothers. Can diplomatic relations be reestablished between the Elvorix and the Vidaar, or will they collapse against the triple onslaught of climate, the Kuld, and the Jaarl? The heroes may be the only chance to restore the Pact of Prolyus.

Adventures At Sea! Elvorix explorers, Vidaar pirates, Jaarl expatriates, forgotten groups of any of these, the possibilities are endless thanks to all these islands. The Flashy approach demands swashbucklers.

Running Game Sessions

Now that your adversary is doing something the PCs will pay attention to, it's time to start them off. Sometimes the best way to do that, especially for the first session of a new story arc, is to put them right in the action. Once the PCs know why they should care about what's going on, you simply get out of the way and let them take care of it.

That said, there are a bunch of tasks the GM needs to perform to run the session:

Run scenes: A session is made up of individual scenes. Decide where the scene begins, who's there, and what's going on. Decide when all the interesting things have played out and the scene's over.

Adjudicate the rules: When a question comes up about how to apply the rules, you get final say.

Set difficulties: You decide how difficult tasks should be.

Play the opposition: Each player controls their own character, but you control all the rest, including the adversaries.

Keep things moving: If the players don't know what to do next, it's your job to give them a nudge. Never let things get too bogged down in indecision or because they don't have enough information—do something to shake things up.

Make sure everyone has a chance to be awesome: Your goal isn't to defeat the players, but to challenge them. Make sure every PC gets a chance to be the star once in a while, from the big bad warrior to the little sneaky thief.

The secret to becoming comfortable doing this at the game table lies in a little preparation and practice.

Preparing

In cooking, *mise en place* means getting all your ingredients measured and utensils prepared, lined near your work area, and generally setting up so you won't have to fumble around looking for something while your hands are covered with flour and egg.

It's the same when you prepare to run a role-playing game: you want to have the information you'll need at your fingertips, organized so you can find it quickly. You don't want to stall, scratching your head, when the players decide they want to find a master mason or the former aide-de-camp of General Bombatio from the spring campaign of 82 AGC.

In order to be ready to improvise, you can create series of lists to crib from as needed. For example, this book supplies suggestions of names for the various factions, but you're probably going to need more, especially if you are focusing on one faction and all your supporting characters come from the same culture. You can also create lists of personality traits to assign, like grumpy, shy, talkative, or suspicious.

Check out websites that offer collections of game-oriented random generators, such as Abulafia at *random-generator.com* or Seventh Sanctum at *seventhsanctum.com*. Sure, they may generate a number of suggestions that don't exactly fit with the War of Ashes setting, but you can adjust them, or cross them out and generate more with one click.

Running Adventures and Scenes

Here is a mini-toolbox for running the game:

Create an Advantage: The GM should place plenty of barriers in the characters' path to make things interesting. The "create an advantage" action will be the players' metaphorical rope ladder to overcoming obstacles: when you can't just accomplish a task easily, start by making the task easier to accomplish.

Scene Aspects: If you want to strongly color a scene in a certain way, give it an aspect and make it visible to the players without requiring discovery through creation of an advantage. For example, if you want to emphasize the climate and the condition at the cold, barren site of an abandoned village, write *Thick Layer of Ice Everywhere* on an index card or a sticky note and put it right there in plain sight for the players.

Compels, Costs, and Consequences: PCs can expect to be taking hard knocks in grimsical Agaptus. The gamemaster should not hesitate to make the heroes' lives difficult, to allow them to succeed at a cost, and generally leave them limping, bruised, and disoriented. It's all part of the experience.

Pre-Compels: To add adversity, you can start your sessions with one or more pre-compels, offering the bribe of fate points to accept beginning the adventure with a compelled aspect.

These may be:

> Character aspects. Example: *Searching for Her Missing Lover* or *Family Trumps Everything. Almost.*
>
> Campaign aspects. Example: *Secrets of the Ice* or *The Seal of Prolyus*.
>
> Adventure aspects. Example: *Kuld Incursion*, *The High Priestess Is Missing*, or *A Series of Gruesome Murders*.
>
> Consequences from Divine Interest or stress left over from a previous adventure. Example: *Still Limping*, or *Marked by Ilunus*.

Ask the players what happened before. If a player doesn't want to accept the compel, don't force them to pay a fate point; instead, try to negotiate another pre-compel they might be interested in.

Adding or Modifying Scenes on the Fly: If the players have come up with something you just never thought about, you may need to insert whole new scenes in your adventure, or change and combine ones you had planned for. Go to the scene aspects first; they provide the cues for what the focus of the scene should be.

*In the adventure "The Mask of Betrayal," the PCs decide to create fake masks which they will slip to the various groups that are trying to acquire the artifact, so they look for a suitable artist capable of creating replicas. Kim hadn't thought of this; she thinks of a few possible scene aspects like **Backup Copy** or **Weird Little Shop of Nightmares**. Since she wants to end the adventure with lots of intrigue threads, she opts for **Gifted Artist With A Great Memory**.*

Setting Difficulties

When another character is opposing a PC, their rolls provide the opposition in a conflict, contest, or challenge. But if there's no active opposition, you have to decide how hard the task is.

Fixed difficulties: Some difficulties are already pre-defined: frothing, casting a ritual, moving multiple zones, etc. For those challenges, use the difficulties already assigned.

Adventure Approaches: If the adventure approach is applicable, use that. The heroes are exploring an island looking for an entrance to the secret temple? Use the Exploration approach for the difficulty. Trying to convince the angry spear-toting locals that they mean no harm? Use the Interaction approach.

If neither of those is applicable, here are some guidelines for making up difficulties on the fly:

Low difficulties are best when you want to give the PCs a chance to show off and be awesome. **Difficulties near their approach ratings** are best when you want to provide tension but not overwhelm them. **High difficulties** are best when you want to emphasize how dire or unusual the circumstances are and make them pull out all the stops.

Rules of Thumb

❋ If the task isn't very tough at all, give it a Mediocre (+0)—or just tell the player they succeed without a roll.

❋ If you can think of at least one reason why the task is tough, pick Fair (+2).

❋ If the task is extremely difficult, pick Great (+4).

❋ If the task is impossibly difficult, go as high as you think makes sense. The PC will need to drop some fate points and get lots of help to succeed, but that's fine.

❋ In **tense situations**, any obstacle's difficulty can be set at two higher than the Approach used to overcome, so it is likely to need an Invoke.

Approaches and Difficulties

Sometimes being Careful makes things a lot easier; sometimes it just takes too long. The GM may wish to adjust the target number up or down by 1 or 2 depending on whether you choose a fitting or a problematic approach.

For example, there should be different difficulties, costs, and repercussions depending on whether the PCs decide to Forcefully break down a door, Sneakily pick the lock, or Cleverly come up with a legitimate excuse to be let in. See how Approaches can be described **descriptively** and **prescriptively** on page 188.

Adjudicating Rules

At the game table, it's one of your jobs to make most of the moment-to-moment decisions about what's legit and what's not regarding the rules. Most often, you're going to decide when something in the game deserves a roll, what type of action that is (overcome, attack, etc.), which approach is most appropriate, and how difficult that roll is. In conflicts, this can get a little more complicated, like determining if a situation aspect should force someone to make an overcome action, or deciding whether or not a player can justify a particular advantage they're trying to create.

Invocations and Compels: You also judge the appropriateness of any invocations or compels that come up during play, and make sure that everyone at the table is clear on what's going on. With invocations, this is pretty easy—as long as the player can explain why the aspect is relevant, you're good to go. With compels, it can get a little more complicated, because you need to articulate precisely what complication the player is agreeing to.

Saying Yes: *Fate* is all about saying "yes" to what the group creates. You can build on each other's ideas, sometimes saying "Yes, and…" or "Yes, but…" to add twists and turns or make the various pieces of the puzzle fit better together.

Every once in a while you'll have to say "no" when a player misunderstands the fiction that has been created so far, misunderstands the rules, is not in tune with the group's idea of where the story should go, or just wants to test the waters and see if they can get away with it. Even then, see if you can turn this into a "No, but…" to use at least some of the idea.

Fiction First: In *Fate*, fiction comes first; the rules are only meant to support this fiction. In our case, the fiction comes with the benchmark of fitting in with the War of Ashes setting, and this will trump generic rules. However, the group's fun and fiction, in turn, trump the official setting.

Connecting The Games

You may want to conduct larger conflicts representing the ongoing War of Ashes. Note that thanks to the Fate ladder, scale can be used to represent group size, from individual opponents to mass combat. In that case, you might enjoy the miniatures combat games SHIELDWALL (larger-scale battles) and SHIELDBASH (skirmish-scale) from ZombieSmith. These books are also great as setting reference, providing details on the world and history that are merely summarized in FATE OF AGAPTUS and could provide good story seeds and enrich the background material.

If you would like to have some mass combat rules but you are a hard-core *Fate* gamer, you might also want to have a look at DROPS IN A POND: MASS COMBAT by Leonard Balsera, which offers optional rules for large-scale warfare in *Fate* and is available as a free download from *evilhat.com*.

Custom-Fitting and Expanding the World

Let's address a few more questions GMs might come up with after playing for some time:

* ❋ How do I use the *Fate* dials to make my game lighter or darker to suit my group?

* ❋ How much can I fill in the setting?

* ❋ How do I re-scale my campaign when the PCs have outgrown the original scope?

We'll go over these briefly here; for advanced discussion of using *Fate* to create new setting material, or modifying system parameters to change the flavor of a campaign, we recommend consulting the resources listed in the appendices, *"Inspirations and Resources."*

The Fate Dials

You'll see the expression "the Fate dials" in the books and in online discussion of the system. What are these dials and how can you use them to adjust the game to your group's preferences?

On the "macro" adjustment level, dials are the campaign-wide parameters which in this book we have presented as fixed for our vision of the War of Ashes, such as number of character aspects and stunts, refresh rate, stress track, etc. Each of those can be changed, but you have to consider the effects. You also need to discuss this with your group and come to a consensus, so everyone comes to the table with compatible expectations of what the mood and tone of the campaign will be like.

Here are some quick sets of adjustments to move the campaign toward either end of the grimsical mood.

Grim: You want to move toward a darker game. You're looking for mayhem and harsh destinies like in a Bernard Cornwell or George R. R. Martin novel, and death is always waiting. Recommended changes:

* ❋ Set the refresh rate at 2 (instead of 3).

* ❋ Starting characters are limited to one free stunt (instead of up to three).

* ❋ Approach bonus improvement with experience is capped at Great (+4) instead of Superb (+5).

In addition, you'll want to push hard with brutal compels, sinister adventure aspects, and harsh consequences resulting from stress; use pre-compels at the start of adventures; minimize the goofiness and maximize the destructiveness of side effects resulting from magic; and emphasize powerful, angry gods straight from a Greek tragedy.

Whimsical: You're looking for a lighter game. You want zany Muppet-like adventures, with a side of Maurice Sendak. Recommended changes:

* ❋ Encourage players to take all five aspects and three free stunts at character creation or by the end of the first adventure. After all, they can always make changes at the end of milestones.

* ❋ Starting characters get four stress boxes (instead of three).

* ❋ Increase refresh rate to 4.

* ❋ Approach bonus improvement with experience is capped at Fantastic (+6) instead of Superb (+5).

In addition, you'll want to select compels, adventure aspects, and consequences that emphasize humorous predicaments rather than mayhem.

Godlike: Hey, you like this idea of incompetent but powerful deities—but let's cut the middleman, you want to play the gods of Agaptus themselves! Recommended changes:

* Starting approach bonuses are +5, +4, +4, +3, +3, and +2.

* Starting characters get five free stunts (instead of three).

* Stunts are worth +3 bonus (instead of +2).

* Starting characters get four stress boxes (instead of three).

* Increase refresh rate to 6.

* Approach bonus improvement with experience is capped at Legendary (+8) instead of Superb (+5).

* You do not attract Divine Interest. You're already a god!

In your adventures, you will have to create suitable opposition, perhaps in the form of other deities, monsters, natural elements, and secret organizations of rebellious mortals.

Expanding the Setting

GMs may also be looking to add setting material to fill in the blanks we have left. The world of Agaptus is big enough that you can expand from the material provided in here without much risk of significant conflict with other games or books set against the backdrop of the War of Ashes. After all, there are hundreds of islands out there still unexplored by Jaarl or Sentians. One might even be Garigla.

You could also set your campaign in a different era; for example, while the FATE OF AGAPTUS and SHIELDWALL are both set three years after the Pact of Prolyus dissolved in the wake of Orvas' Folly and the Jaarl counter-strike, the novel OUT ON A YLARK is set a few decades earlier.

FATE OF AGAPTUS is intended to be a framework that you will fill with your own adventures, not a detailed atlas. As you plan scenarios, you may want to create:

* New cultures or nations for the existing species.

* Entirely new species.

* New islands and continents.

* New gods.

* New magic.

Let's work through a few examples of how you might do this, starting with adding new cultures of Sentians, Jaarl, or Kuld.

New Cultures: You could easily decide that a certain region of the Elvorix has remained isolated enough that they retained a distinctive culture. They have their own dialect of the Elvorix language, their own mode of dress, naming patterns, customs, etc. Maybe they grumble about the King and city folk, but they're still basically Elvorix, or at least enough to belong to the same faction. All you need to do is jot down a little description of what distinguishes them from other Elvorix.

This is even easier for the Vidaar, who have wandered the seas for centuries and touched down on countless islands. If fact, we even created a catch-all Vidaar culture, the Late-Comers, that can cover a wide range of distinct subcultures. (More details about Late-Comers in "*The Savage Vidaar*," under "*People*" on page 48.)

The Jaarl are generally more unified, which is why we described their Guilds in terms of function in Jaarl society, but it's not unreasonable to imagine that they too might have straggler refugees who wandered for a long time before catching up with the rest of their people.

Example 1: New Culture

Kim imagines a pocket culture of Elvorix in the eastern mountains of Sentia called the Mountaineers, who have been largely isolated because of their remote location. In recent decades they have had more contact with the rest of the kingdom, but before that they developed their own dialect, traditions, legends, and so forth.

To make them distinctive, Kim decides that visually, they will be based on mountain cultures of South America. In the mountains, it makes sense that they would herd gromal instead of ylark, so their primary economy will be based on gromal herding, gromal wool weaving, and small-scale terrace farming.

Kim adds a distinctive naming custom: gendered names. Mountaineer bucks' names tend to end in -o, does' in -i: Basello, Corteo, Darani, Flavi, Gurado, Jevano, Lilei, Murani, Seguro, Tanno, Utali, Vanni.

In terms of religion, Kim thinks they would favor Atronia, deity of agriculture and farming. Mount Atronia is also nearby, and all Sentians have their origins on its slopes, so that makes sense. Instead of flaming ylark, they sacrifice part of their harvest. However, since Atronia is a merciful god—they say—they sacrifice the unused part of the harvest: chaff, stems, husks, etc. After burning them, they ceremonially spread the ashes over their terrace fields and mix them with gromal dung. Atronia must appreciate this, since their tiny fields' productivity is much higher than any outsider would suspect—or the Mountaineers would not have been left alone this long.

New Nations: What if you want more than cultural differences within an existing faction? You could go one step further and envision a splinter group that constitutes their own nation. They don't recognize the authority of the Elvorix or Vidaar kings nor the Jaarl council; they have their own governing body, agenda, interests, and strategy in the War of Ashes.

Example 2: New Nation

Kim thinks about the way the Vidaar and Elvorix cultures have interacted in recent centuries, and thinks maybe a little nation of rogues and rebels from both factions has formed on one of the southwestern coastal islands, refusing the authority of kings. She calls it the Sentian People's Republic of Eedonia and imagines an earnest but fractious little experiment in direct democracy which grew from an old lawless pirate haven formerly known as Port Eedonia.

Eedonia's general agenda is to remain independent as the greater factions tear each other apart for dwindling resources. Thanks to its southern location, Eedonia still has a relatively temperate climate, and is buffered from the Kuld and the Jaarl by the Elvorix and Vidaar.

Kim thinks the inhabitants would be very protective of their independence and insist on putting just about every important decision to popular vote, but as descendants of pirates would also be practical and savvy enough to pull together against outsiders.

Eedonians are eclectic in matters of religion, but have a lot of obscure customs honoring their nautical and piratical heritage. Eedonian names are usually common Elvorix or Vidaar ones, but accompanied by a descriptor: Elwo Broken-Tooth, Gubba Blacksmith, Handsome Aart, Red Brutila, Semela the Stubborn, Villd Baker, etc.

New Species: Continuing up the ladder of detail, we could make up a whole new intelligent species that is also fleeing the advancing ice. You could draw visual inspiration from any number of sources, including some of the ones we list in the appendices, *"Inspirations and Resources."*

If you decide to allow the new species as player characters, or unorthodox PC types such as those discussed on page 153, you have a little extra work ahead of you. You need to create one or more aspects and stunts that will represent the unique flavor of the new faction you're creating; you may want to work with the players to make sure the result will be interesting to them and won't undermine other PCs. Remember that aspects need to be interesting both when they're invoked and compelled, and that stunts typically provide a +2 bonus to one action under narrow circumstances, or provide a once-per-session special effect.

Example 3: New Species

Kim takes a look at another game set in the world of Agaptus, WAR OF ASHES: SHIELDBASH, and finds an image of six-armed warriors which she likes. She decides to create a whole new species for her game, which she names the Ghitamaru.

Based on the image, she decides they must come from an island that had a warm climate until recently. But since there has been much focus on the glaciers' advance, she decides to tie them to the eruption of Mount Murmadon instead. She comes up with the following:

Although they don't know the source of the catastrophe, their island of Ghita-Roka, located southeast of Murmadon, was covered in a thick layer of volcano ash after the eruption. Since then, the Ghitamaru have struggled to clean up their island and recover their food sources, but it has been a losing battle; they have since sent scouting parties in all directions in their sea-worthy long-boats. (Kim pictures the outrigger boats used by native peoples of the Pacific Islands.) Now they come to the islands of Iradon and Sentia, looking for fertile lands and perhaps hardier crops to bring back to Ghita-Roka.

*Kim is not sure whether she wants them available as player characters, though, because that's a **lot** of weapons they can carry! She begins by giving them NPC stats as she would any adversary, starting with an ordinary specimen:*

GHITAMARU

Weight: 2 (Bigger than a Sentian)
High Concept: *Six-Armed Islander.*
Trouble: *Poor Sense of Boundaries.*
Other Aspects: *Inquisitive Nature, Skilled Mariner.*
Skilled (+2) at: Multi-tasking, tasks requiring dexterity.
Bad (-2) at: Enduring cold climates.

STRESS
○○(○), +1 mild consequence

She thinks about them a little more and decides to add the following details on their culture, trying to make them different from the existing factions:

Ghitamaru religion centers on reverence for their ancestors and mistrust of natural spirits. They ask their ancestors to guide them and protect them from the mischievous or downright hostile nature spirits that hide in every rock, tree, or land feature. The role of shaman receives much respect, because they are the ones brave enough to risk the ill will of spirits for the sake of their people. Priests are covered in elaborate tattoos, wear bright and ornate garments, and for ceremonies wear magnificent masks representing their ancestors. All this is intended to focus the attention of the spirits on them rather than on the rest of those present. A healing ceremony, for example, consists of essentially taunting the evil spirit afflicting the sick individual into attacking the shaman instead.

Ghitamaru names are polysyllabic and usually composed of three parts: one for the personal name, one for the lineage, and one for the clan. Very important individuals may receive an additional syllable indicating their accomplishment. Sample names: Au-Ya-Pak, Ku-Tha-Ru, Ni-Mo-Reh, etc.

Kim likes this, and thinks maybe she wants to open this to player characters if there is a good in-game justification. They will need to have a faction stunt that represents their weight of 2 but otherwise are just as playable as the other races.

New Lands: Creating new islands and continents for your group to explore should be relatively straightforward by comparison. If they are going to feature as notable locations in your campaign, give them a couple of aspects each to distinguish them from other places; we suggest, just like in scenes, using an environmental aspect and an obstacle aspect.

Example 4: New Island

Kim decides to add an island that was visited by the Vidaar a long time ago, say the Thirty-First-or-Thirty-Second-Island-That-Wasn't-Garigla. She wants it to look different from Sentia, Iradon, and Matriga, and to present danger and mystery. She pictures a volcanic environment, but very different from the one that used to exist on the jungle island of Murmadon, with smooth lava flows that solidified eons ago into long rounded slopes, fumaroles, hot water springs, geysers, hollow caverns that sometimes open to the sea, and sounds like the low call of a wind instrument when the wind moves through some of the volcanic chimneys. She gives it the following aspects:
Environmental Aspect: **Cave-Ridden Volcanic Island.**
Obstacle Aspect: **Hidden Troglodyte Tribe.**

New Gods: The Vidaar only worship Akka-Maas, their variation of Agaptus; the Kuld revere the Source; and the Jaarl have an on-and-off relationship with Murmadon, still resentful about the destruction of their homeland. The Elvorix, however, are firm in their belief in sixteen (or maybe seventeen) gods, only a handful of which any two scholars agree on. That gives you the chance to invent any number of deities, to decide whether the Source and Murmadon are different entities altogether or just different guises of the gods in the Elvorix pantheon, and to make up new gods for new factions you create.

All you really need for a god is a high concept representing its domain, although a flaw and maybe a few other aspects will be useful if you plan of the god showing up a lot. A god should have extensive ability to use free invocations of its high concept aspect, say one or two free invocations per scene.

Example 5: New God

Kim decides to create a god of knowledge, now largely forgotten because King Vidaarus the First spent so much effort to eradicate this cult. She creates the following:

KARILA, GOD OF KNOWLEDGE
High Concept: *God of Knowledge*.
Trouble: *Bitterly Resentful to Be Forgotten*.
Other Aspects: *I Gotta Try This PR Thing*, *Hoarder*.

She assigns no skills, stunts, stress, or consequences because she figures the god is too powerful compared to Sentians to need to worry about such details.

If You Stat It, They Will Kill It...

You may have noticed that an ordinary NPC tends to be less powerful than a starting player character. That's because the PCs are exceptional characters about whom stories will be told in generations to come—if there are more generations to come for the the world of Agaptus, that is. They are well above average.

But we also gave you suggested starting stats for playing gods as PCs. Does that mean that player character gods are more powerful than NPC gods? In a word: No. Just the opposite. The stats we gave you are for beginner, wet-behind-the-ears deities, because otherwise how will your PCs be challenged by the story? The gods of the Agaptan canon are much more powerful, if not wise, and don't have a definite number of check boxes and consequences. If you decide you want the PCs to be able to go toe-to-toe against them, you need to assign their vital statistics to suit your idea of the difficulty. A 100-foot-tall embodiment of Agaptus should probably be at least weight 12 and an entire zone himself!

New Magic:

Magic is the most complex element to expand, because it's an entire subsystem and needs to be balanced against the other elements. Going through the creation of a whole new magic system, for example to represent a completely different take on magic which the Ghitamaru might use, goes beyond the scope of this book; you can find some discussion in *"Magic"* on page 260 and extensive analysis in *"Inspirations and Resources,"* listed in the appendices, particularly the FATE SYSTEM TOOLKIT.

However, you can adapt the general magic system presented earlier in this book and give it a different flavor by requiring a different form of ritual, such as meditating, making offerings to the ancestor spirits, undertaking physical challenges, using hallucinogenic substances, and so forth.

Re-Scaling the Campaign

You have plenty of breathing room before the player characters start pushing the default limits through milestones. Still, if you play a continuing campaign for long enough, you'll end up with PCs that are vastly more powerful than when they started. A rule of thumb for this might be when all the PCs have either:

* Doubled the total of their approach bonuses, from +9 (+3 +2 +2 +1 +1 +0 = +9) to +18.

* Raised three or more of their approach bonuses to Superb (+5).

When this happens, it's time to think about what you need to do to maintain the group's interest, keep everyone challenged and engaged, and give the heroes a suitably epic story. Here are some ideas for gamemasters:

Retire the Campaign in Style: Maybe the campaign has reached its natural end, story-wise, and all you need to do is give the heroes a graceful exit, then play something new. If you decide that is the proper course, it remains for you to give your campaign a fitting ending, one that will provide a satisfying conclusion.

Look at the campaign aspects—they may have evolved in play—and the current PC aspects; think about the overarching plots and how they have developed; talk to your players. Use this to extrapolate what would be a fitting final scenario or story arc for the heroes, perhaps resolving some of the dramatic hooks embodied by their high concept and flaw aspects, giving them with a well-earned retirement—or even a heroic death.

Scale Forward—Take It Into the Future: Ice ages aren't known for their blinding speed or short duration, relatively speaking. You can move forward by years, decades, even centuries to show the impact of the heroes' actions on the world of Agaptus and the War of Ashes.

Even if somehow the heroes have managed to find a way to stop or reverse the climate effects, the world will continue to change in dramatic ways; perhaps the heroes retired after a job well done, only to be called to serve the greater good again; or they went deep into hiding after making too many enemies, but the consequences of their actions finally catch up with them.

This is a good time to adjust the cap on approach bonuses, refresh rate, number of stress boxes, and so forth, not only for PCs but also for the opposition. It's not just a matter of increasing the numbers either; re-scaling the campaign means changing the scope of the issues and adversaries.

Scale Wide—Play Factions: Perhaps instead of playing single characters, your group needs to start thinking in terms of power factions in Agaptus: noble houses, armies, religious orders, secret organizations, etc.

Thanks to the Bronze Rule discussed on page 288 in *Gamemaster Advice*, you can move to playing entire factions, either as extras for your characters *or as the characters themselves.*

As a result, challenges, contests, and conflicts will be on a whole new scale, but here is the happy news: it doesn't change how they are resolved. We'll still use the same actions, aspects, stunts, stress tracks, and consequences we've been using all along.

After a lot of play and advancement, Kim's PCs have grown so much that it's time to rescale; the group discusses options and decides that it would be fun to move on to world-spanning plots. Each player gets to create a faction or detail one already created in play, negotiated with the GM to provide some balance.

> » *Sharlene's character Rustica has become involved with a Scholar House in play, House Kalamus; this makes a fine faction.*

> » *Ian decides he wants to create a pirate—ahem, "freebooter"—league operating among the western islands with Ulf as its leader, and calls it "The Brotherhood of the Claw."*

> » *Ben, who plays Iva, would like to control the Virian Order; Kim says that's a bit much since she has plans for the Order, but suggests that he control the Stone-Seekers, which Ben agrees to.*

Note that the original PCs don't have to be the official leaders of these factions, merely aligned with them. Another charm of this approach is that you can re-scale again later by picking umbrella organizations operating at yet a higher level.

For more ideas on creating and playing such wide-ranging entities, refer to Mark Diaz Truman's supplement "Factions," which can be downloaded free from *evilhat.com*.

Scale Down—Play the Little People: You can choose to scale *down* instead by playing the PCs' allies and supporters that have been created in the story. In this case, you're essentially creating them as your new player characters, and the former PCs are now high-powered allies that only appear occasionally. This option is very easy to use because the only thing you have to do is fill in new character sheets!

If Kim's group opted to scale down, Sharlene could play Rustica's research assistant, Ian could play one of Ulf's former sailors, and Ben could play Iva's fawn Kuri, grown up to an adventurous adolescent.

Scale Up—Play Gods: If you want to go big, you can always re-visit the option we discussed earlier under *"Custom-Fitting and Expanding the World"* on page 316, and move on to play deities of Agaptus. Like the faction option, this means moving challenges, contests, and conflicts to a new world-spanning scope, but one look at real-world mythologies will reassure you that divine plots can also be petty, silly, and absurd!

Forward! The Fate of Agaptus

Matia: "So what did you do?"

Ulf: (bellowing) "Do? DO? We looked for it, of course!"

Rustica: "Searched the ship, searched the surviving crew, even tried reversing course and searching the ocean."

Iva: "Nothing."

Matia: "So the mask simply…"

Rustica: "Vanished."

Iva: "Disappeared."

Ulf: "Was claimed by Akka-Maas."

Rustica: "Don't start."

Ulf: "How else can you explain it? The mask was in a locked trunk, sealed with chains, in a locked storeroom on a ship in the middle of the ocean! Who could possibly have taken it but Akka-Maas!"

(The two begin to bicker.)

Iva: "Honestly, I think Kuri probably got it and broke it. You know how good children are at that sort of thing…"

Kuri: "HEE!"

Iva: "If we had managed to retrieve the mask, we certainly wouldn't have time to be doing this interview. We would be doing more important work. Perhaps unifying the various races into a peaceful society."

Rustica: "Or leading armies into battle to defeat the Kuld for good!"

Ulf (bellowing): "OR DESTROYING THE TREACHEROUS KI-KAK BEFORE THEY KILL US ALL!"

(A long silence follows. The explorers seem a bit ill at ease.)

Ulf: "Oops. Spoilers!"

From interview notes for the volume "The Explorers," by Matia Bibulus. Transcribed by Bibulus Ven Proudheart, 88 AGC.

The fate of the world is now in your hands. Will Agaptus perish under ashes and ice as the inhabitants of the imperiled islands wrestle for dwindling resources? Will one faction triumph over the others in time to carve out its future? Will capricious and clumsy gods finish destroying this world, or will they be its saviors? And how will your heroes' adventures shape this future?

Play and find out!

Appendices

Inspirations and Resources

The world of Agaptus began with ZombieSmith's **War of Ashes: Shieldwall**, a miniatures combat game showcasing innovative mechanics to do something no other miniatures game had done: provide the experience of armies clashing with classic shieldwall tactics—as seen in our early Middle Ages. The rules explicitly marry a simple, streamlined system with narrative objectives, and the world was created to express a "grimsical" aesthetic—gritty, yet whimsical.

Agaptus was too large to stay contained in a single game!

ZombieSmith created a second miniatures game building on **Shieldwall** but adapted to smaller, skirmish size conflicts, called **War of Ashes: Shieldbash**. Licensed "Young Adult" fiction was the next step, and author Carrie Harris wrote **Out On a Ylark**.

Soon the meeting of the minds between ZombieSmith's approach and Evil Hat's *Fate Core* roleplaying system generated a new project, the **War of Ashes: Fate of Agaptus**, which you now hold.

When imagining the "grimsical" flavor of **War of Ashes**, think of the whimsy of Jim Henson's television shows like *Fraggle Rock* and *The Muppet Show*, married to dark, gritty military fantasy like Bernard Cornwell's *Warlord Chronicles*, *Saxon Tales*, and *Grail Quest* series, or Glenn Cook's *Chronicles of the Black Company*. In my experience, a lot of gamers resonate with a campaign that unfolds with humor and silliness, but also with actual drama and dire consequences.

The creatures are funny-looking, Muppet-like, and have amusing or offbeat abilities—but at the same time, we're reminded of the British Isles in the Early Middle Ages after the Romans had left, leaving marvels of architecture the locals cannot replicate. There are also hints of the folly of societies who keep right on doing what led to their near extinction (think of the French, English, or Russian royal courts at the time of their respective nations' revolutions, or the original inhabitants of Easter Island).

So here are the inspirations that came to mind as I was writing
WAR OF ASHES: FATE OF AGAPTUS.

Illustrations and books by Dr. Seuss, Maurice Sendak, Edward
Gorey, and Andy Hopp.

Movies like *Monsters Inc.* (Pete Docter, Pixar), *Princess
Mononoke* (Miyazaki Hayao, Studio Ghibli), *Antz* (Eric
Darnell, DreamWorks), *The Dark Crystal* (Jim Henson
Studios), and *The Nightmare Before Christmas* (Tim Burton,
Touchstone Studios).

Games like the original *Warhammer 40,000: Rogue Trader*,
Bloodbowl (both from Games Workshop), *OmegaZone*
(Brooklyn Indie Games), and *Low Life* (Andy Hopp, Pinnacle
Entertainment).

Any soundtracks by Danny Elfman, Camille Saint-Saens'
"Carnaval des animaux," Edvard Grieg's *"Peer Gynt Suite,"*
Johann Sibelius' *"Finlandia"* and *"The Tempest."*

However, my primary source of inspiration was the stunning art created by
ZombieSmith's Josh Qualtieri, Jonathan Hoffman, Noah Bradley, Jennifer
Bach, and the rest of their team.

The second part of my sources were the tools for tinkering with FATE
ACCELERATED EDITION. Fortunately, several high-quality resources are at
hand, both among official publications and fan-written essays:

Publications

The FATE CORE SYSTEM book vastly expands FATE
ACCELERATED EDITION's capabilities and provides the rationale
for the way various parts of the system are designed. Both FATE
ACCELERATED EDITION and FATE CORE are available as pay-
what-you-want downloads from Evil Hat Productions' website:
evilhat.com.

The FATE SYSTEM TOOLKIT turbo-charges this with in-depth
analysis of *Fate*'s "dials." Also available from the link above.

I also drew from the excellent advice found in Robin D. Laws'
ROBIN'S LAWS OF GOOD GAMEMASTERING (Steve Jackson Games).
Available for purchase and download at *jgames.com/robinslaws/*.

Essays

Leonard Balsera's optional rules for large-scale warfare in *Fate* in his book **DROPS IN A POND: MASS COMBAT**, available as a free download from *evilhat.com*.

Ryan M. Danks' thoughts on the *Fate Core* Fractal in designing adventures: *ryanmdanks.com/?p=507*.

David Goodwin's "Approaching Approaches" on Google+.

Google+ *Fate Core* and *Fate Accelerated (FAE)* communities.

Jack Gulick's "Supported Suspension of Disbelief and Fate" on Google+.

Robert Hanz's "Fate Core: Calibration" and "Fate Fractal and Aspect" on Google+.

Wil Hutton's "Locations, Fate Core Style"—Part I: *rivetgeek. blogspot.com/2013/09/locations-fate-core-style-part-i.html* and Part II: *rivetgeek.blogspot.com/2013/09/locations-fate-core-style-part-ii.html*.

Jeremy Kostiew's series of *Fate* tutorials:

bblgcast.com/tag/fatetutorials/.

Mark Kowalizzinn's "Weapons and Armour in Fate": *rollforcritical.com/2013/09/weapons-and-armour-in-fate.html*.

Mark Diaz Truman's supplement, "Factions," which explores creating and playing wide-ranging entities and is available as a free download from *evilhat.com*.

Additional Products

If you're looking for nifty new Fate or War of Ashes products, look no further!

Deck of Fate produced by Evil Hat, available at *evilhat.com*.

Fate Dice™ produced by Evil Hat, available at *evilhat.com*.

Fate Tokens produced by Campaign Coins, available at *campaigncoins.com/store/fate.html*.

War of Ashes miniatures produced by ZombieSmith, available at *zombiesmith.com/pages/war-of-ashes*.

Additonal Online Resources

For quick inspiration, check out game-oriented random generators, and adjust accordingly for the War of Ashes setting:

Abulafia at *random-generator.com*.

Seventh Sanctum at *seventhsanctum.com*.

Rules:
Quick Reference

Value	Adjective
+9	Miraculous
+8	Legendary
+7	Epic
+6	Fantastic
+5	Superb
+4	Great
+3	Good
+2	Fair
+1	Average
+0	Mediocre
-1	Poor
-2	Terrible
-3	Awful
-4	Abysmal

Rolling the Dice
(page 198)

Result = Dice Roll

+ Approach Bonus
+ Bonuses from Stunts
+ Bonuses from Invoked Aspects

Aspects *(page 190)*

» Invoke *(page 192)*: Spend a fate point to get a +2 or a reroll for yourself, or to increase difficulty for a foe by 2.

» Invoke for effect *(page 194)*: Spend a fate point or a free invocation to create a specifically defined mechanical effect.

» Compel *(page 195)*: Receive a fate point when an aspect complicates your life.

» Establish facts *(page 197)*: Aspects are true. Use them to affirm details about you and the world.

Types of Aspects

Character Aspects *(page 191)*

» Written when you create your character.

» May be changed when you reach a milestone *(page 240)*.

Situation Aspects *(page 191)*

» Established at the beginning of a scene.

» May be created by using the create an advantage action.

» May be eliminated by using the overcome action.

» Vanish when the situation ends.

Zone Aspects *(page 210)*

» Established at the beginning of a scene or as the terrain (zone) is encountered in play.

» May be discovered or modified by using the create an advantage action.

» Each pre-defined zone aspect starts the scene with one free invocation.

» Aspects "discovered" by the players (by creating an advantage) start with one or two free invocations, as usual.

» May be eliminated by using an appropriate overcome action.

Boosts *(page 192)*

» May be invoked once (for free), then they vanish.

» May be eliminated by an opponent using an overcome action.

» Unused boosts vanish at the end of the scene.

Consequences
(page 192 and 231)

» Used to absorb shifts from successful attacks.

» May be invoked by your opponents as if they were situation aspects.

Approaches *(page 188)*

» **Careful:** When you pay close attention to detail and take your time to do the job right.

» **Clever:** When you think fast, solve problems, or account for complex variables.

» **Flashy:** When you act with style and panache.

» **Forceful:** When you use brute strength.

» **Quick:** When you move quickly and with dexterity.

» **Sneaky:** When you use misdirection, stealth, or deceit.

Actions *(page 180)*

Create an advantage when creating or discovering aspects:

» **Fail:** Don't create or discover, or you do but your opponent (not you) gets a free invocation.

» **Tie:** Get a **boost** if creating new, or treat as success if looking for existing.

» **Succeed:** Create or discover the aspect, get a free invocation on it.

» **Succeed with Style:** Create or discover the aspect, get two free invocations on it.

Create an advantage on an aspect you already know about:

» **Fail:** No additional benefit.

» **Tie**: Generate one free invocation on the aspect.

» **Succeed:** Generate one free invocation on the aspect.

» **Succeed with Style:** Generate two free invocations on the aspect.

Overcome:

» **Fail:** Fail, or succeed at a serious cost.

» **Tie:** Succeed at minor cost.

» **Succeed:** You accomplish your goal.

» **Succeed with Style:** You accomplish your goal and generate a **boost**.

Attack:

» **Fail:** Attack doesn't harm the target and you take one point of stress.

» **Tie:** Attack doesn't harm the target, but you gain a **boost**.

» **Succeed:** Attack hits and causes damage.

» **Succeed with Style:** Attack hits and causes damage. You also gain a **boost**.

Defend:

» **Fail:** You suffer the consequences of your opponent's success.

» **Tie:** Look at your opponent's action to see what happens on a tie.

» **Succeed:** Your opponent doesn't get what they want.

» **Succeed with Style:** Your opponent doesn't get what they want, and you get a **boost**.

Getting Help *(page 187)*

» An ally can help you perform your action.

» When an ally helps you, they give up their action for the exchange and describe how they help.

» You get a +1 for each ally that helps in this way.

» GM may place limits on how many may help.

Challenges, Contests and Conflicts *(page 206)*

» **Challenges:** A series of overcome and create an advantage actions used to resolve an especially complicated situation, with each action dealing with one task or part of the situation. Look at the sequence of rolls to describe the resolution.

» **Contests:** When two or more characters are competing against one another for the same goal, but not directly trying to hurt each other. Compare the competing characters' rolls.

» **Conflicts:** Used to resolve situations where characters are trying to harm one another morally, socially, physically, or through some other means using attack and defense rolls.

Turn Order *(page 215)*

» **Physical Conflict:** Compare Quick approaches—the one with the fastest reflexes goes first.

» **Mental Conflict:** Compare Careful approaches—the one with the most attention to detail senses danger.

» **Everyone else goes in descending order:** Break ties in whatever manner makes sense, with the GM having the last word.

» **The GM may choose to have all NPCs go on the turn of the most advantageous NPC.**

Roar Phase *(page 215)*

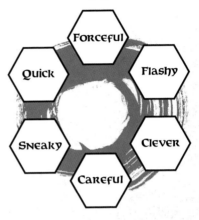

In initiative order, everyone declares whether they are Roaring or not.

Everyone who is Roaring rolls to create an advantage against a difficulty of +2. Depending on roll result:

» Fail: Create a froth aspect at a cost with one free invocation and gain a related consequence.

» Tie: Create a froth boost.

» Success: Create a froth aspect with one free invocation.

» Success with style: Create a froth aspect with two free invocations.

While in froth, you are limited to using the approach you used to create the froth advantage, and the two closest approaches (see diagram).

The froth aspect lasts until you use a non-adjacent approach or until the end of the scene, whichever comes first.

Weight *(page 222)*

- » If you outweigh your opponents in the zone by at least 2 to 1, replace any one of the dice rolled with a ⊞ .

- » If you outweigh the zone opposition by at least 4 to 1, replace two results with ⊞ .

- » Swarms come in three sizes: small is weight 1, big is weight 2, huge is weight 4.

Stress & Consequences
(page 231)

- » Severity of hit (in shifts) = Attack Roll – Defense Roll

- » **Stress Boxes:** You can check one stress box to handle some or all of the shifts of a single hit. You can absorb a number of shifts equal to the number of the box you check: one for Box 1, two for Box 2, three for Box 3.

- » **Consequences:** You may take one or more consequences to deal with the hit, by marking off one or more available consequence slots and writing a new aspect for each one marked.

  - » Mild = 2 shifts

  - » Moderate = 4 shifts

  - » Severe = 6 shifts

- » **Taken Out:** If you can't (or decide not to) handle the entire hit, you're taken out and your opponent decides what happens to you.

- » **Giving In:** Give in before your opponent's roll and you can control how you exit the scene. You earn one or more fate points for giving in *(page 238)*.

- » Recovering from Consequences:

  - » **Mild consequence:** Clear it at the end of the *next* scene, provided you get a chance to rest or get appropriate help.

  - » **Moderate consequence:** Downgrade to mild at the end of the next session, provided it makes sense within the story.

  - » **Severe consequence:** Downgrade it to moderate at the end of the scenario or the next major milestone *(page 234)*, whichever comes first, provided it makes sense within the story.

Divine Interest *(page 256)*

Functions like a set of consequences for the entire group of heroes, recording how much attention they have attracted among the gods.

- » **Attracting Divine Interest:**

  - » Rolling ⊞⊞⊞⊞ or ⊟⊟⊟⊟ on the dice. Even if a fate point is used to re-roll, the point will be incurred although the result of the action will be changed.

  - » Obtaining a Miraculous (+9) or better result—a.k.a. succeeding catastrophically.

» Obtaining an Abysmal (-4) or worse result—a.k.a. heroic calamity.

» Performing a magic ritual.

» Certain costs associated with magical stunts *(page 269)*.

» Doing something extravagant, extraordinary, eccentric, or otherwise distinguishing you from those around you, in place of taking a personal consequence.

» Choosing to take a Divine Interest consequence in place of a stress consequence.

» **Recovery from Divine Interest:**

  » **Mild Divine Interest consequence:** A minor milestone *(page 241)* allows one mild consequence to be cleared.

  » **Moderate Divine Interest consequence**: Lasts at least two sessions and until a significant milestone *(page 241)*, at which point it can be reduced to mild.

  » **Severe Divine Interest consequence:** Will last at least through one significant milestone and until the next major milestone *(page 242)*.

» **Being Taken out by Divine Interest:** When all four Divine Interest consequence slots are full and you get one more, you are taken out. At the end of the session, the group takes a Divine milestone *(page 243)*.

Magic *(page 260)*
(Requires an appropriate character aspect.)

» Choose a ritual and perform the required chanting, dancing, and so forth.

» Make an appropriate approach roll to overcome against the target of the ritual.

» The GM marks a Divine Interest consequence.

» Cast the ritual:

  » **General ritual:** Use to create a temporary stunt on a target individual or item.

  » **Battle ritual:** Use during Roar phase to create an aspect appropriate to a curse or blessing on the target group.

Character Advancement
(page 240)

Minor Milestone: After a minor milestone, you can choose to do one (and only one) of the following:

» Switch the ratings of any two approaches.

» Rename one aspect that isn't your high concept.

» Attach an existing equipment stunt to a new, similar piece of equipment to replace one that was lost or damaged.

» Exchange one stunt for a different stunt.

» Choose a new stunt (and adjust your refresh, if you already have three stunts).

» Clear one mild Divine Interest consequence *(page 258)*.

» If you've had a chance to recover: rename a moderate consequence that has been around for at least one full session and change it to a mild consequence.

Significant Milestone:

In addition to the benefit of a minor milestone, you also gain *all* of the following:

» If you have a severe consequence that's been around for at least two sessions, and you've taken action to recover from it, you can rename it and downgrade it to a moderate consequence.

» Raise the bonus of one approach by one.

» The group as a whole may clear one mild Divine Interest consequence OR reduce a moderate Divine Interest consequence that has been around for at least two sessions to mild. (See *"Divine Interest"* on page 256.)

» "Flag" an aspect that you intend to change, including your high concept. This is letting the GM know you intend to make the change, so talk to the GM about what direction you're thinking of taking it.

» Change a previously flagged aspect (with GM approval).

Major Milestone:

Achieving a major milestone confers the benefits of a significant milestone *and* a minor milestone. In addition, you may do *all* of the following:

» Take an additional point of refresh, which you may immediately use to purchase a stunt if you wish.

» Rename your character's high concept (optional).

» If a Divine Interest consequence has been around since at least the previous significant milestone, you can reduce it from severe to moderate.

Divine Milestone:

» At the end of any session in which you are taken out by Divine consequences, clear all the Divine Interest consequences and decide on a new permanent group aspect *(page 243)*.

Glossary

Action: Specific ways to get things done: create an advantage, defend, overcome, or attack.

Adventure: Also called a "scenario." A short story arc that can usually wrap in one to three game sessions.

Agaptus: (1) The god of the sky for the Elvorix; (2) the land encompassing the islands of Sentia, Matriga, and Iradon.

Ancients: Another term for Sentians, from which both Elvorix and Vidaar are descended.

Approach: Descriptions of how you accomplish tasks: Careful, Clever, Flashy, Forceful, Quick, and Sneaky.

Aspects: Little bits of fiction that encapsulate an idea or theme that can be used to produce a mechanical effect.

Aspect extra: An aspect that can be invoked for powerful special effects beyond the usual bonus or re-roll.

Bookworms: Vidaar term for the Elvorix.

Boost: A temporary aspect can be invoked once for free, then it goes away.

Broke-Backs: Jaarl term for the Vidaar.

Bronze Rule: Also called the "Fate Fractal." The method of treating anything in Fate as a character and assigning it aspects, approaches, stunts, stress tracks, consequences.

Buck: Adult male Elvorix, Vidaar, or Jaarl.

Bucky: Underage male Elvorix, Vidaar, or Jaarl. Similar to "kid" or "kiddo."

Campaign: A series of games you play with the same characters, where the story builds on what happened in earlier sessions.

Challenge: A series of overcome and create an advantage actions that you use to resolve an especially complicated situation.

Character advancement: The ability to change aspects, add or change stunts, or raise your approach bonuses. See "Milestones."

Combat: When a conflict turns physical.

Concede: Also called "giving in." Rather than being taken out, you give in before dice are rolled, and get a say in what happens to you. Your opponent gets some major concession from you.

Conflict: When characters are trying to hurt each other, either morally, socially, or through any other means except physically.

Contest: When two or more characters are competing against one another for the same goal, but not directly trying to hurt each other. Examples include a foot chase, a public debate, or an archery tournament.

Consequence: A new aspect that you take to reflect being seriously hurt in some way—mentally or physically.

Corduu: The Second Sword presented to a particularly worthy Jaarl soldier with the promotion to the rank of Valani. It is a great honor to wield two swords of Jaarl steel.

Create an advantage: Anything you do to try to help yourself or one of your friends.

Deck of Fate: A deck of cards that mimics the probability of Fate dice.

Doe: Adult female Elvorix, Vidaar, or Jaarl.

Divine Interest: A measure of the level of cosmic trouble one has attracted.

Fail: When you fail a roll, your total is less than your opponent's total.

Fate dice: Also called Fudge dice, a special kind of six-sided die that are marked on two sides with a plus symbol ➕, two sides with a minus symbol ➖, and two sides are blank ⬛.

Fate Fractal: Also called the "Bronze Rule." The method of treating anything in Fate as a character and assigning it aspects, approaches, stunts, stress tracks, consequences.

Fawn: Young Elvorix, Vidaar, or Jaarl.

Froth: A higher state of consciousness that can allow a character to transcend their usual physical or mental limitations.

Froth aspect: A specific aspect that can be gained while frothing.

Gamemaster: GM for short; the person who acts as an arbitrator of dice rolls, provides details of the world in which the players explore, and represent any non-player characters.

Give In: Also called "concede." Rather than being taken out, you give in before dice are rolled, and get a say in what happens to you. Your opponent gets some major concession from you.

GM character: A character portrayed by the gamemaster to interact with the player characters. Often called a non-player character or NPC.

Golden Rule: The guideline for GMs that you should decide what you're trying to accomplish first, then consult the rules to help you do it.

Great Catastrophe: A global event 86 years ago in which the world's climate changed and has brought on a new ice age. Many believe it is an effect of divine wrath.

High Concept: A single phrase or sentence that neatly sums up your character, saying who you are, what you do, what your "deal" is.

Houselord: Head of an Elvorix House; responsible for administering and enforcing local authority.

Invoke: Using an appropriate aspect to give a re-roll or +2 to a roll.

Iradon: The easternmost island of Agaptus, currently claimed by the Jaarl but disputed by both Elvorix and Vidaar forces.

Lethal: When damage bypasses stress points and goes straight to consequences.

Marhn: A race of fierce trolls used by the Kuld as heavy troops.

Major milestone: Occurs at the end of a big story arc, the final defeat of a main NPC villain, or any other large-scale change. Players have additional options to choose from when choosing how to modify their character.

Maneuver: Feats in combat based on the four basic actions.

Matriga: The island that forms the southwestern part of Agaptus, currently occupied by the Vidaar despite Elvorix resistance.

Milestone: When a particular story-line in your game has been   wrapped up.

Minion: An unnamed brute, monster, or goon that is there to make the PC's day a little more difficult.

Minor cost: After a tie on an overcome action, a player may elect to succeed and accept something that will complicate the PC's life.

Minor milestone: When a piece of a story has been resolved, your character can adjust in response to whatever's going on in the story by making minor changes to their character sheet.

Murmadon: The island from which the Jaarl migrated after its central mountain, Mount Murmadon, exploded and made it uninhabitable.

Murmadon rock: The stone from the core and slopes of Mount Murmadon, imbued with unusual magic-amplifying properties.

Nhilde: A race of trolls found on a distant island and brought back by the Vidaar to serve as shock troops.

Non-player character: NPC for short; a character being portrayed by the GM to interact with the player characters.

Outweigh: When one side's total weight is greater than the other. See "Weight."

Player: Those who represent the protagonists of a game and make the decisions that their character would make.

Player character: PC for short; the character being portrayed by the player.

Range: The distance in zones at which a weapon can be effective.

Refresh: The number of fate points you begin each game session with. By default, this starts at 3.

Ritual: A little bit of magic to allow a blessing or a curse to be placed on someone or something.

Roar: The first phase of combat in which characters can froth to create special aspects.

Scenario: Also called an "adventure." A short story arc that can usually wrap in one to three game sessions.

Sentia: The largest of the three isles of Agaptus, from which the Elvorix and Vidaar originate and is currently disputed between all four factions.

Sentian: The species from a common stock originating on the island of Sentia from which both Elvorix and Vidaar are descended.

Serious cost: After failing an overcome action, a player may elect to succeed by making a tough choice or accepting a consequence.

Shift: A way to measure the severity of an attack; the difference between the attack roll and your defense roll.

Significant milestone: Usually occurs at the end of a scenario or the conclusion of a big plot event. The characters can learn new things and players have added options to choose from.

Skirra: A heavy double-bladed polearm carried by a Jaarl monster-hunter (Cospico).

Silver Rule: The guideline for GMs that you should ever let the rules get in the way of what makes narrative sense.

Stress: If you get hit and don't want to be taken out, you can choose to take stress. Stress represents you getting tired or annoyed, taking a superficial wound, or some other condition that goes away quickly.

Stress track: A row of three boxes to track your stress.

Stunt: A special trait, trick, maneuver, or piece of equipment that changes the way an approach works for your character.

Subject: A person, place, group, or thing which will be the focus of a ritual's effect on the target.

Succeed with style: When you succeed with style on a roll, your total is at least three greater than your opponent's total.

Success: When you succeed on a roll, your total is greater than the difficulty or your opponent's total.

Swarm: When creatures with a weight of 0 attack in a group. A small swarm is weight 1, a big swarm is weight 2, and a huge swarm is weight 4.

Taken out: Because of the severity of an attack you received, you're out of the action for a while, and can re-enter in the next scene. Whoever takes you out narrates what happens to you.

Target: The person, place, group, or thing that a ritual will affect.

Tie: When you tie on a roll, your total is equal to your opponent's total.

Trouble: Something that causes complications for your character, such as a personal weakness, a recurring enemy, or an important obligation.

Tyromancy: Augury and prophecy based on the study of cheese.

Volcanium: The Jaarl steel that used to be forged in the fires of Mount Murmadon, but can no longer be worked for lack of sufficiently hot fires.

Weaklings: Jaarl term for the Elvorix.

Weight: The size of a fighter or group of fighters in a zone, which has a mechanical effect on their attack.

Zone: A loosely defined area that tells you where characters are.

Zone aspect: A specific aspect assigned to a zone that tells you what's in it, such as Trees, Steep Slope, Kitchen, Crumbling Stairway.

Sample Names

Elvorix:
[Title] [Personal name] [Occupation name] ix [City of origin] co [Adopted city of residence]

Occupation names: Aedituus (priest), Agrius (farmer), Bibulus (scholar), Gladius (soldier), Nummus (merchant), Parvulus (child), Usus (laborer).

Personal names: Aart, Aguros, Atronia, Baseros, Biblius, Bluum, Brojan, Brutilus, Caperna, Elani, Elantrix, Elvora, Elwo, Evrard, Ficca, Flautul, Garigla, Gicca, Ggorll, Hlarn, Homarus, Huudos, Hyllva, Ilunas, Kalamus, Killim, Kiptus, Kiriko, Kkahl, Lilia, Lukkus, Maladros, Matia, Mauro, Mearios, Monru, Naril, Nyllo, Orvas, Pallo, Rogus, Seadros, Semela, Sentius, Sigurod, Tera, Tomlin, Toranus, Torvus, Ven, Wiccar, Yladuur.

Vorix Clan Names: Arrowflight, Deathsong, Proudheart, Quickstrike, Shadowstep, Two-Blades.

Vorix: [Title] [Personal name] [Clan name]

Vidaar:
[Title] [Personal name] [Possible Nickname] [Possible Clan Name]

Personal names: Aenwubba, Blagaard, Forlad, Gholas, Gubba, Kraka, Krula, Nhilde, Offrus, Ragnhild, Sverra, Tahrynn, Ulryg, Vaad, Vaett, Valeran, Vendela, Venks, Vidaarus, Vigdis, Villd, Volo, Vulgg, Ylwa.

Clan Names: Black Raiders, Death Singers, Piercing Lances, Red Hammers, Skull Crushers, Wave Riders, White Wights.

Jaarl:
[Title] [Personal Name] [Possible Nickname]

Personal names: Agirix, Arabaldo, Arduino, Asdrubale, Azzone, Bodo, Burlanda, Ezzo, Ghinga, Harrie, Hgglar, Illinani, Jusipio, Khugg, Lele, Meloria, Morenus, Mortox, Nofri, Rigarda, Rocco, Rolius, Tedaldo, Tenghi, Tybal, Ugolina.

Kuld:

Given Names: Aaaagrrblah, Aargh, Ack, AhhhWuun, Blubbous, Clubfoot, Dank Cave, Goola, Grrsnikt, Grunt, HnnHnn, Kagaar, Maaahaunn, Mossback, Old White-Scar, River-Berries, Shambla, Waaanoooo, Ylark Sweat.

Scent-Names: Brood-Bearer, Flatulent Hero, Horde-Leader, Inspiring Perfume, Meal-Finder, Old Odoriferous Retcher, Powerful Pungency, Rock-Eater, Source-Scented.

Campaign Title

Setting/Scale (PAGE 143)

Issues (PAGE 144)

CURRENT ISSUES | IMPENDING ISSUES

Faces & Places (PAGE 144)

OTHER

ISSUES/ASPECTS

OTHER

ISSUES/ASPECTS

OTHER

ISSUES/ASPECTS

OTHER

ISSUES/ASPECTS

OTHER

ISSUES/ASPECTS

OTHER

ISSUES/ASPECTS

Dials (PAGE 316)

NUMBER OF ASPECTS	5
BONUS IMPROVEMENT CAP	Superb +5
FACTIONS ALLOWED (PAGE 148)	
REFRESH RATE	3
NUMBER OF INITIAL STUNTS	3
DEFAULT # OF STRESS BOXES	3
CONSEQUENCE SLOTS	2/4/6

Divine Interest (PAGE 256)

MILD

MILD

MODERATE

SEVERE

GROUP ASPECT

Group Concept (PAGE 148)

War of Ashes

Roleplaying Game

CHARACTER SHEET

FATE

Refresh

Name

Description

Weight

ASPECTS

HIGH CONCEPT

TROUBLE

FACTION

APPROACHES

Forceful

Quick

Flashy

Sneaky

Clever

Careful

STRESS

1   2   3

STUNTS

FACTION

EQUIPMENT

OTHER

CONSEQUENCES

2 MILD

4 MODERATE

6 SEVERE

War of Ashes

Roleplaying Game

CHARACTER SHEE

NAME **Rustica Bibulus ix Atronia**

FATE

Refresh **3**

Description

Elxorix scholar showing too much originality for her elders at the Academy. Rustica studies the mystery of the Great Catastrophe and the connections with the eruption of Mount Murmadon.

Weight

1

ASPECTS

HIGH CONCEPT
Overachieving Elvorix Scholar

TROUBLE
I'm Convinced That the Theory is Sound

FACTION
Bookworm

The Collected Notes of Peony the Elder

Owes Valius Nummus a Favor

APPROACHES

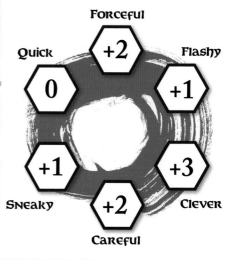

FORCEFUL **+2**

Quick **0**

Flashy **+1**

Sneaky **+1**

Clever **+3**

Careful **+2**

STRESS

1 **2** **3**

STUNTS

FACTION
BECAUSE I AM ATRONIAN, once per game session I can pass myself off for Vidaar.

EQUIPMENT

OTHER
WELL-READ: Because I am Well-Read, once per scene I get +2 to Cleverly create an advantage involving my book learning.

(May take one more stunt without reducing refresh!)

CONSEQUENCES

2 MILD

4 MODERATE

6 SEVERE

War of Ashes
Roleplaying Game

NAME Ulf LongTeeth

Description

Young Vidaar with a love for the old heroic sagas who longs to return to the life of swashbuckling seafaring adventures instead of this inhospitable land. He and Rustica are distantly related.

Weight

1

Aspects

HIGH CONCEPT
Nostalgic young Vidaar Privateer

TROUBLE
Out to Make A Name for Himself!

ACTION
A True Vidaar Acts First and Asks Questions Later!

The Good Ship *Blagaard*

Family Trumps Everything. Almost.

Stunts

ACTION
BECAUSE I AM FROM THE VYGGORAN LATECOMER CLAN, I get +2 to Cleverly create advantages by improvising repairs on technology I understand.

EQUIPMENT

OTHER
BORN SAILOR: Because I am a Born Sailor, I get +2 to Cleverly overcome when sailing, climbing, maintaining my balance, or swinging from a line.

(May take one more stunt without reducing refresh!)

Fate

Refresh 3

Approaches

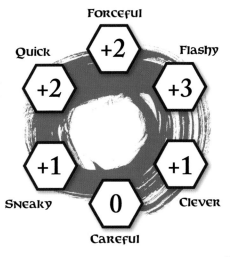

- **Forceful** +2
- **Quick** +2
- **Flashy** +3
- **Sneaky** +1
- **Clever** +1
- **Careful** 0

Stress

1 2 3

Consequences

2 MILD

4 MODERATE

6 SEVERE

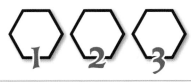

CHARACTER SHEET

FATE

Refresh **3**

Name Iva the Stubborn

Description

Jaarl Virian mother torn between fulfilling her duty to the Virian Order and the Stone-Seekers by assisting Rustica's quest, and the wish to go looking for her banished lover, who lost his sword.

Weight **1**

APPROACHES

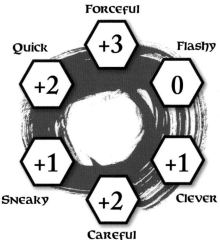

FORCEFUL **+3**

Quick **+2**

Flashy **0**

Sneaky **+1**

Clever **+1**

Careful **+2**

ASPECTS

HIGH CONCEPT
Jaarl Wandering Virian Master

TROUBLE
Single Mother With A Fawn

FACTION
Discipline Is the Core of a Jaarl's Soul

Searching for Her Banished Lover

Sponsored by the StoneSeekers

STRESS

1 **2** **3**

STUNTS

FACTION
ATTUNED TO THE SACRED ROCK: Because I am Attuned to the Sacred Rock, once per session I can find the direction of the closest Murmadon rock.

EQUIPMENT
MORNINGSTAR FLAIL: When I use my morningstar flail in physical conflicts, my weight counts as 2 when defending against multiple opponents.

OTHER
(May take one more stunt without reducing refresh!)

CONSEQUENCES

2 MILD

4 MODERATE

6 SEVERE

War of Ashes

Roleplaying Game

Adventure Sheet

Title _____

Trouble Overhanging

ASPECT _____

Approaches

Combat

Interaction

Exploration

Lore

Scenes

ENVIRONMENTAL ASPECT	ENVIRONMENTAL ASPECT
OBSTACLE ASPECT	OBSTACLE ASPECT
NOTES	NOTES

ENVIRONMENTAL ASPECT	ENVIRONMENTAL ASPECT
OBSTACLE ASPECT	OBSTACLE ASPECT
NOTES	NOTES

ENVIRONMENTAL ASPECT	ENVIRONMENTAL ASPECT
OBSTACLE ASPECT	OBSTACLE ASPECT
NOTES	NOTES

ENVIRONMENTAL ASPECT	ENVIRONMENTAL ASPECT
OBSTACLE ASPECT	OBSTACLE ASPECT
NOTES	NOTES

War of Ashes
Roleplaying Game

Adventure Sheet

Title
The Mask of Betrayal

Trouble Overhanging
The wrong hands, or at least some wrong hands…

ASPECT
The Seal of Prolyus Is On the Trail!

Approaches

Combat +2
Interaction +4
Exploration 0
Lore +2

Scenes

The Theft

ENVIRONMENTAL ASPECT
Topsy-Turvy Shop

OBSTACLE ASPECT
The City Watch Doesn't Like "Help"

NOTES
City Watch: Skilled (+2) at: Asserting their authority, arresting people. Bad (-2) at: Making friends.
Valius Nummus: Clever +1, Careful +2, Flashy +1

The Stone Seekers' Interest

ENVIRONMENTAL ASPECT
Shadowy Ruins on the Outskirts of Town

OBSTACLE ASPECT
Our Purpose Is Greater

NOTES
Jusinio, Virian Master: Clever +1, Sneaky +2, Forceful +1
Note: Optional, intended to motivate one PC

Race for the Prize

ENVIRONMENTAL ASPECT
Race for the Prize

OBSTACLE ASPECT
We Need to Get Out of Port First…

NOTES
Captain Volo TrollAxe (see character sheet).
Vidaar Sailor: Skilled (+2) at Sailing, fighting with boarding axes, climbing in the rigging. Bad (-2) at: Planning, social situations.

The Forbidden Temple

ENVIRONMENTAL ASPECT
Even the Boobytraps Are Boobytrapped…

OBSTACLE ASPECT
The Goddess Curses Trespassers!

NOTES
Cultists: Good (+2) at: Stabbing, ganging up, dark magic; Bad (-2) at: Strategy. Vicious: +2 to backstab in the dark.
Temple Guardian: Skilled (+2) at: Appearing suddenly, crushing stragglers, scaring trespassers. Bad (-2) at: Resisting magic.

Recovering the Manuscript

ENVIRONMENTAL ASPECT
Dark Waterfront Alleys

OBSTACLE ASPECT
Cheap Hired Thugs

NOTES
Thugs: Skilled (+2) at: Ganging up, scaring innocent people. Bad (-2) at: Thinking ahead, fighting outnumbered.
Run Like Rats: +2 to disappear on the waterfront.

Researching the Mask

ENVIRONMENTAL ASPECT
The Records Are Patchy at Best

OBSTACLE ASPECT
Angry Elvorix Scholars

NOTES
Scholars: Skilled (+2) at: Obstructionism, politics, lore; Bad (-2) at: Everything else. Voice of Authority: +2 to get lone characters thrown out of the library.
Laetitia Bibulus (see character sheet)

Nautical Adventures

ENVIRONMENTAL ASPECT
Is It Always Like This?

OBSTACLE ASPECT
They Said It Was an Easy Trip!

NOTES
Tentacled Sea Monster: Skilled (+2) at: Grabbing people off ships, sinking small boats; Bad (-2) at: Everything else.
It's Everywhere: No penalty for up to 3 attacks per turn.

Who Gets the Mask?

ENVIRONMENTAL ASPECT
Fragile Alliances and Sudden but Inevitable Betrayals

OBSTACLE ASPECT
All Factions Converge

NOTES
Let the chips fall where they may. Even if the PCs get the mask, they have to decide who they will give it to.

INDEXES

How to use these indexes:
We've organized our indexes into two conceptual frameworks, divided between game setting (**WORLD OF AGAPTUS INDEX**) and game rules (**RULES INDEX**).

Page numbers in **bold** contain the most important information for the use or understanding of the term in that given context.

Example of a cross-reference within the same index: —See VIDAAR: Military Structure

Example of a cross-reference to another index: —See **RULES INDEX:** VIDAAR: Military Structure

WORLD OF AGAPTUS INDEX

RULES INDEX

In Short

Rolling the Dice *(page 189)*

Result = Dice Roll

+ Approach bonus
+ Bonuses from stunts
+ Bonuses from invoked aspects

Four Actions *(page 180)*

» **Overcome** an obstacle.
» **Create an Advantage** (aspect).
» **Attack** another character.
» **Defend** against attacks or advantages.

Four Outcomes *(page 179)*

Versus opponent's result or target number.

» **Fail** if your result is lower. Take appropriate fallout or succeed at serious cost.
» **Tie** if your result is equal. Gain appropriate benefit or succeed at minor cost.
» **Success** if your result is higher by 1 or 2.
» **Success with Style** if your result is higher by 3 or more. Gain appropriate benefit.

Turn Order *(page 215)*

» **Physical Conflict:** Highest Quick goes first.
» **Mental Conflict:** Highest Careful goes first.
» **Everyone else** goes in descending order.
» **NPCs** go on the turn of the most advantageous NPC.

Roar Phase *(page 215)*

Create an advantage against a difficulty of Fair (+2).

» **Fail:** Create a froth aspect and gain a consequence.
» **Tie:** Creates a froth **boost**.
» **Success:** Create a froth aspect with one free invoke.
» **Success with Style:** Create a froth aspect with two free invokes.

While frothing, you are limited to the approach you used and the two adjacent approaches.

The froth aspect lasts until you use a non-adjacent approach or the scene ends.

Weight *(page 222)*

» If you outweigh your opponents in the zone by at least 2 to 1, replace any one of the dice rolled with a ⊞.
» If you outweigh the zone opposition by at least 4 to 1, replace two results with ⊞.

Stress & Consequences

(page 231)

» Check one **stress box** to handle some or all of the shifts of a hit.
» Take one or more **consequences** to deal with the hit.
  » Mild = 2 shifts
  » Moderate = 4 shifts
  » Severe = 6 shifts
» If you don't handle the entire hit, you're **taken out** and your opponent decides what happens.
» **Give in** before your opponent's roll to control how you exit the scene and earn one or more fate points.

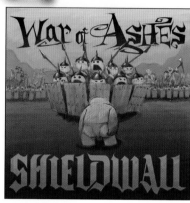